VOICES OF TOMORROW

by Contemporary Art Curator Magazine

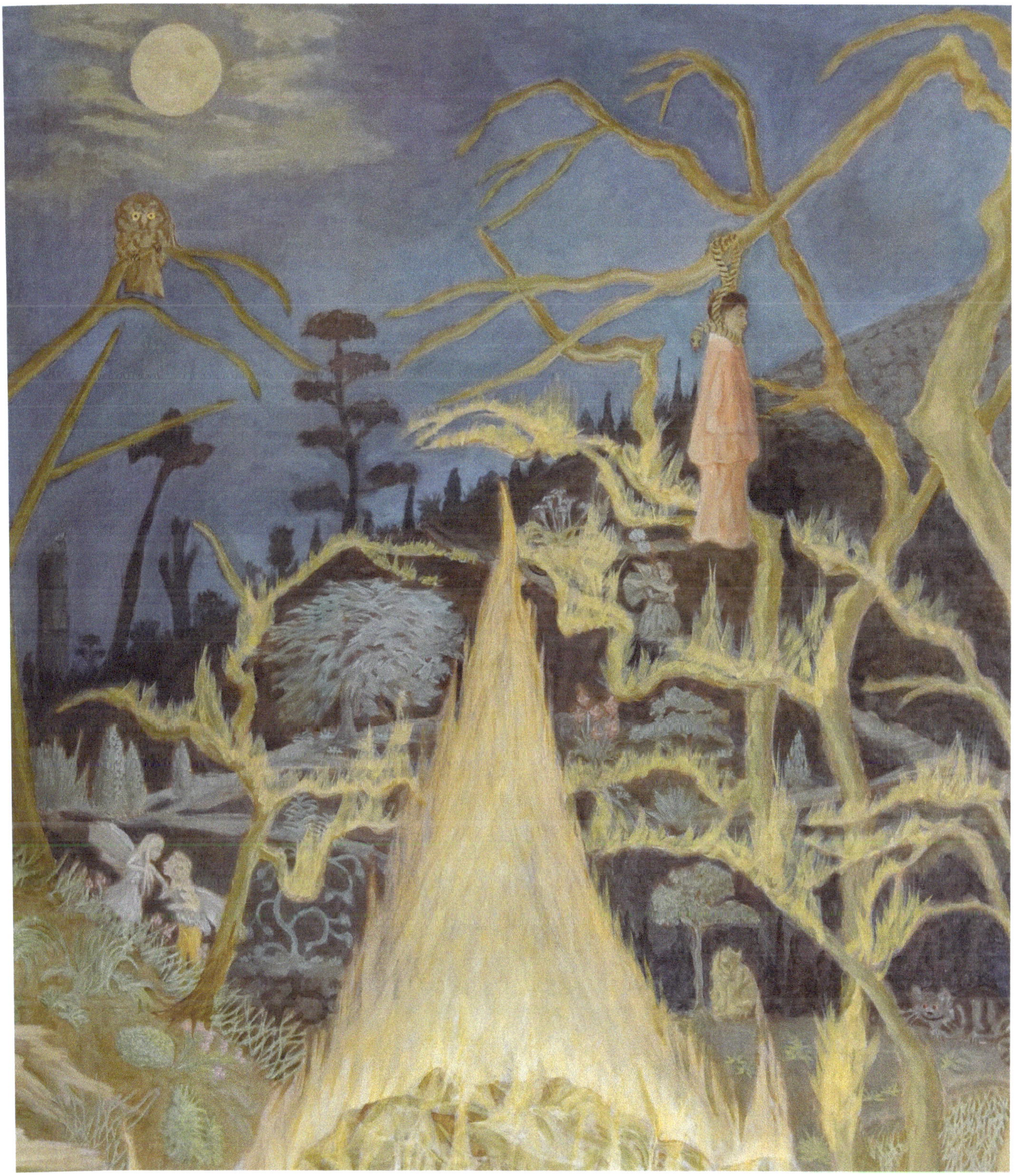

Cover by Li Ning.

VOICES OF TOMORROW

by Contemporary Art Curator Magazine

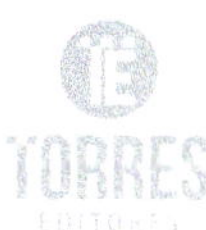

Cover by Li Ning.

Published by the Contemporary Art Curator Magazine.
All of the images are subject to copyright by the artists represented in the book.
2023 © Contemporary Art Curator Magazine.

ISBN: 978-84-19526-48-9
DL: GR 163-2023

Imprime: Lozano Impresores S.L.
Distribuye: TORRES EDITORES
Tel.: 958 80 05 80 - Fax: 958 29 16 15
www.torreseditores.com
info@torreseditores.com

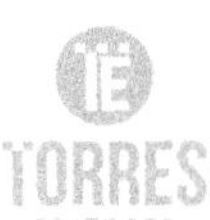

VOICES
OF TOMORROW

by Contemporary Art Curator Magazine

VOICES OF TOMORROW

Voices of Tomorrow is a new art book featuring the work of outstanding
artists from around the world.
This collection showcases the diversity of styles and perspectives of
these talented individuals, and provides a glimpse into the future of the
art world.
From thought-provoking paintings to striking photography, the pages of
Voices of Tomorrow are filled with breathtaking imagery that will inspire
and delight art lovers and collectors.
Voices of Tomorrow is a must-have for anyone looking to discover new
and exciting talent in the world of art. It is a powerful reminder that the
future of art is bright, and countless voices are waiting to be heard.

Voices of Tomorrow Art Book Concept

Humanity has arrived at a crossroads, and all signs point to a new era.
The Voices of Tomorrow Art Book examines the society we live in today
and explores the creation of a new one with space for our voices,
opinions, and ideas as an alternative to the deluge of
gloomy narratives.
Art has the potential to impact the world!
Art has the power to make people feel, and this feeling can inspire them
to think and act.
Art can help individuals overcome the numbing effect of today's
information overload by inspiring them to act on their ideas.
Art is a powerful tool for social change because it tells a story that can
change and positively influence people's futures and beliefs.
The Voices of Tomorrow urges poetic reinvention, asserting that art
has the power to engage with the issues and complexities of the world
around us. The Voices of Tomorrow Art Book seeks alternative acts,
thoughts, and tales from the perspective of common futures, changing
fear into opportunity and peril into vitality.

by Contemporary Art Curator Magazine

ALEKSANDRA CIĄŻYŃSKA
ANDREW BINDER
AOMI KIKUCHI
BARBARA PALKA WINEK
BRITTA ORTIZ
CAROLINE BOFF
CEVIGA
CLAIRE DAVENHALL
CLAUDIA HABRINGER
DAVE THOMAS
DAVID TANNER
DOMINIE CHAN
EDDA GYLFADÓTTIR
EVELINE GÖLDI
FATINHA RAMOS
FRANCO SMITH
FRÉDÉRIC DEMEUSE
GAYLE PRINTZ
GM SACCO
GUSTAVS FILIPSONS
HANNA RHEINZ (HRZ)
HILARY THURSFIELD
HOWARD HARRIS
IRINA HOWARD
JEONG-AH ZHANG
JOJO HUXFORD
JULIE REBY WAAS
JULIET PETRARULO
KAITLYN WALLACE
KAT KLEINMAN
KATHY STANLEY
KLAUS BILICZKY

KOQUI HANDAL
LENE KLOVBORG
LI NING
LINGMUKI
LUANA STEBULE
LUCIE BOSWELL
MAGDALENA FASCHING
MARCELLE MANSOUR
MARIA GRANADINO
MARINA CHISTY
MARÍA ISABEL DE LINCE
MIRO FREI
MONIKA GLOVICZKI
NANCY ANNE WOOLF-PETTYJOHN
NATHA OUT OF THE BLUE
NATHANAEL COX
PATRICIA SPOON
PAV SZYMANSKI
RAMÓN RIVAS
REINER BINSCH
REYDEL ESPINOSA
REZAUL HOQUE
ROBERT VAN DE GRAAF
SHIR ZALCMAN
SHUAI XU
STEFFI RODIGAS
SUSAN PLATT
TINA CORRALES-MADER
TOTI CUESTA
WENDY COHEN
WERONIKA RACZYNSKA
WOWSER NG

VOICES OF TOM

ORROW

LI NING

China

Li Ning (b.1994) graduated from Royal College of Art major in painting, tutored by Emma Talbot. In his Painting degree show 'A Room of One's Own' was well received with strong recognition from the college and wider public. Following graduation, Li Ning has actively continued his practice as artist. This is evident by his participation in several exhibitions in the art world. These include work exhibited in Royal Society of Portrait Painters 2021 annual exhibition at Mall Galleries, Jingdezhen Ceramic University 110th anniversary exhibition at Museum of Jingdezhen Ceramic University. In addition, his work has appeared in media publications for example Aesthetica magazine, Contemporary art curator magazine and Contemporary art collectors platform. Li's works represent subjects under allegorical and fantastic imagination. His sources of inspiration come from both mythical forms and ordinary objects. Deeply influenced by Renaissance painters such as Titian and Botticelli, Li realized figurative paintings contain infinite possibilities. By embracing Renaissance painters, he incorporates their style to depict his subjects in a contemporary art construct His works manifest allegorical and spiritual meanings beyond subjects' original physical forms. His sensitive observation combined with spiritual imagination gives the work a sense of idiosyncratic temperament.

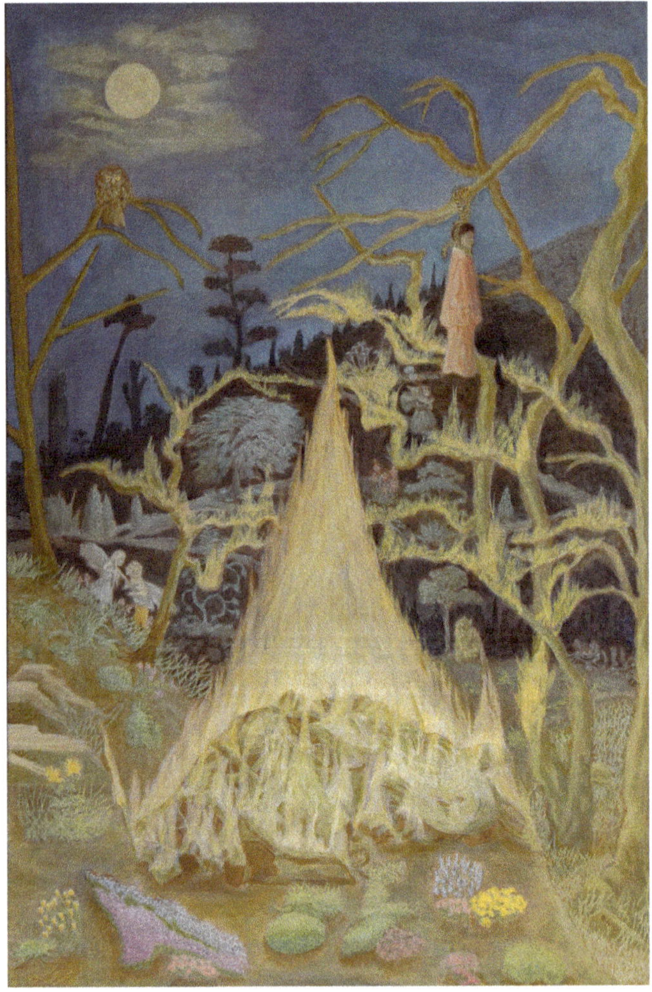

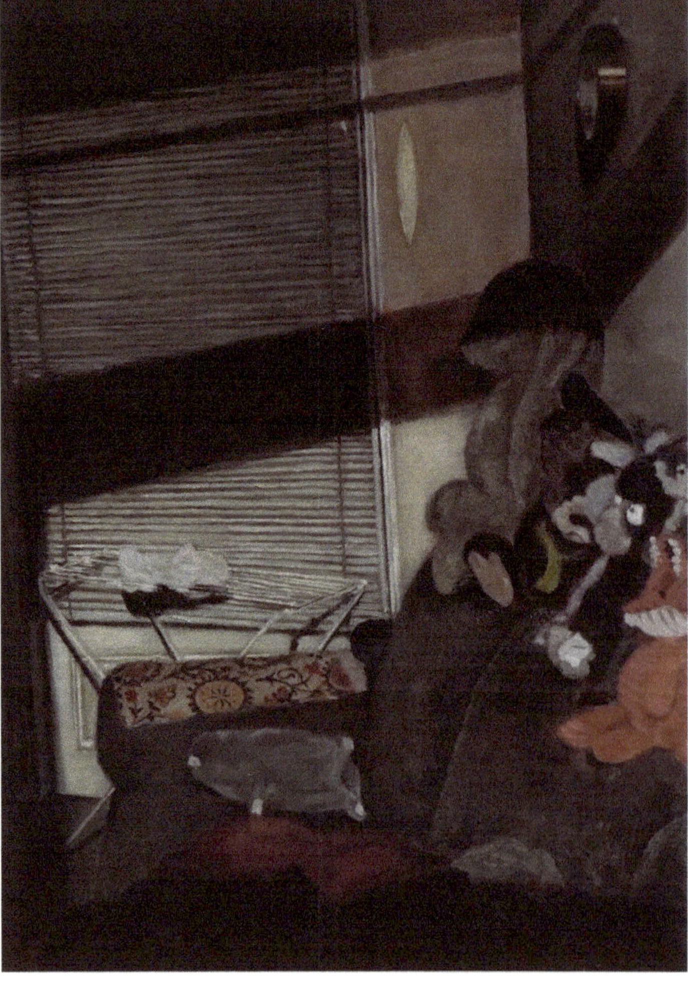

Bonfire - Secret Garden, 2021, Oil on canvas, 150 x 100 cm

A Room of One's Own, 2019, Oil on canvas, 70 x 50 cm

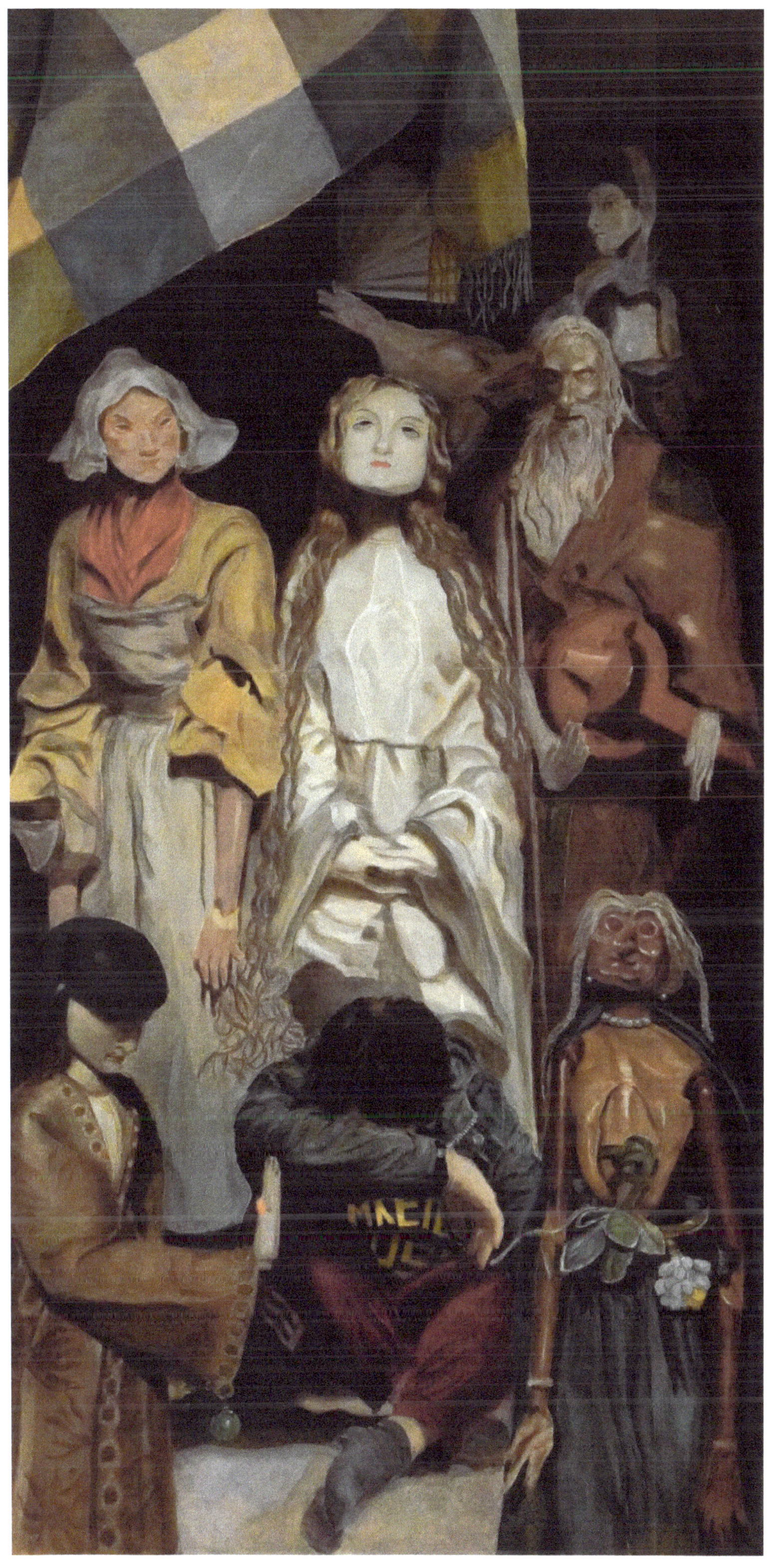

Viennese Somniloquist – puppet drama, 2019, Oil on canvas, 120 x 60 cm

LI NING

China

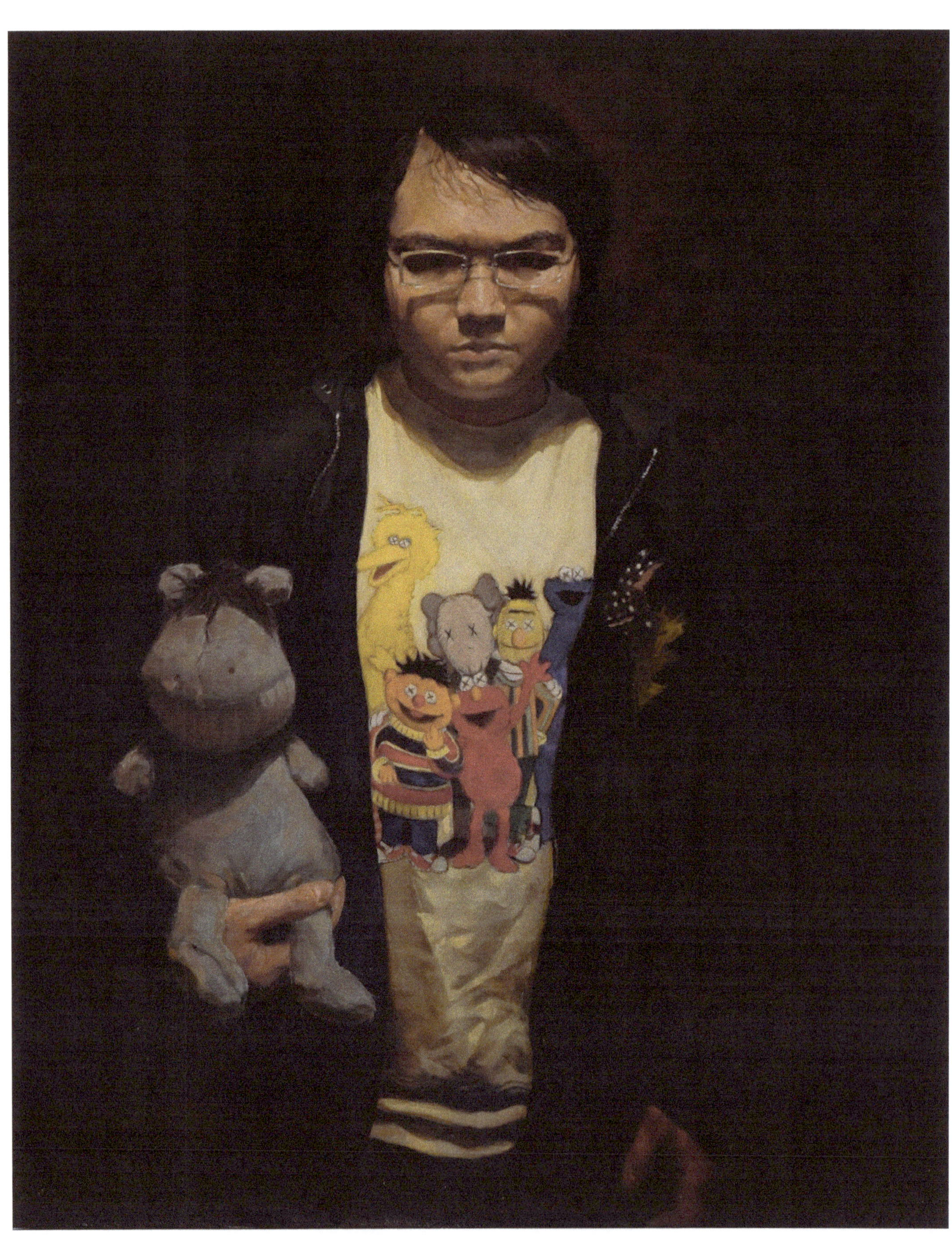

Stranger, 2019, Oil on canvas, 100 x 80 cm

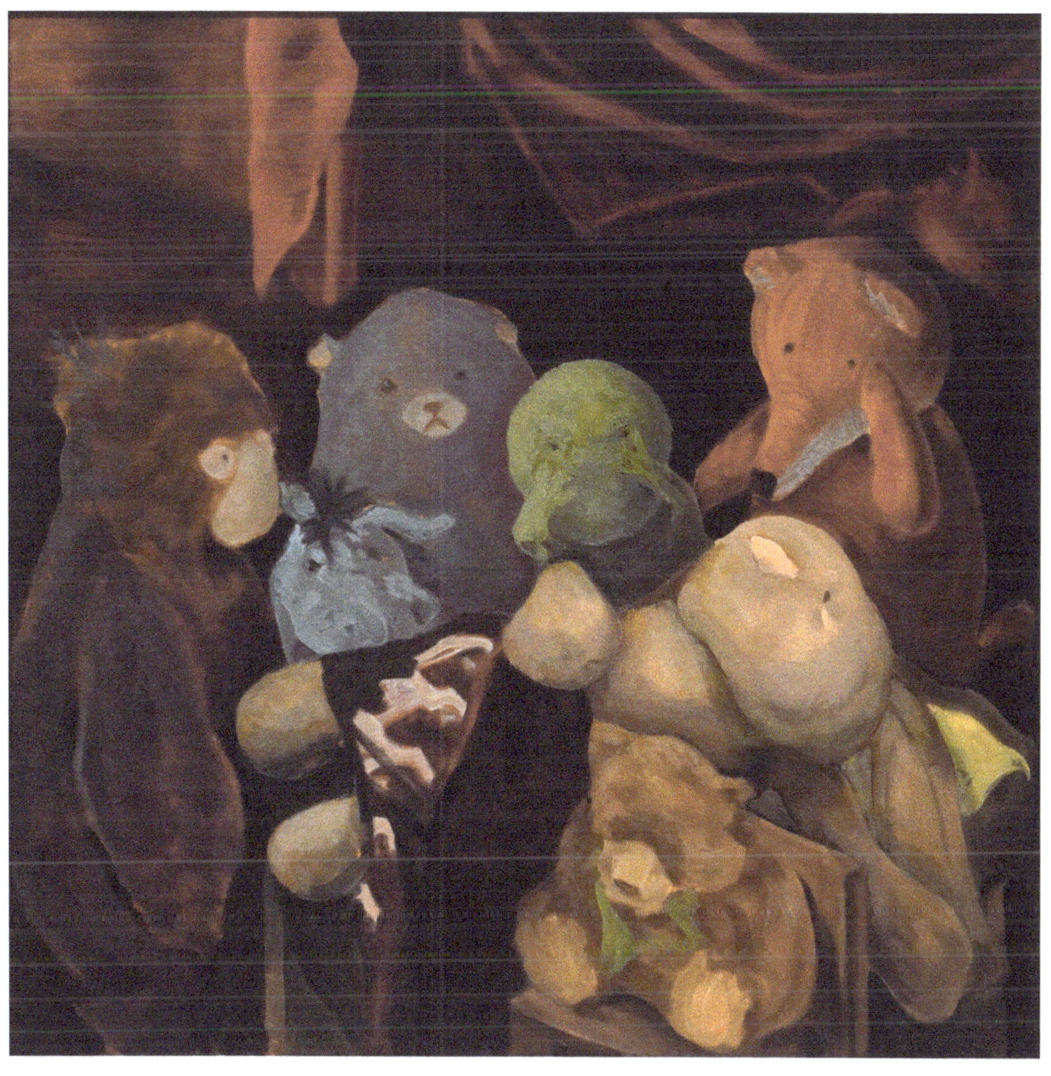

Delirium, 2019, Oil on canvas, 100 x 100 cm

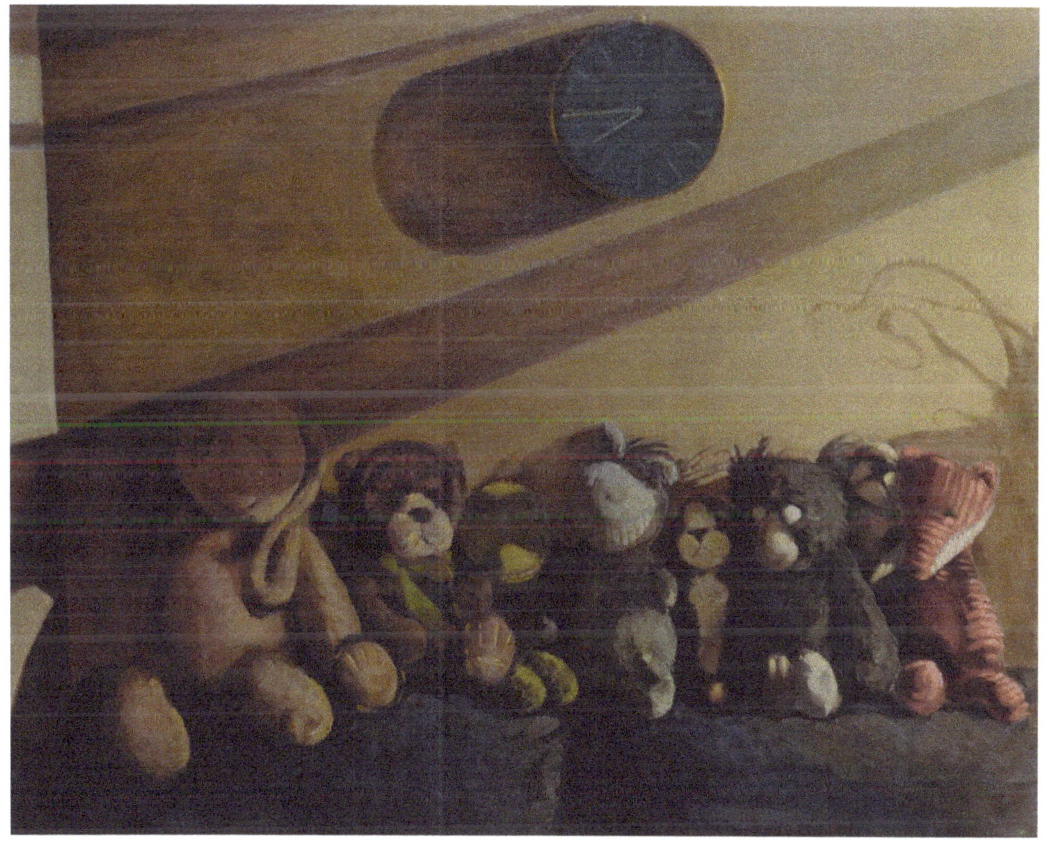

Party, 2019, Oil on canvas, 100 x 80 cm

LUANA STEBULE

United Kingdom | luanastebulefineart.co.uk

From 2013 Luana Stebule have been living and creating in the United Kingdom. Artist was born in Lithuania in 1962. She finished A.Martinaitis Art School and Academy of Art. Her artistic career starts from 1988. Since she created 11 stage's projects for the theatrical performances, mural paintings, together with 24 solo and 44 shared exhibitions in Europe, England, Canada and the United States.In 2018 she created Luana Stebule Paintings website in English language and became more accessible and appreciable in the Art World around the globe. Luana Stebule received several recognitions. In 2019 by the International Art Market Magazine, she was selected to be on the Gold List as one of the Top Artists of Today. In 2020 painter was awarded the 3rd International Leonardo Da Vinci Prize and the with New York City Prize. Her paintings included into the Art Anthologies "Important World Artists 2020" and "International Contemporary Masters 2021" publisher is Artavita, US. Also, into books "Masters of Contemporary Art 2020" and "Best 2021 Modern and Contemporary Artists" In 2022, in New York she was awarded with the ATIM's Top 60 Masters Award and the Collector's Choice Award. Also, in 2022 her paintings published in the Art Anthology V, Madrid Edition, curated by the Guto Ajayu Culture and in the book "La Biennale di Venezia 2022"

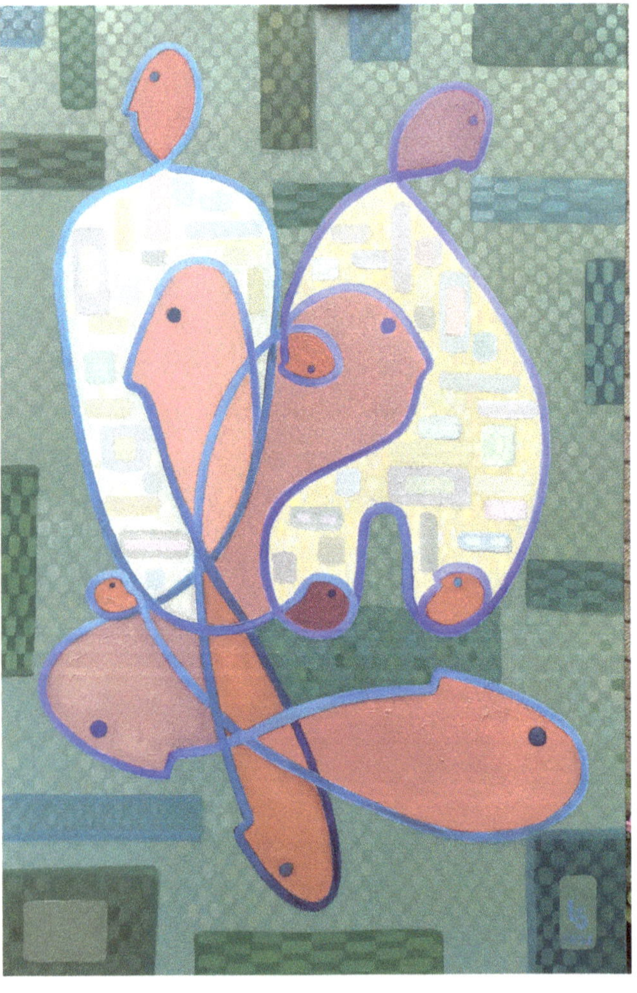

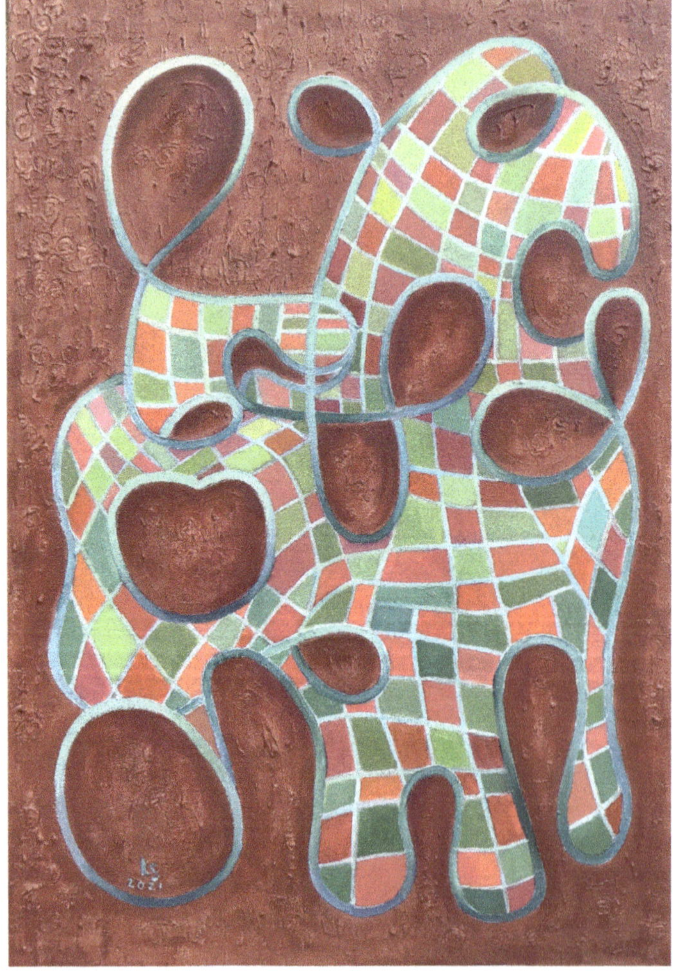

Behind you,2021.Oil on canvas, 76 x 51 cm

Oxford street, 2021. Oil on canvas, 61 x 46 cm

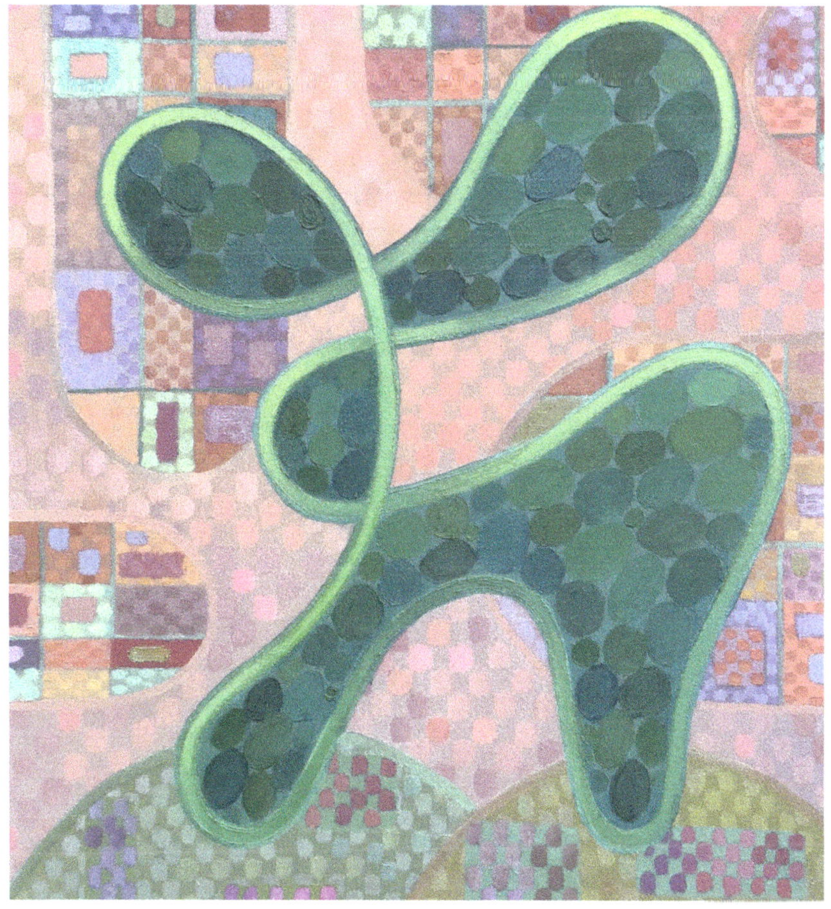

Transformation from the toy, 2021. Oil on canvas, 61 x 51 cm

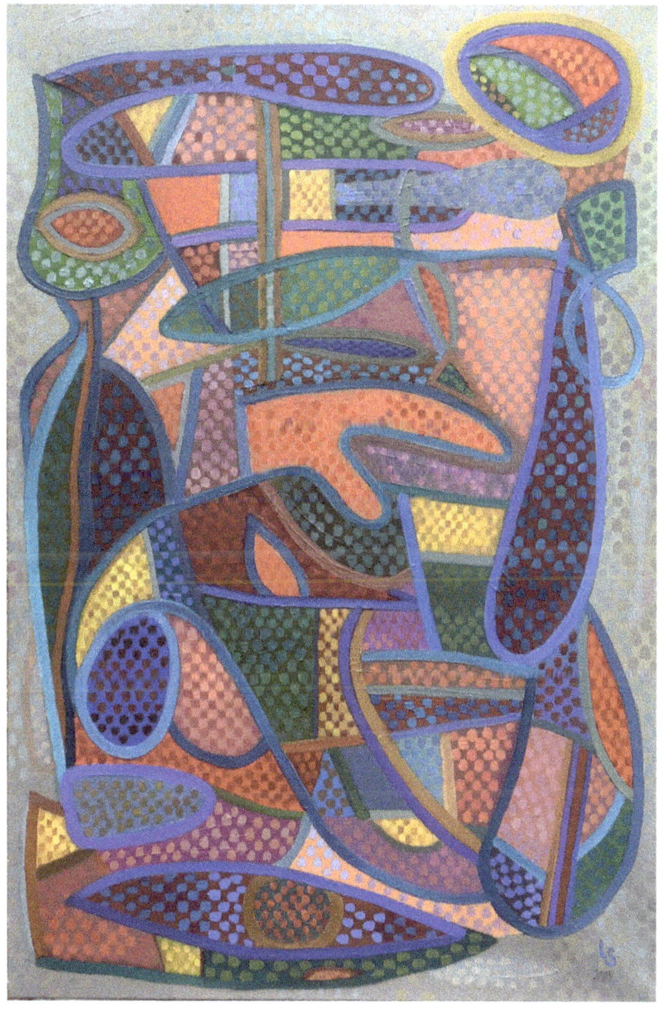

Round the clock, 2019. Oil on canvas, 91 x 61 cm

LUANA STEBULE

United Kingdom | luanastebulefineart.co.uk

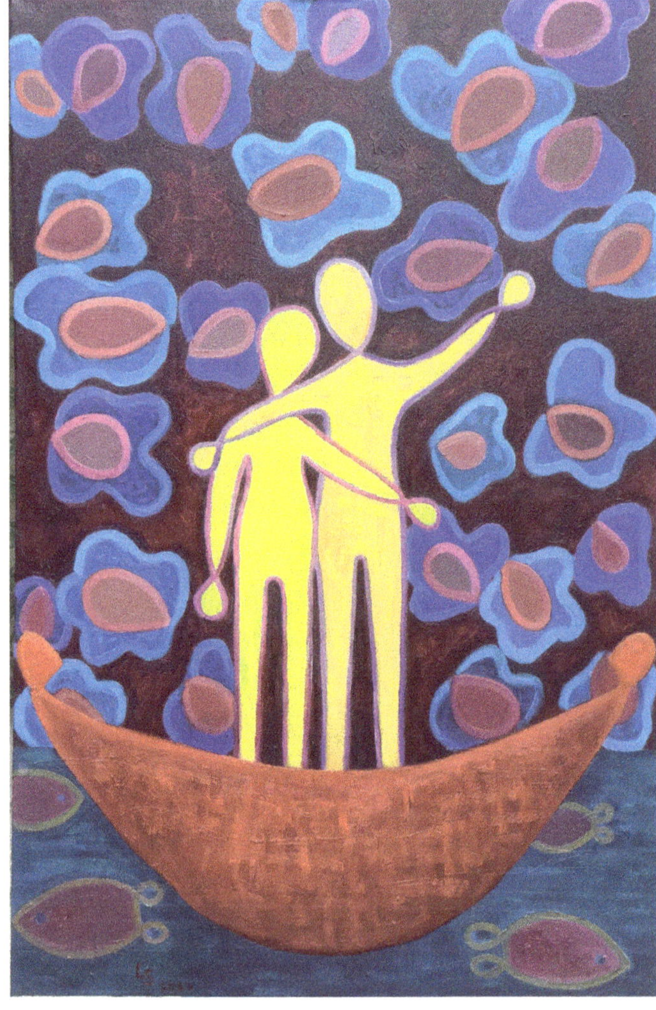

Gondola for two, 2022.Oil on canvas, 91 x 61 cm

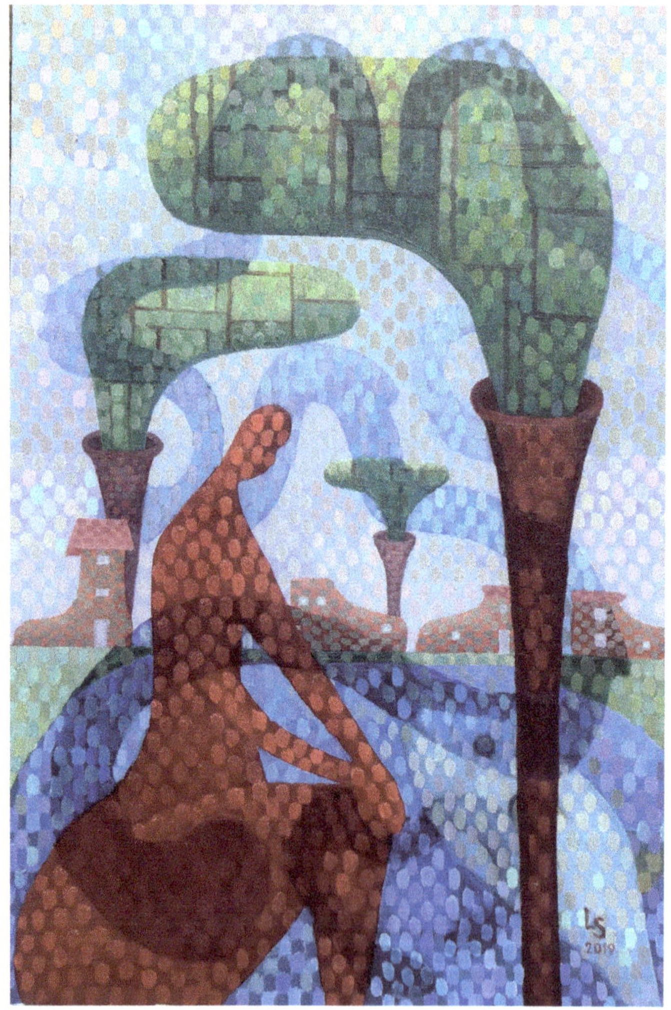

"The keeper of the lost dreams,2018. Oil on canvas, 76 x 51 cm

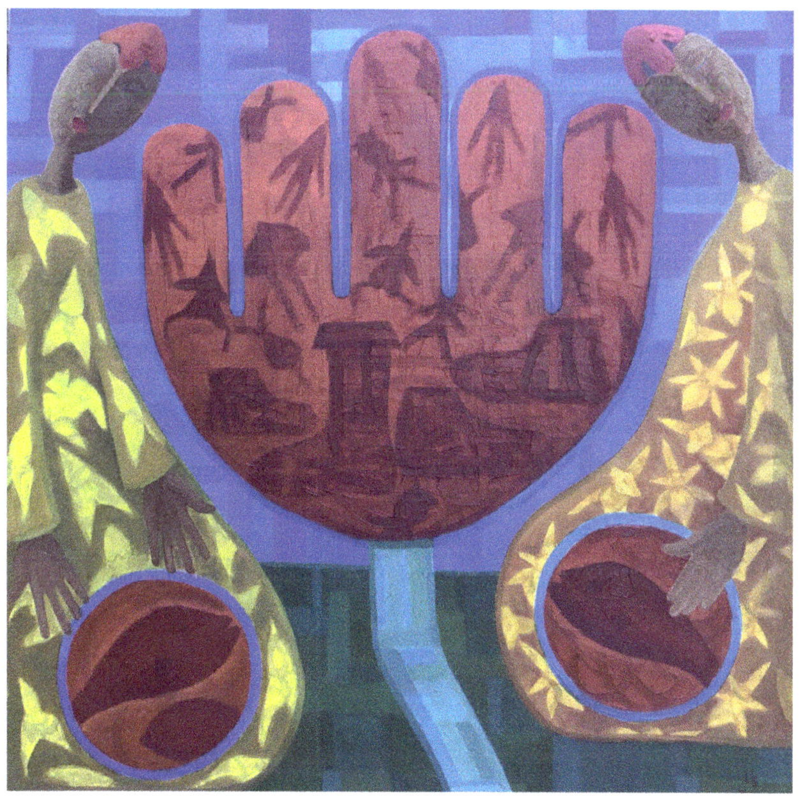

Magical about Majestic, 2018. Oil on canvas, 102 x 102 cm

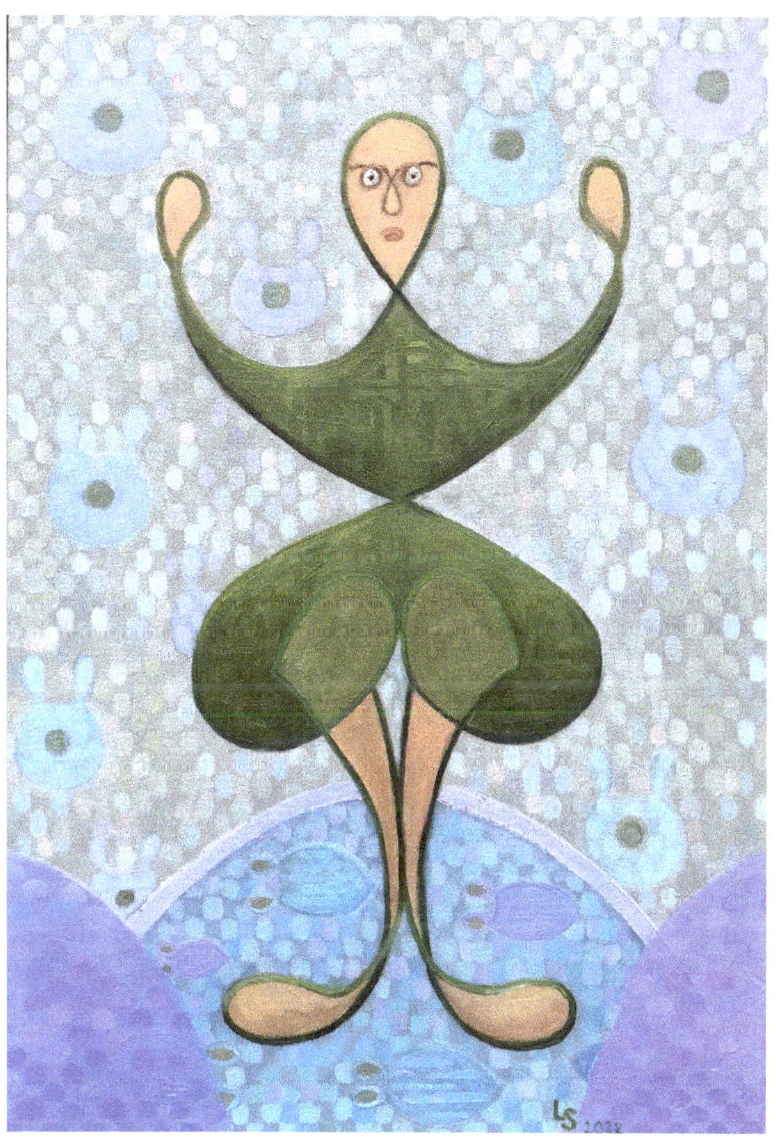

"Primadonna, 2022. Oil on canvas, 61 x 46 cm

ALEKSANDRA CIĄŻYŃSKA

Poland | ciazynska.pl

Aleksandra was born in 1987 in Poland. She is a graduate of the Faculty of Economic Sciences at the University of Warsaw and a passionate painter. She has loved to paint since she was a child. For many years she participated in classes conducted by prof Paweł Lewandowski-Palle. It was there that she fell in love with art even more, especially painting. She loves the diversity of the world and it is from this diversity that she draws inspiration. This is why her paintings are so diverse, both in terms of themes and techniques. Her paintings are just as diverse as the world is. Aleksandra took part in many exhibitions. Her paintings have been in, among others, New York, Rome, Venice, Barcelona, Vienna, Munich, Paris, Heidenreichstein, Ajdovščina, Ciechocinek, Milan and Fuerteventura. She received many awards, e.g. Woman Art Award 2022 by Musa International Art Space in Paris and ATIM's Top 60 Masters in New York. Her paintings have also appeared in many publications. Many articles have been written about her art, in, among others, Today in New York, Warsaw Tribune, The European Gazette, Economic News Observer, International World Times, Fox 28, US National Times, etc.

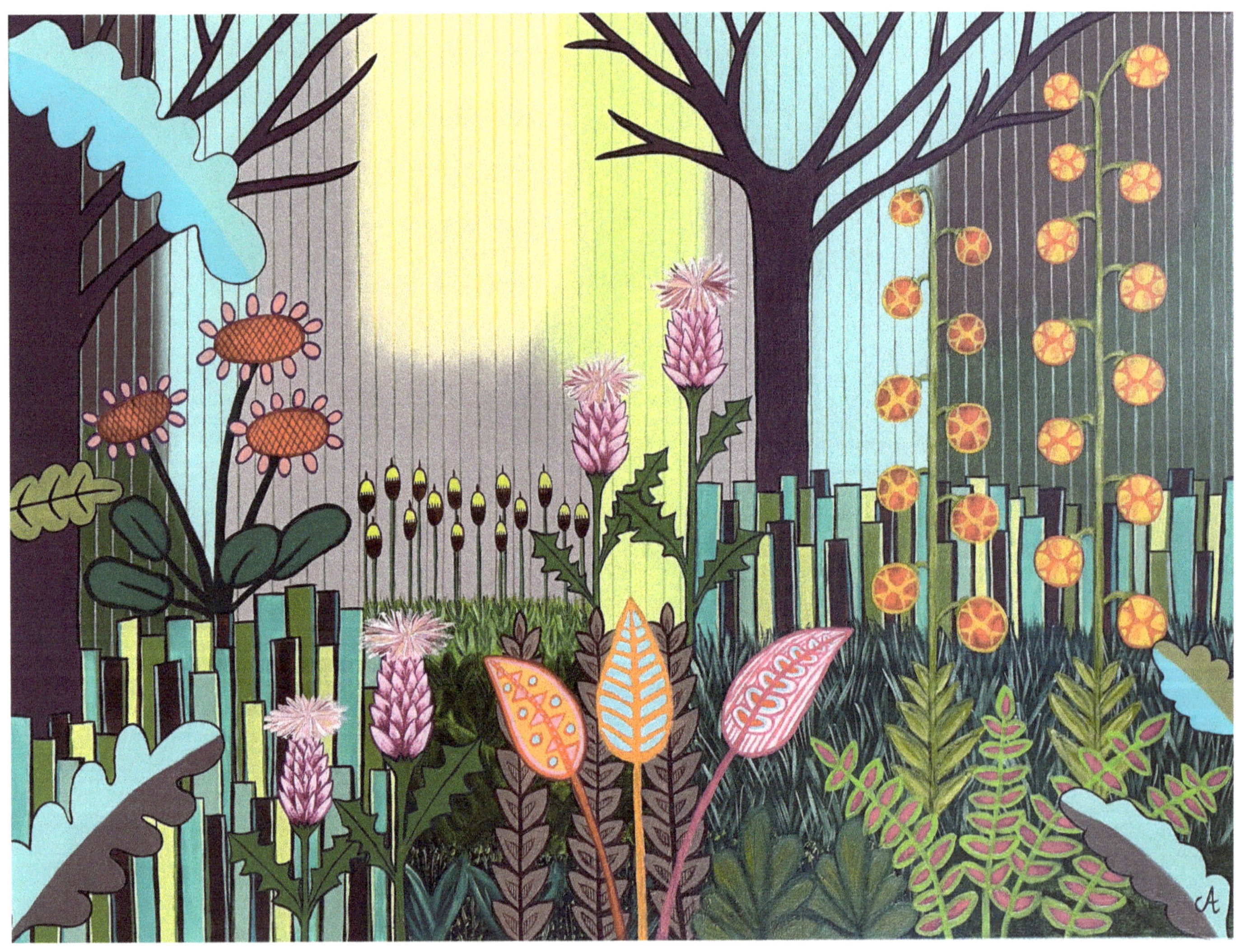

Garden of Eden VII, 2022, oil on canvas, 80 x 60 cm

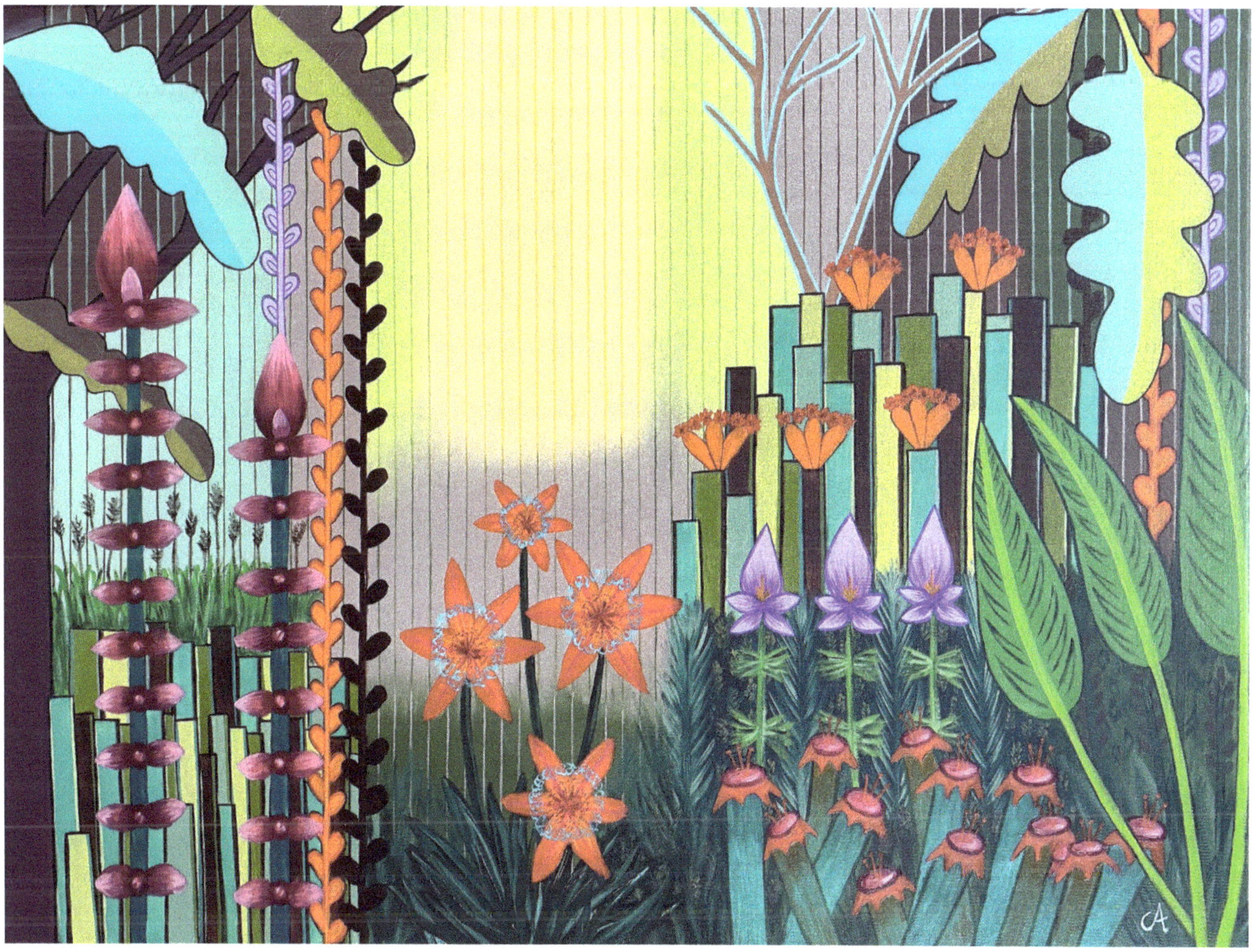

Garden of Eden VIII, 2022, oil on canvas, 80 x 60 cm

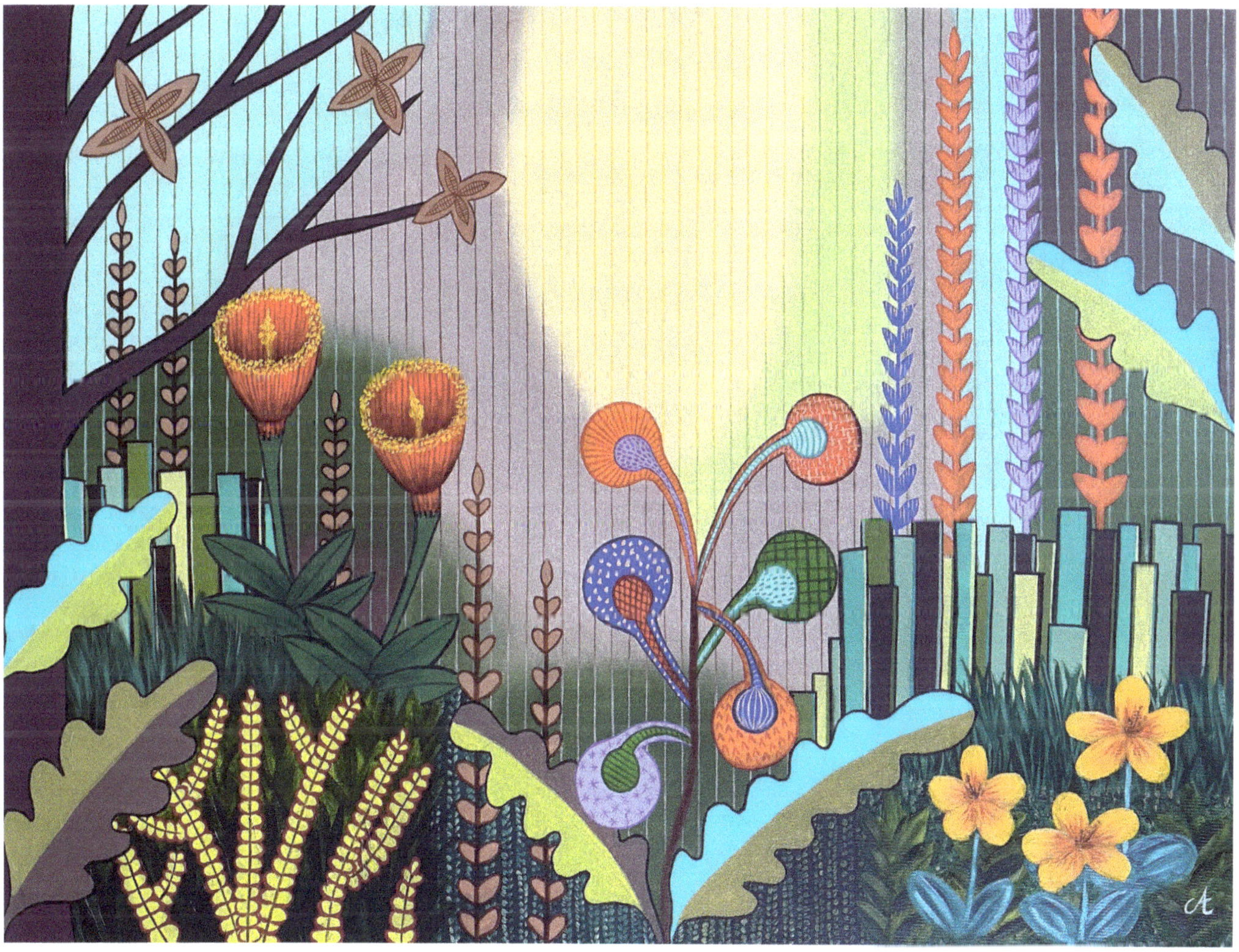

Garden of Eden IX, 2022, oil on canvas, 80 x 60 cm

REINER BINSCH

Germany | atelier-binsch.de

In many of my paintings I reflect our environment. But especially I am concerned with constructed landscapes. Cities and houses live their own lives and they give our lives space. Buildings arise, grow and change. Sometimes they cave in or are being torn down. We work and live inside of them and share a close relationship with them. We change and form our houses. Sometimes it's the other way around. Houses are like the stage of our lives. Here stories are told, dramas are played out or ballads are sung. In my pictures the buildings are mostly changed or even invented. They are more than a scenery to me. People are often lonely or fade into the background.

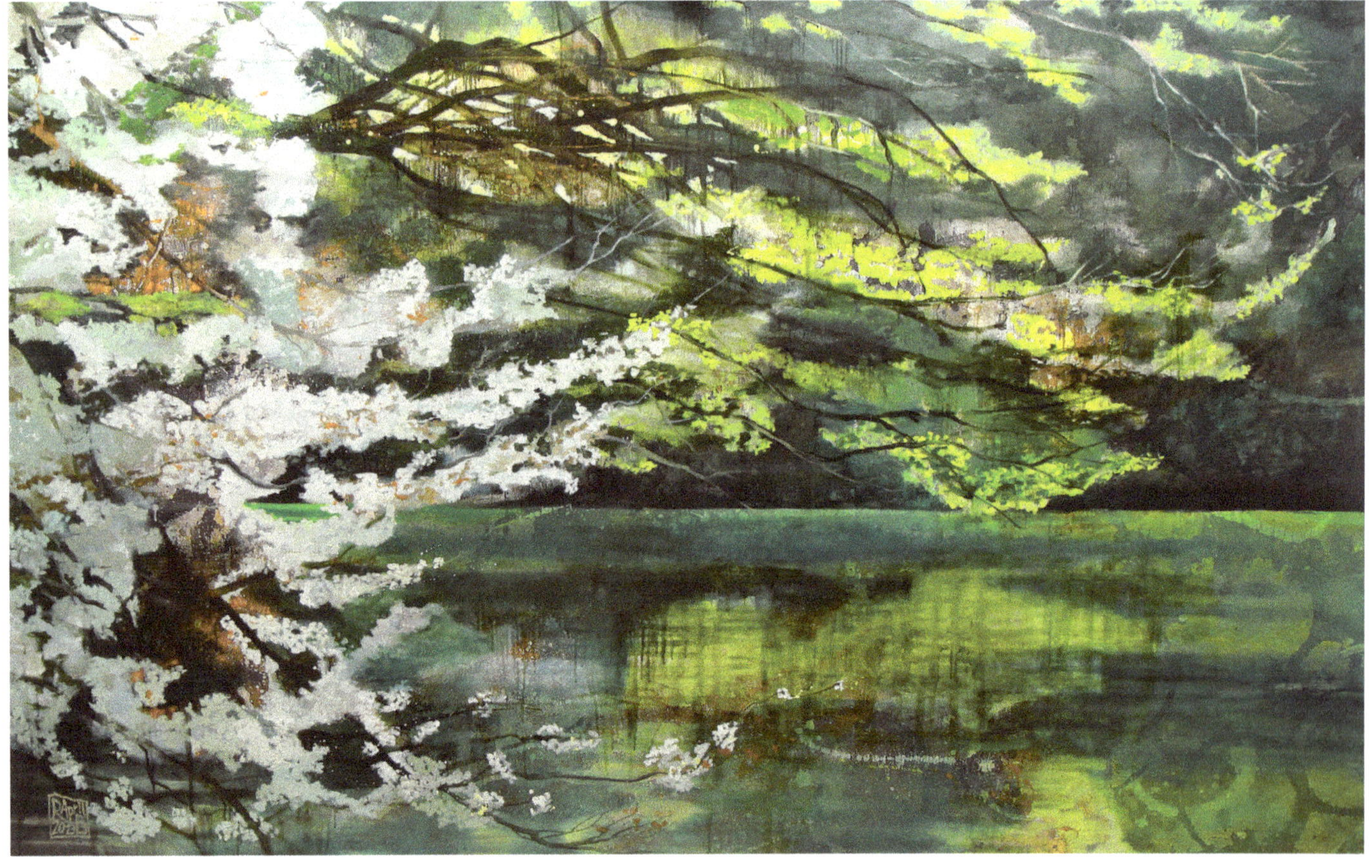

Blossom at the Imperial Palace.

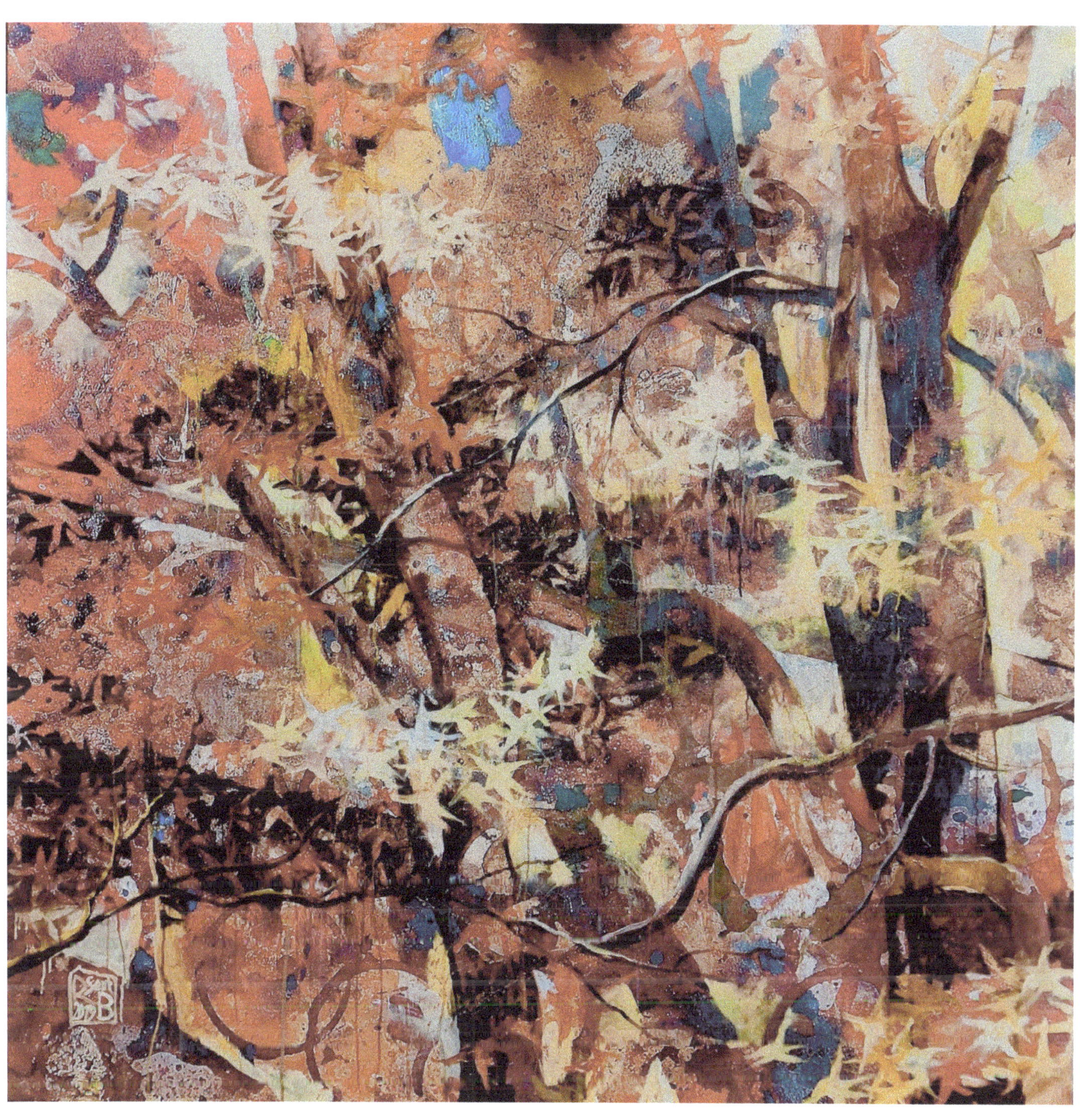

Autumn in Japan.

KLAUS BILICZKY

Germany | biliczky.de

Klaus Biliczky is an award-winning visual artist. He was born in Dinkelsbühl, Germany's most beautiful old town, according to Focus and lives in Neuendettelsau, Bavaria. As early as his school years, he inquisitively absorbed everything related to art and published his first drawings in school newspapers. Personal traumatic events and experiences shaped his childhood, adolescence and time of growing up, which he processed in expressive surrealist pen and pencil drawings. Klaus Biliczky decided to pursue a professional education, especially since he had not originally thought of becoming an artist. For many years he worked as a graphic designer and held leading positions in the packaging industry. Through a chance encounter with an action artist, who encouraged him in his artistic work, he discovered his lifelong passion for art. He decided to study advertising and commercial art and continued his education self-taught and in workshops. Abstract painting and object art are now his preferred means of visual expression. In his current themes he explores with sensitive perception the connections between fantasy and reality and traces the mystery of the hidden. His works reflect the beauty and vulnerability of our world and testify to the transience of our being. Klaus Biliczky's works can be seen regularly in exhibitions, nationally and internationally.

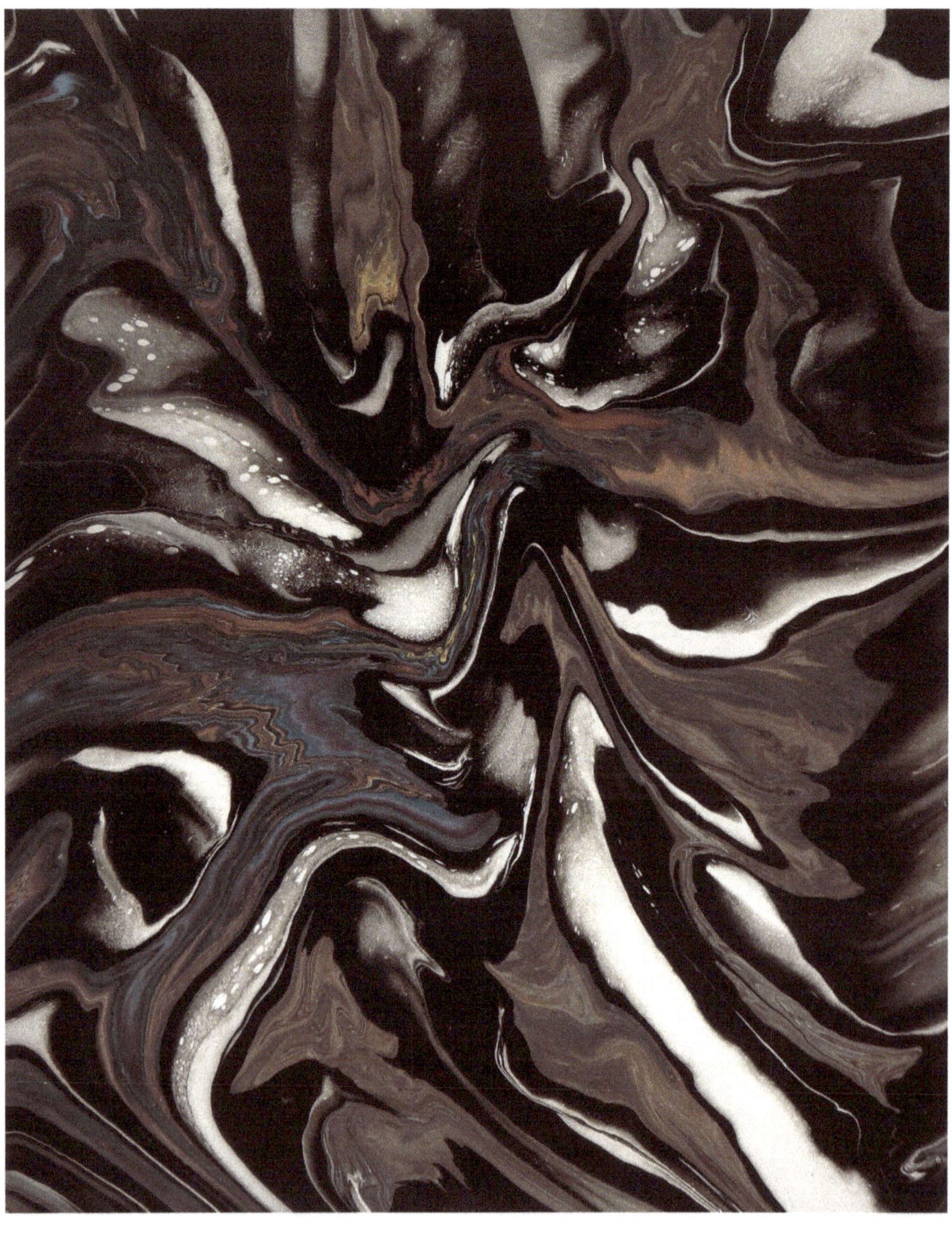

Compressed, 2021. Acrylic on canvas, 100 x 80 cm.

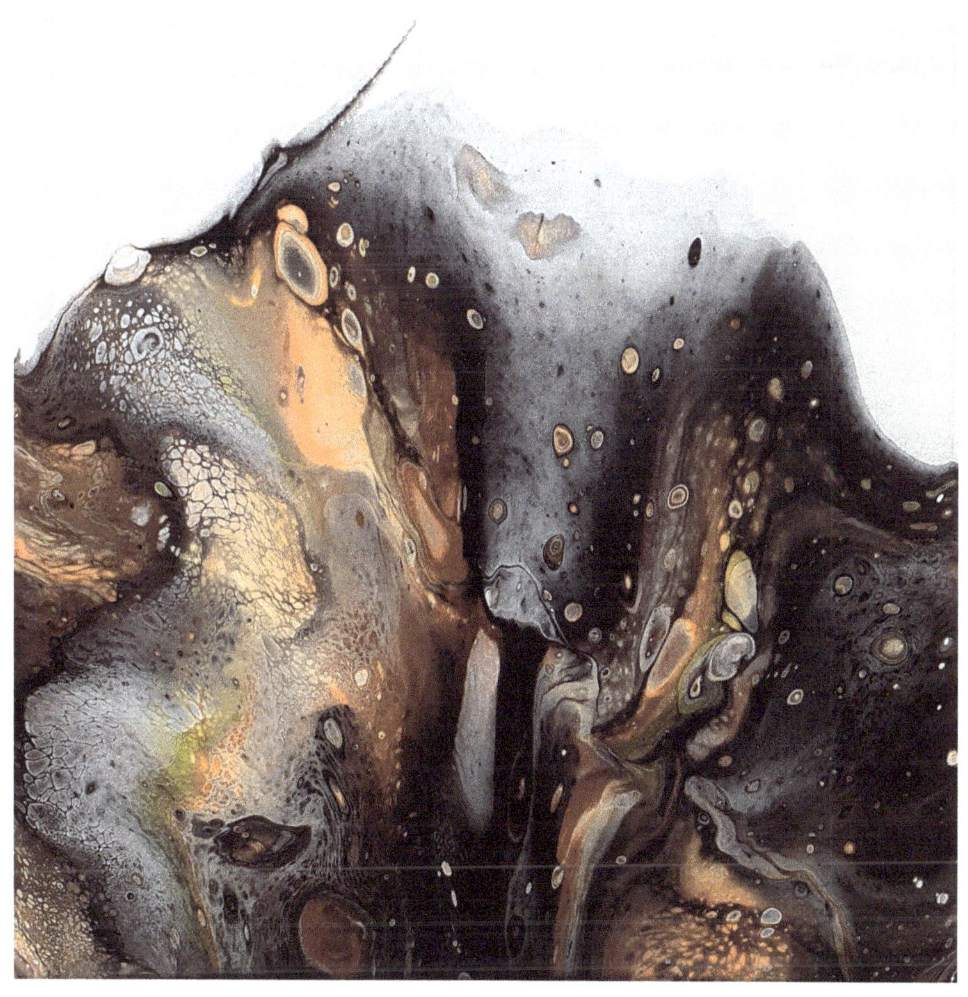

Glacier retreat, 2022. Acrylic on canvas, 30 x 30 cm.

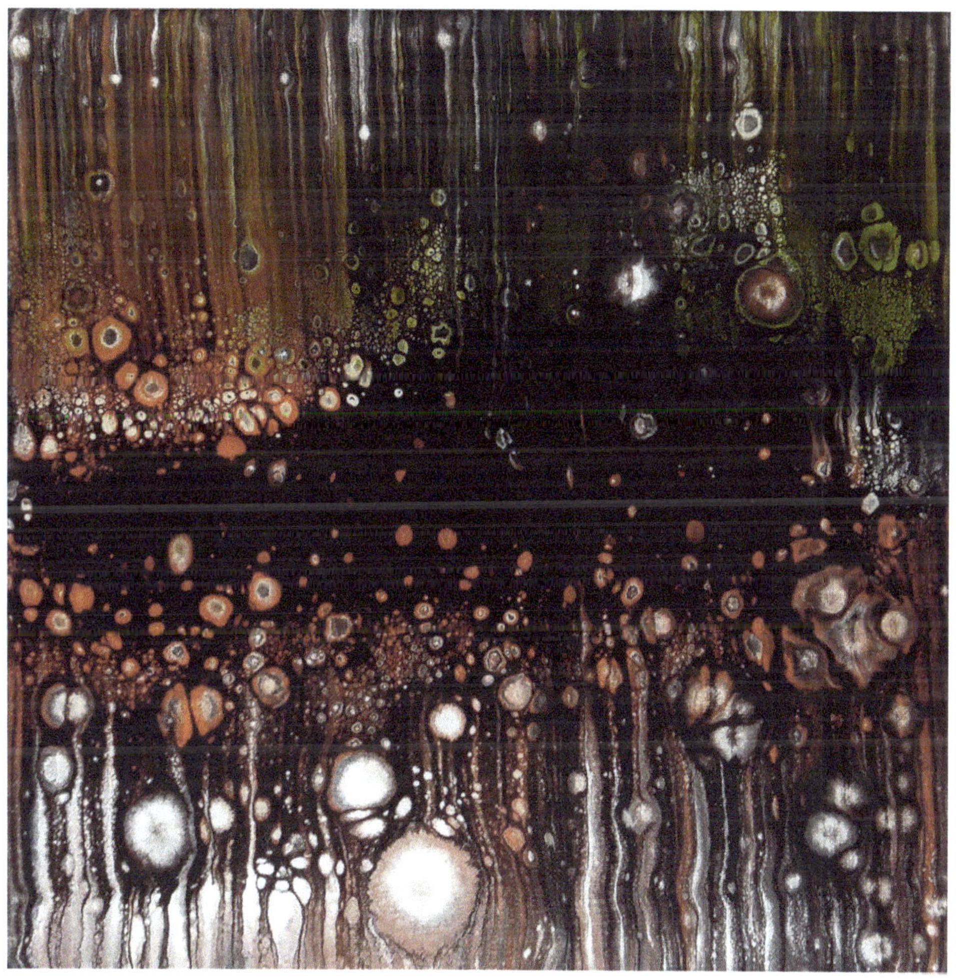

Raised bog, 2022. Acrylic on canvas, 30 x 30 cm

TINA CORRALES-MADER

United States | tinamader.com

Tina Corrales-Mader is an American artist born and raised in Los Angeles, California. She began her love of visual arts at a very young age mesmerized by Mexican folk art all around her. Tina graduated from The Art Institute of Los Angeles with a BFA in Graphic Design 2005. She worked as an Illustrator and Designer for Japanese American Publishing Company, Tokyopop. Tina participated in several group art shows in Los Angeles, CA while working as a Graphic Designer. She eventually moved to Dusseldorf, Germany with her husband where she began to study millinery design and later founded a small bridal millinery business (Velvet Owl Bridal) in 2009 and participated in group collaborative art exhibitions in Berlin as well. Tina has been steadily showing her work in NYC, Europe, and most recently in Asia. She uses a wide variety of mediums including oils, acrylic, pen and ink, watercolors, pressed flowers, metallics, and gold leaf. She paints on canvas, wood panel, and paper. Tina feels the most inspired during restless periods just before falling asleep. With thoughts and images invading her mind during that time. She attributes the evolution and style of her work to her multifaceted journey through life in all its complexities with her children and husband of 16 years. "Creation and expression are truly amazing gifts." "Feeling the days, breathing in the colors, and spaces are so important to living with gratitude and that's inspiring." Tina Luz Corrales- Mader

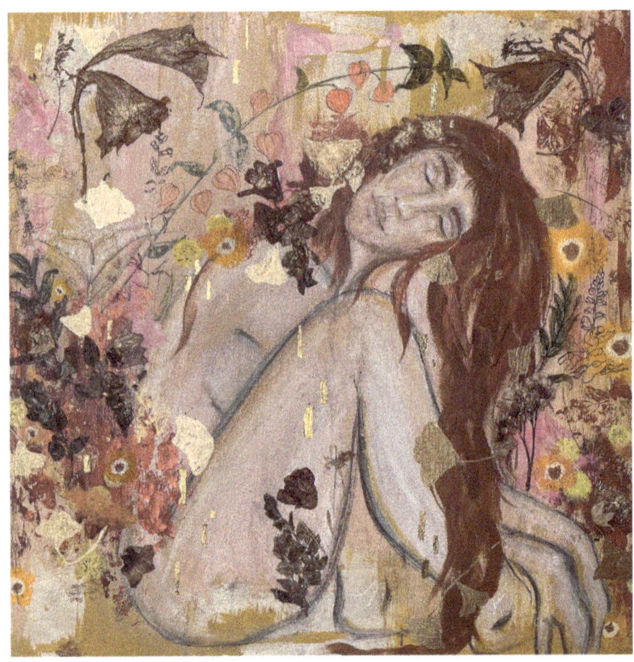

Daybreak, 2022. Acrylic on wood panel, 58 x 58 cm

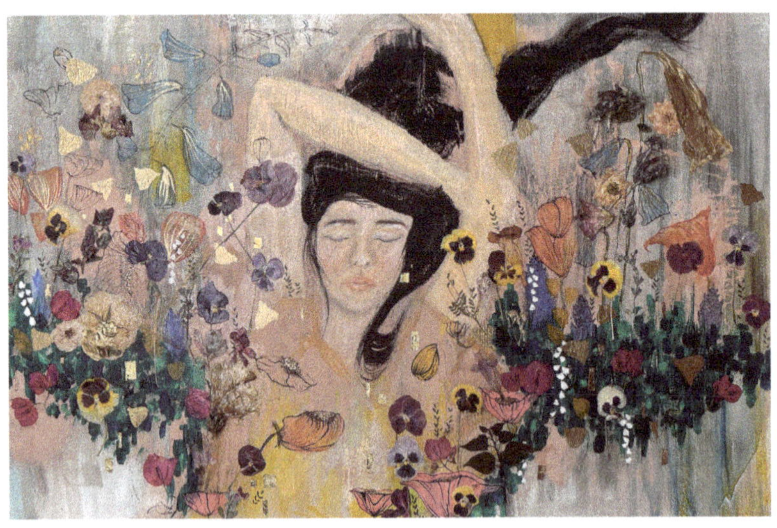

Always Endeavor, 2022. Acrylic on canvas, 88 x 60 cm.

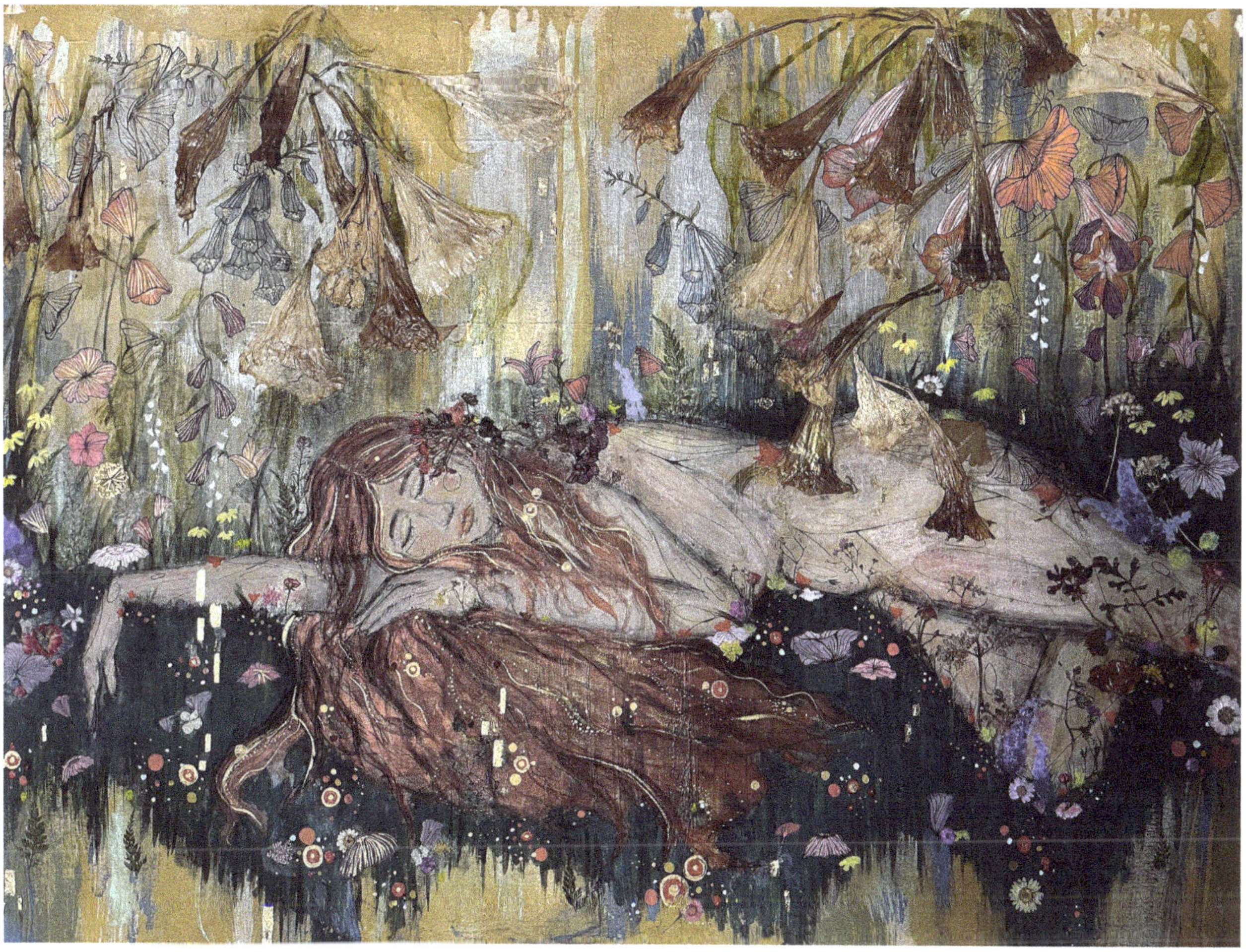

Garden gift, 2021. Acrylic on wood panel, 76 x 101 cm

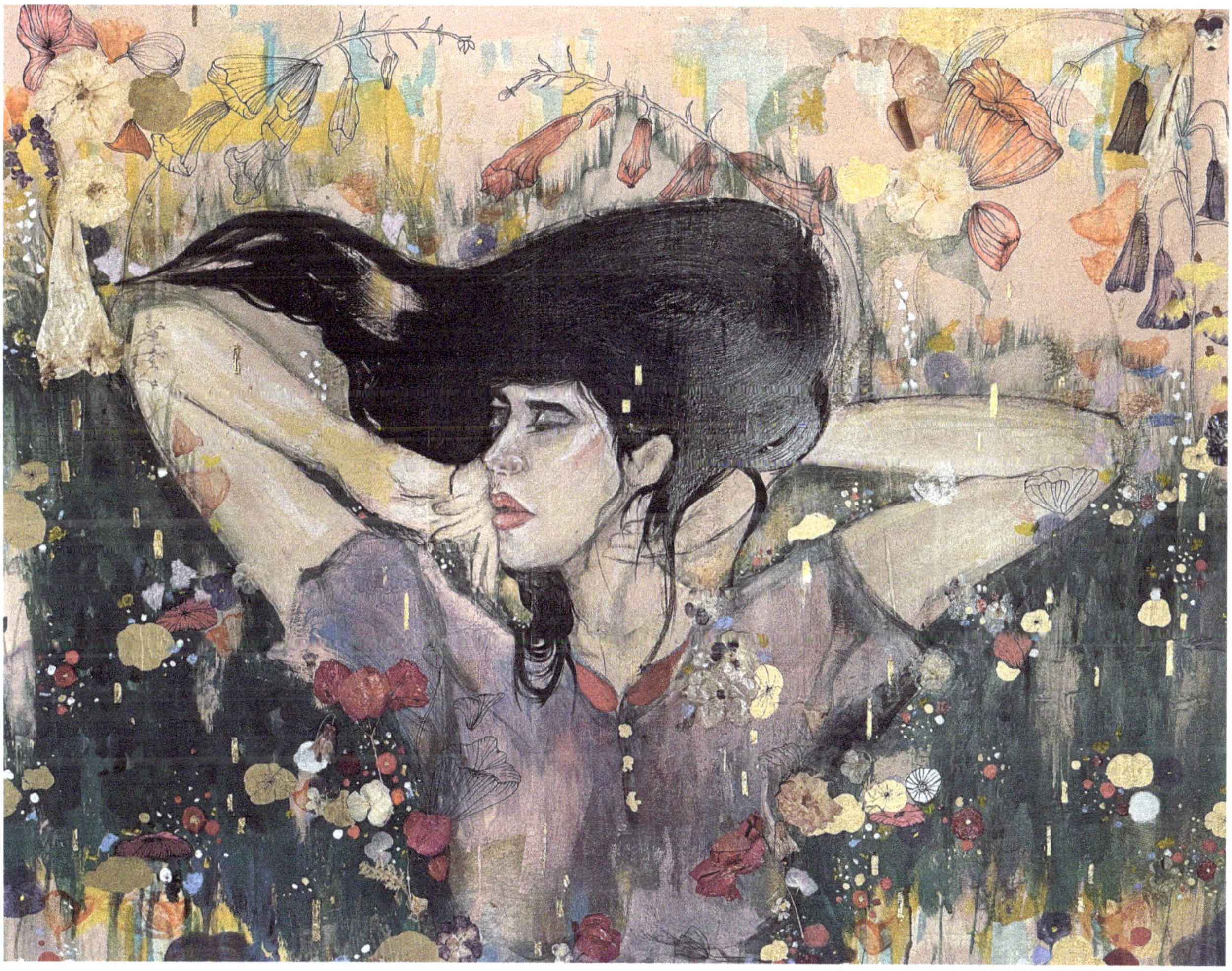

The Longing, 2021. Acrylic on wood panel, 76 x 101 cm

NATHANAEL COX

United States | natecphotography.com

Nathanael Cox is a New Jersey based photographer. He originally learned 35mm photography in the late 2000s when dark rooms were still prevalent and digital photography hadn't yet completely dominated the landscape. After a taking a long break, and a few detours, he started to learn digital photography and resumed exploring the world through his lens. Nathanael lists Stephen Wilkes and Peter Lik as major influences/inspirations. His style leans towards breathless landscapes and sprawling cityscapes.

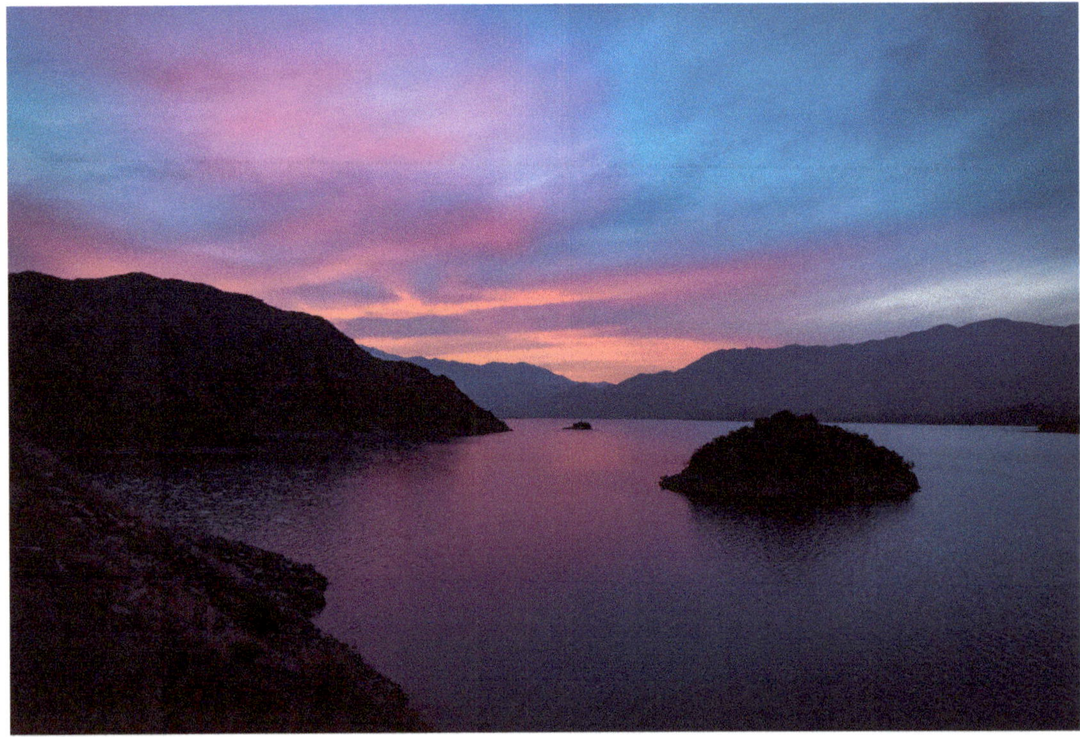

Cotton Candy, 2019

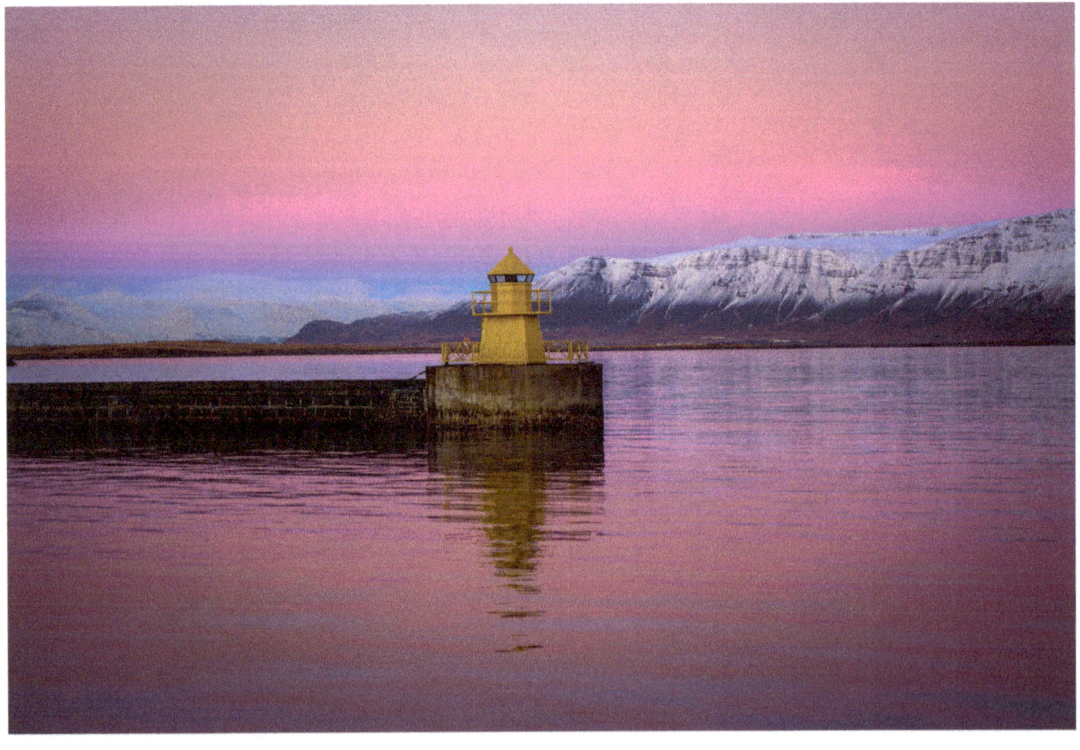

Iceland Lighthouse, 2018

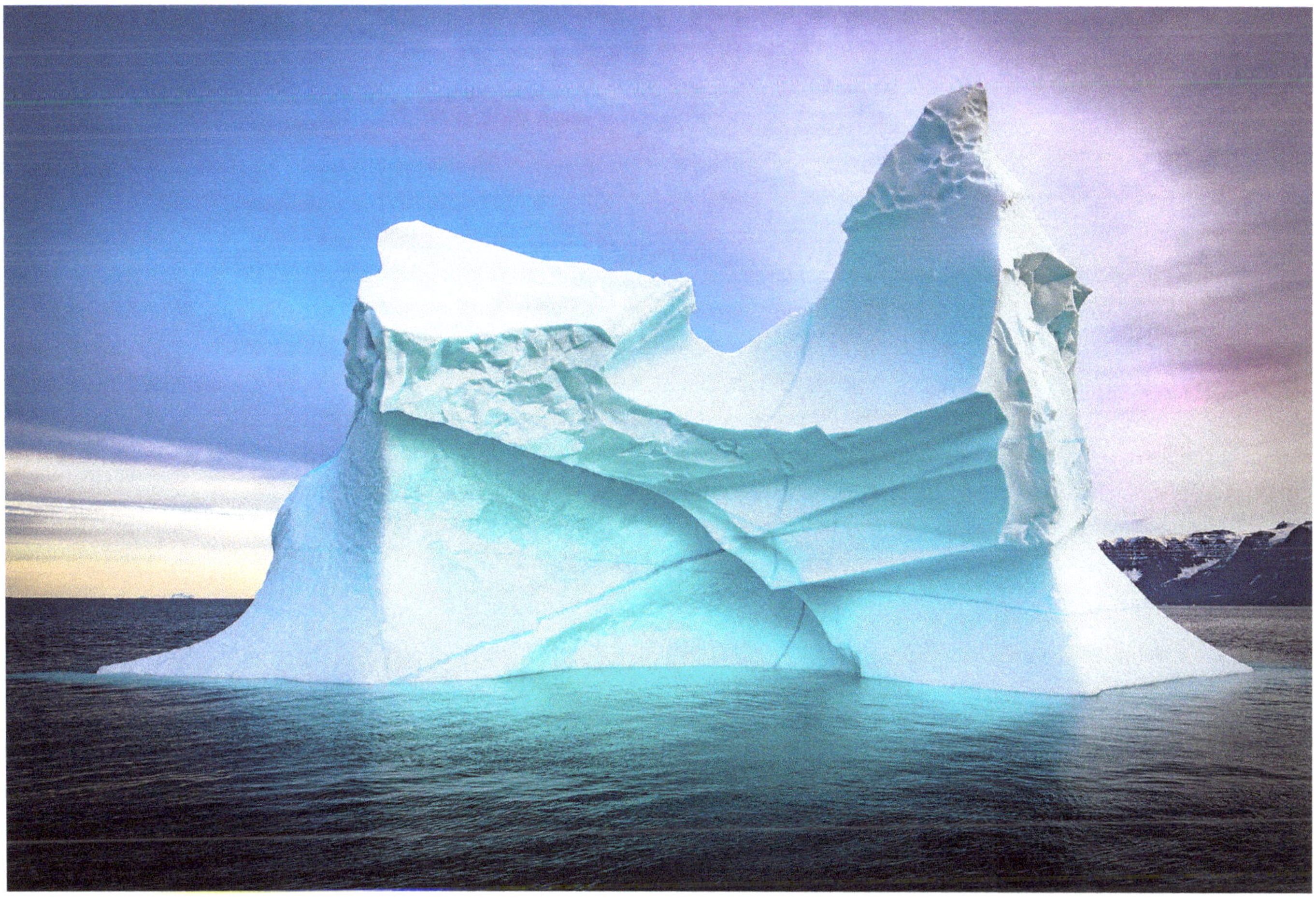

Crown Of Ice, 2022

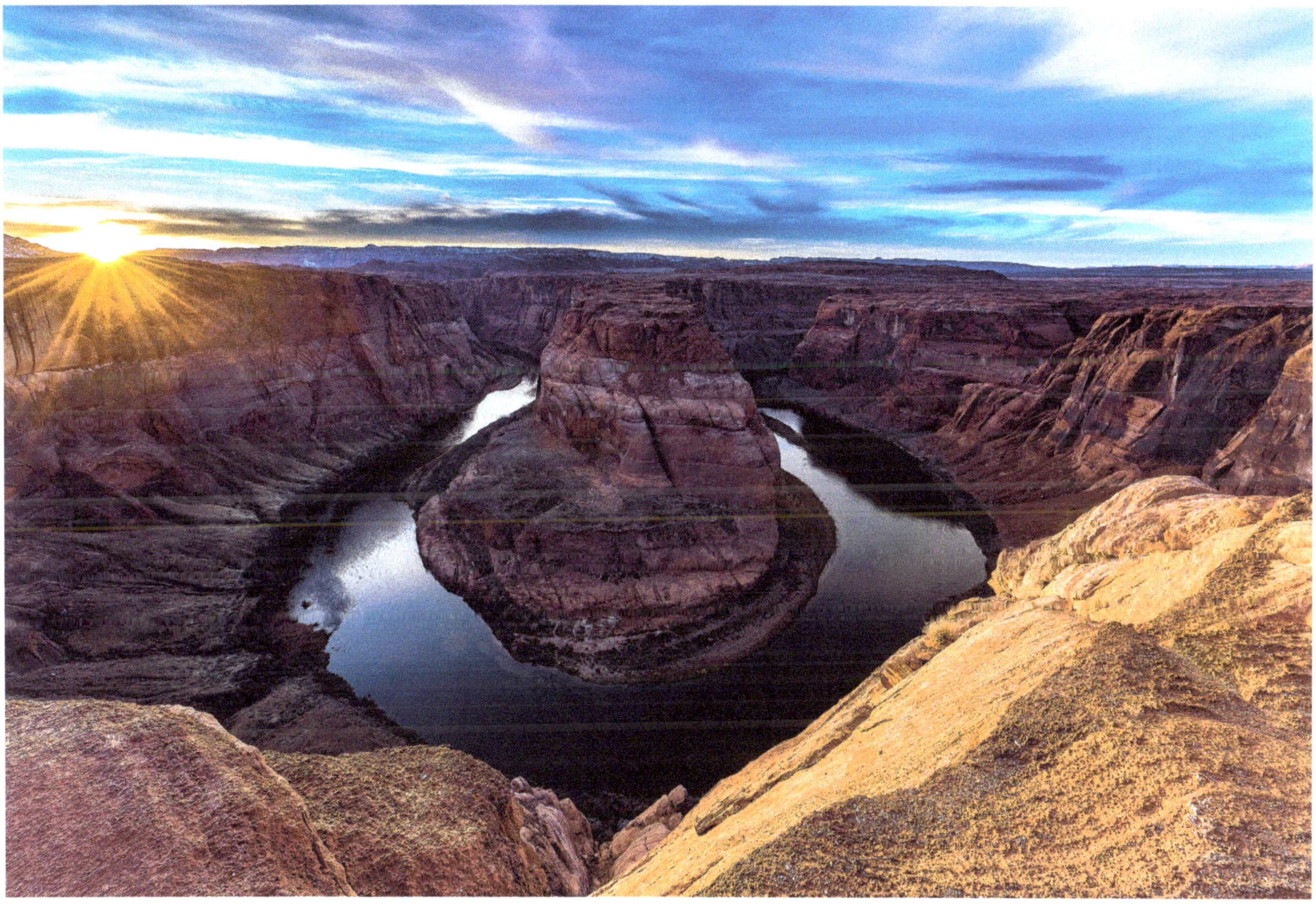

Horseshoe Canyon, 2020

CEVIGA

United Kingdom | ceviga.com

Ceviga is a Korean female artist with a nomadic soul. Her London studio is a compact space which concentrates inspiration and memories drawn from her various experiences of living and working internationally. It is the origin of light. Ceviga is a prolific artist who creates with extraordinary vitality, passion and physical involvement as well as showcasing her artwork frequently in high-profile contexts, such as Palazzo Mora (Venice) during the 59th Venice Biennale, START Art Fair at Saatchi Gallery (London) and more. 'Sunshine Soul' is a recent series of works visualising new perspectives on Ceviga's key themes of exploration: birth, in-betweenness and the relation of body - consciousness -spirit. Deeply introspective yet highly sensitive to society-wide issues, the artist is envisioning a state of liberation and newfound energy in tandem with the world's emergence out of the Covid-19 pandemic. Her canvases are the background upon which life spirals out of a simple dot in a mesmerising dance.

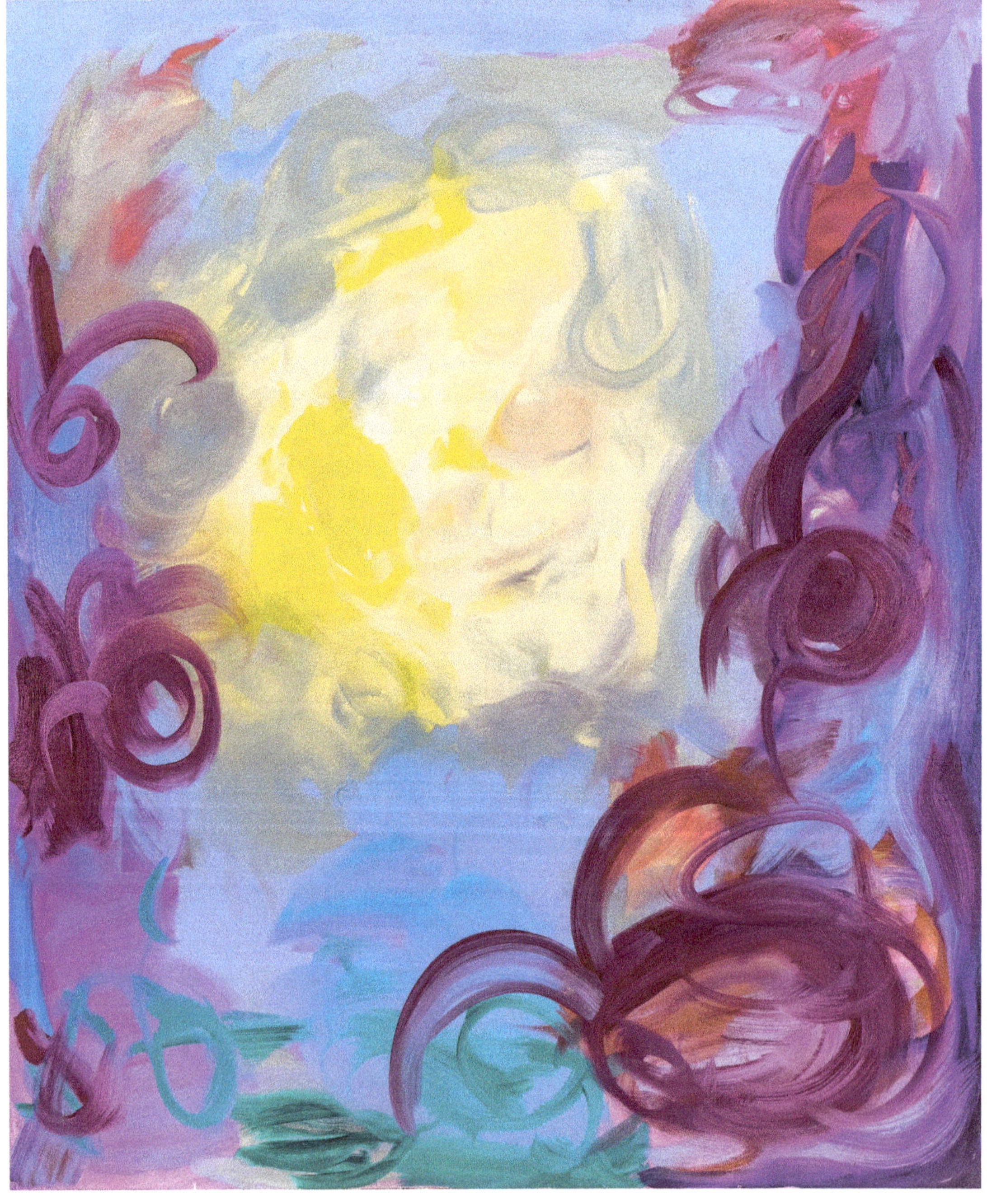

Sunshine Soul, 2022 (oil on canvas, 186x155cm)

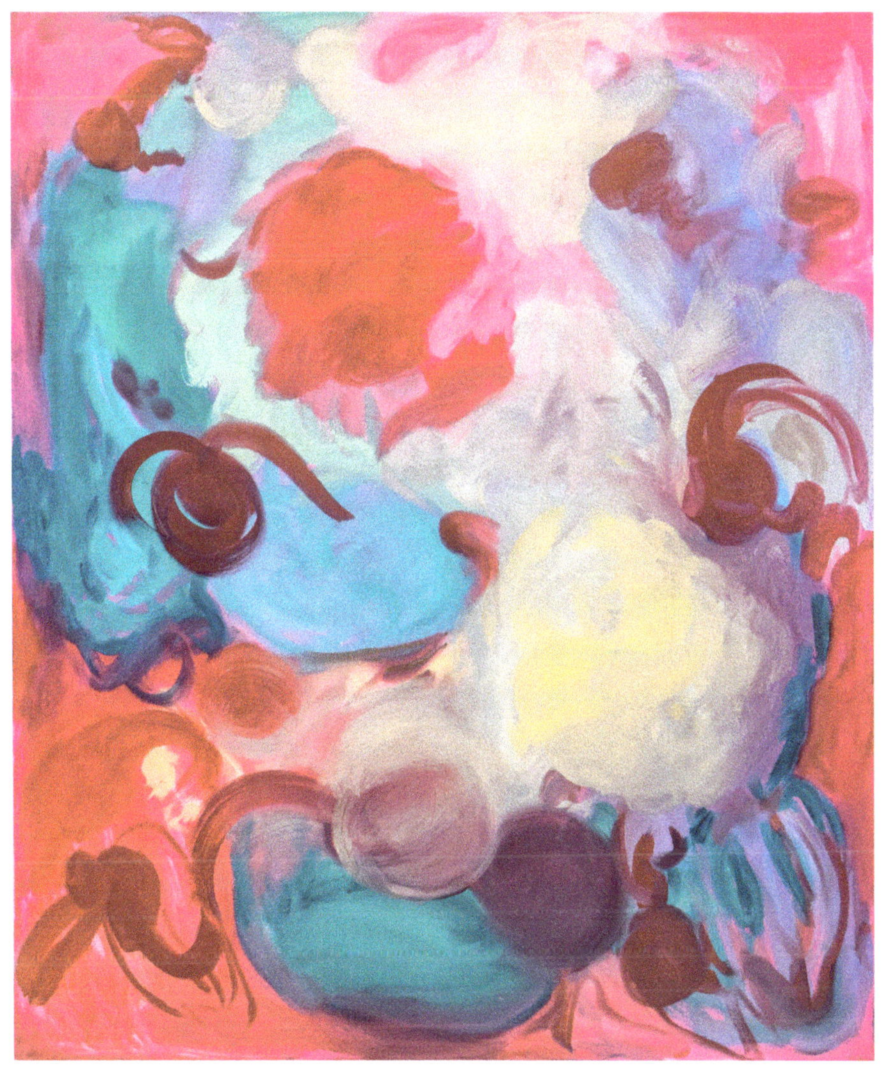

Sunshine Soul, 2022 (oil on canvas, 186x155cm)

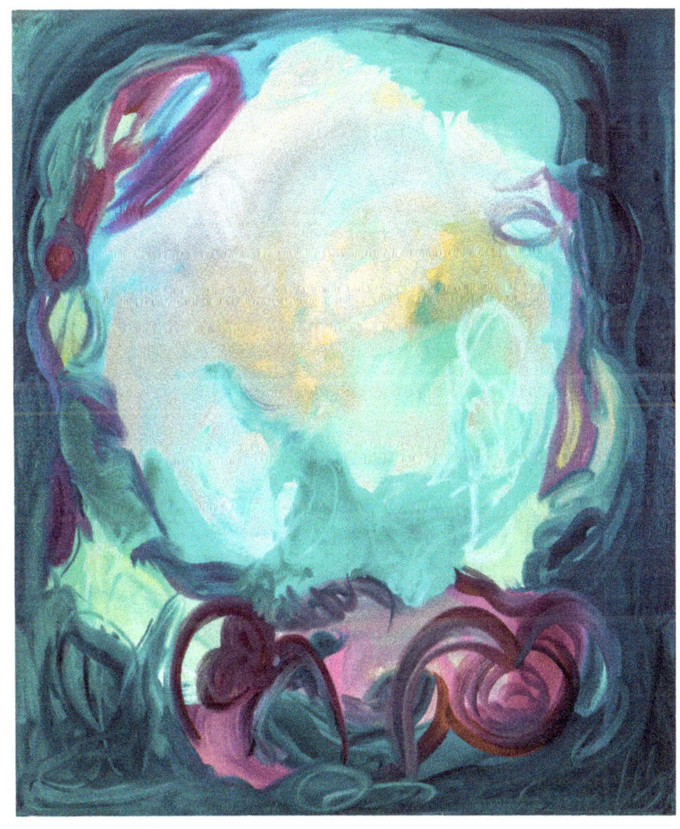

Sunshine Soul, 2022 (oil on canvas, 186x155cm)

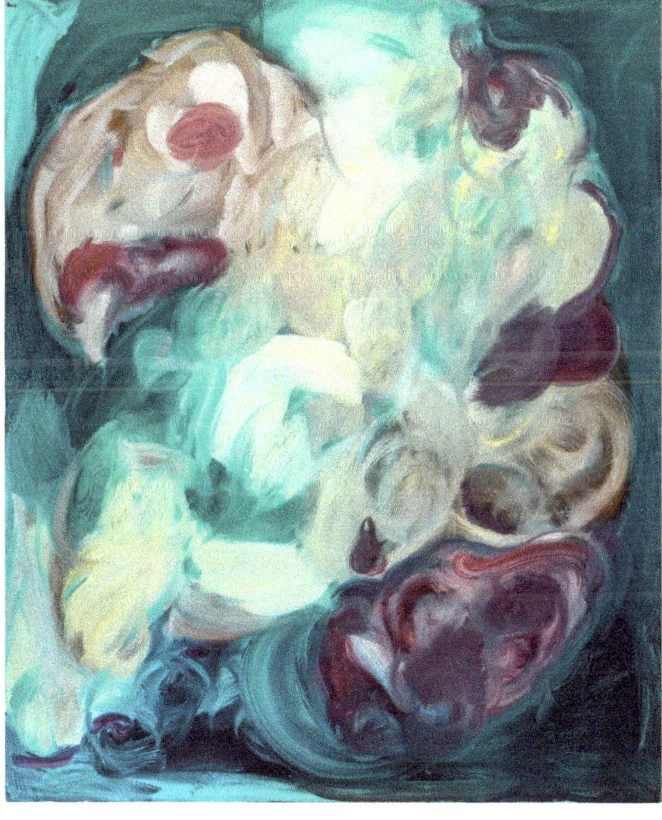

Sunshine Soul, 2022 (oil on canvas, 186x155cm)

JULIE REBY WAAS

United States | intuitiveabstractart.com

Julie Reby Waas has been creating abstract drawings for as long as she can remember. It was only during the isolating, stressful time of the coronavirus pandemic, however, that Waas began turning her original designs into artwork. Waas felt a desire to bring joy into her life and the lives of others through creative expression, using bright color and compelling patterns to stimulate the viewer's spontaneous reaction to each one of her pieces. Her geometric shapes and patterns serve as a way to bring order to her sometimes disordered life, and Waas identifies three recurring symbols in her work: vines, Venn diagrams, and jigsaw puzzle-like designs. To her, these symbols represent friendship, connection, common ground, and fragments coming together to create a bigger picture, which all relate to Waas's belief that everything and everyone is interrelated in some way, and when we come together in friendship and strength we create a beautiful tapestry. In addition to creating her art, Waas also works as a labor and employment lawyer at Baptist Health South Florida. She exhibits her work in galleries in New York, London, Madrid and Miami, and is influenced by other geometrically-inclined predecessors like Plet Mondrian and Joan Miró. Most potently, Waas is inspired by her autistic son, Jonathan, who as a little boy would mix plaid shorts with bright, geometric t-shirts to create his own bold and unique style. Waas's unique style successfully achieves her goal of bringing happiness and enthusiasm to her viewers.

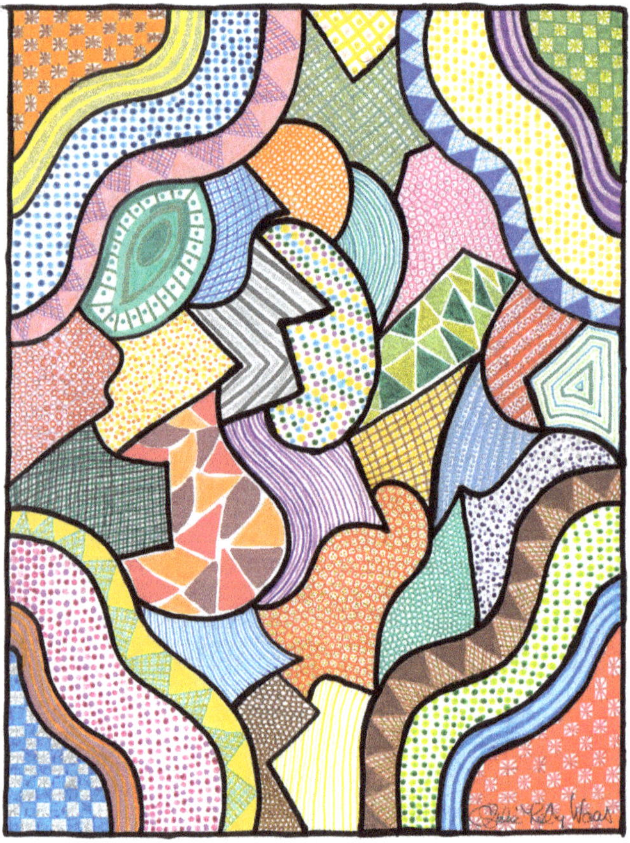

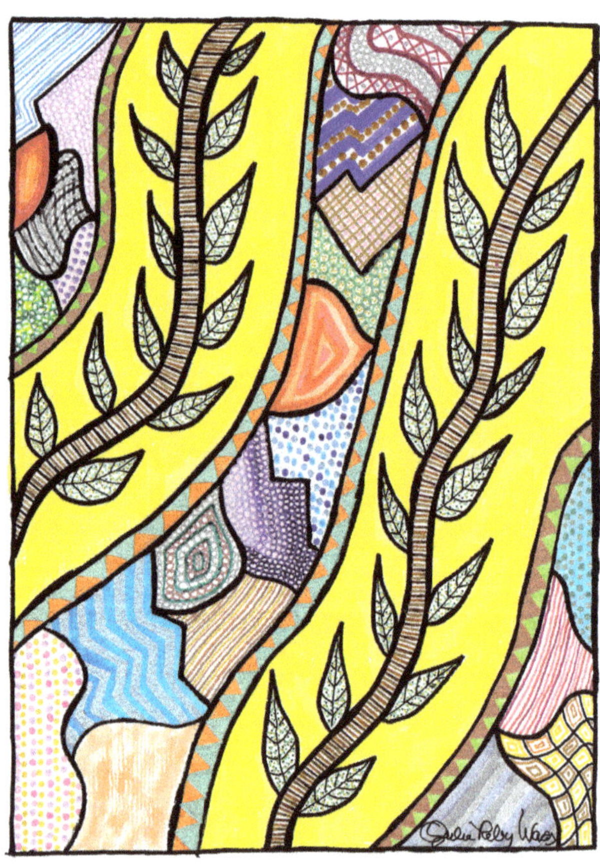

Jigsaw, 2022, Acrylic on paper, 27.95 x 35.56 cm

Leave It Be, Watercolor & Acrylic Drawing on Art Paper;
14.25" X 17.5" (Including Frame)

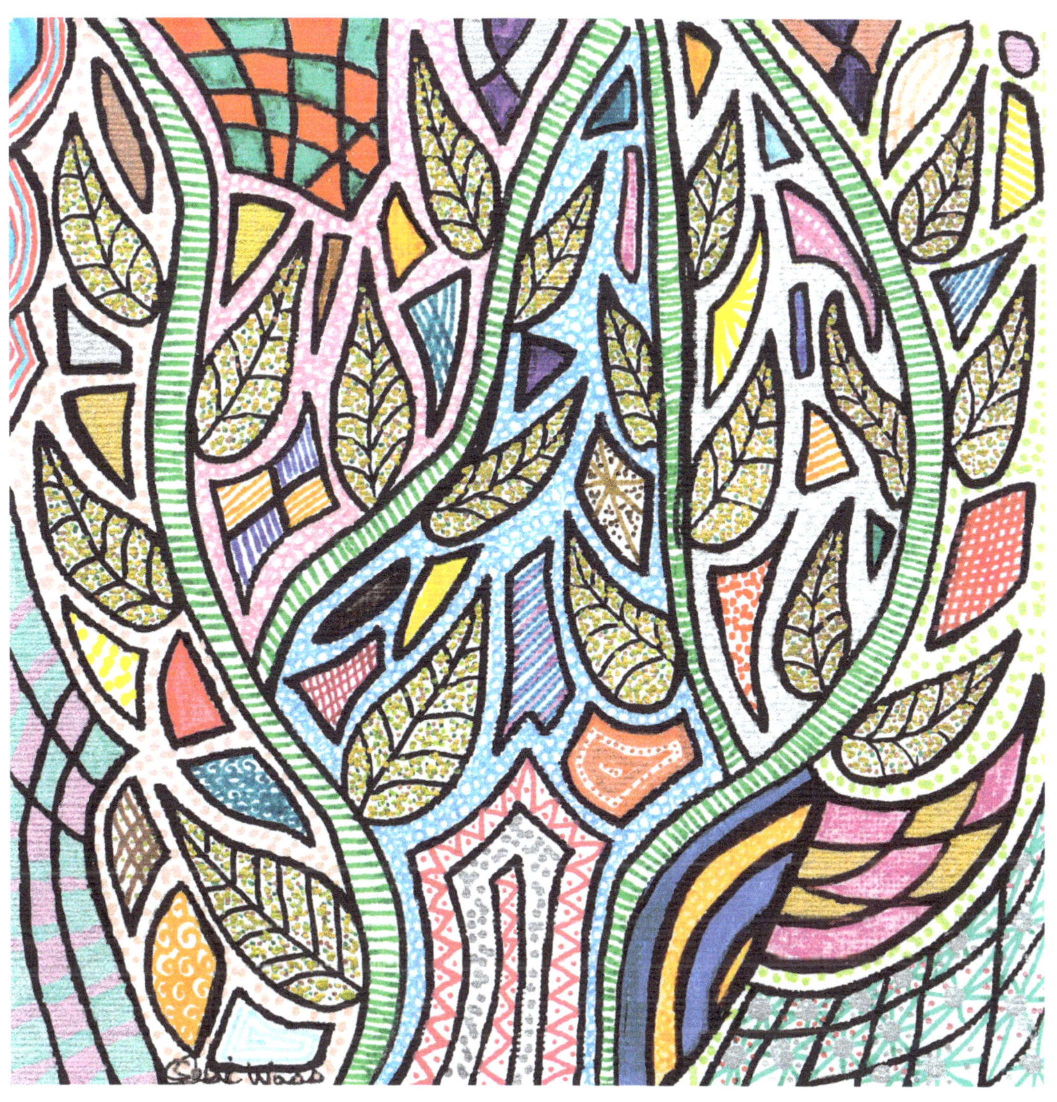

Autumn, 2021, Acrylic on paper, 15.24 x 15.24 cm

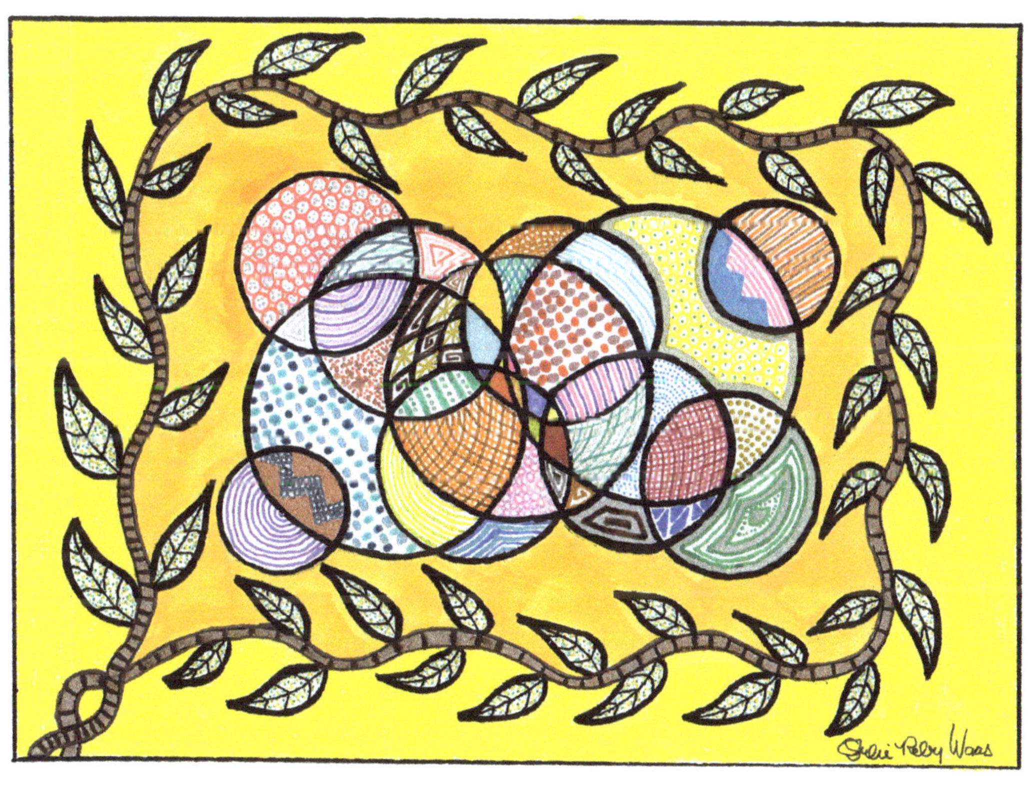

Venn on the Vine, 2021, Acrylic and Watercolor on paper, 22.86 x 27.94 cm

DOMINIE CHAN

Hong Kong - China | dominieandartworks.com

Dominie is inspired by her emotional responses to Nature. For her, the seas that surround Hong Kong are her nature and she finds inspiration in her sojourns to the many beaches around the island. With her senses and sensibilities, she has discerned the patterns and textures with which Nature expresses herself and Dominie's work resonates with the synchronicities that she has sussed through her many intimate interactions with Nature. Inspired by the myriadity of Nature, she works across a multitude of media and materials to create art that hopes to instigate a deeper dialogue about / with Nature.

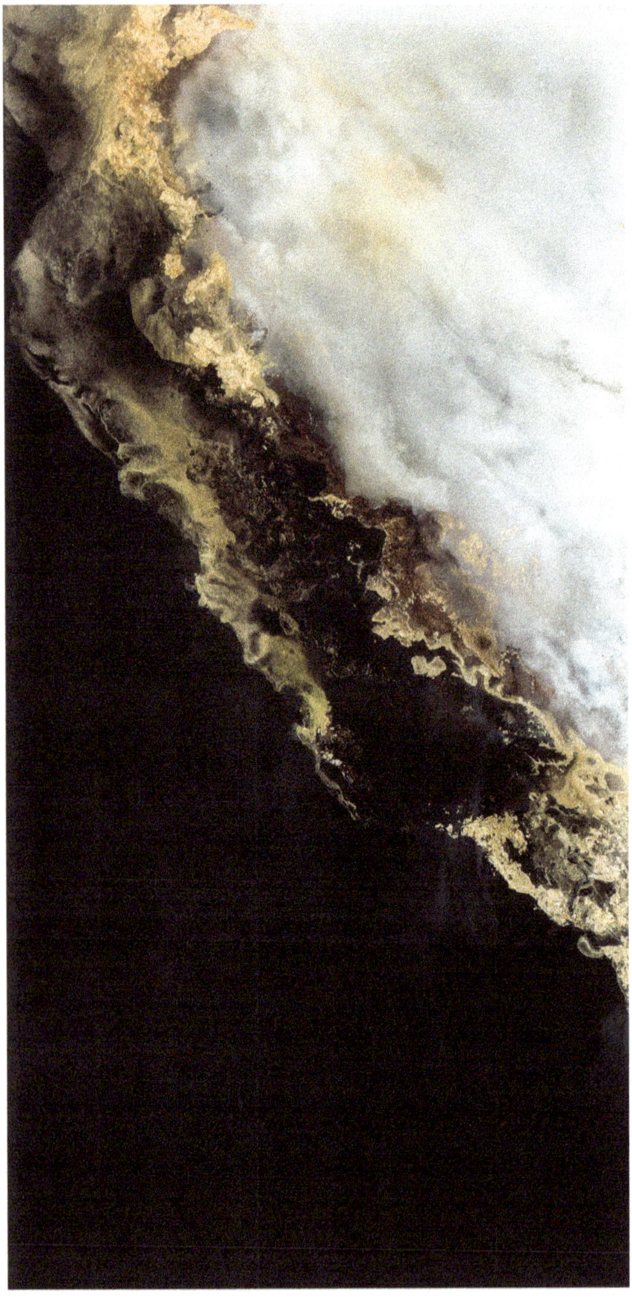

Mer Dorée, 2022. Layered pure 24k gold, acrylic, ink on mounted canvas, 1220 x 610 mm

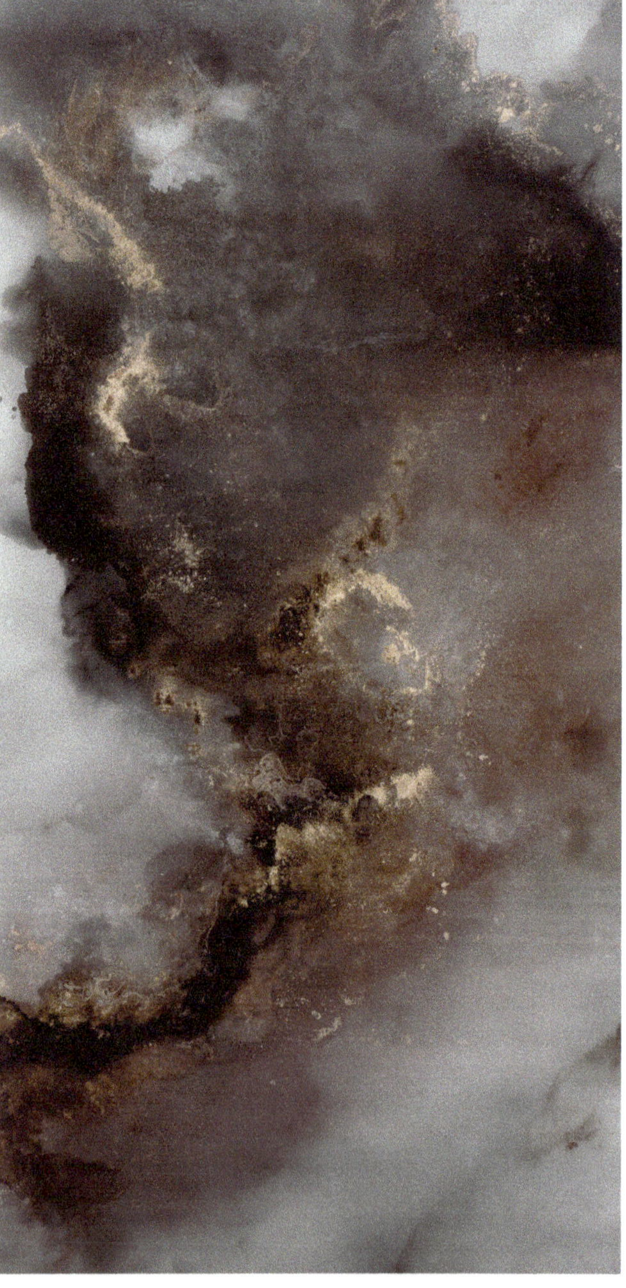

Dance of Dusk, 2022. Ink on mounted canvas, 600 x 900 mm

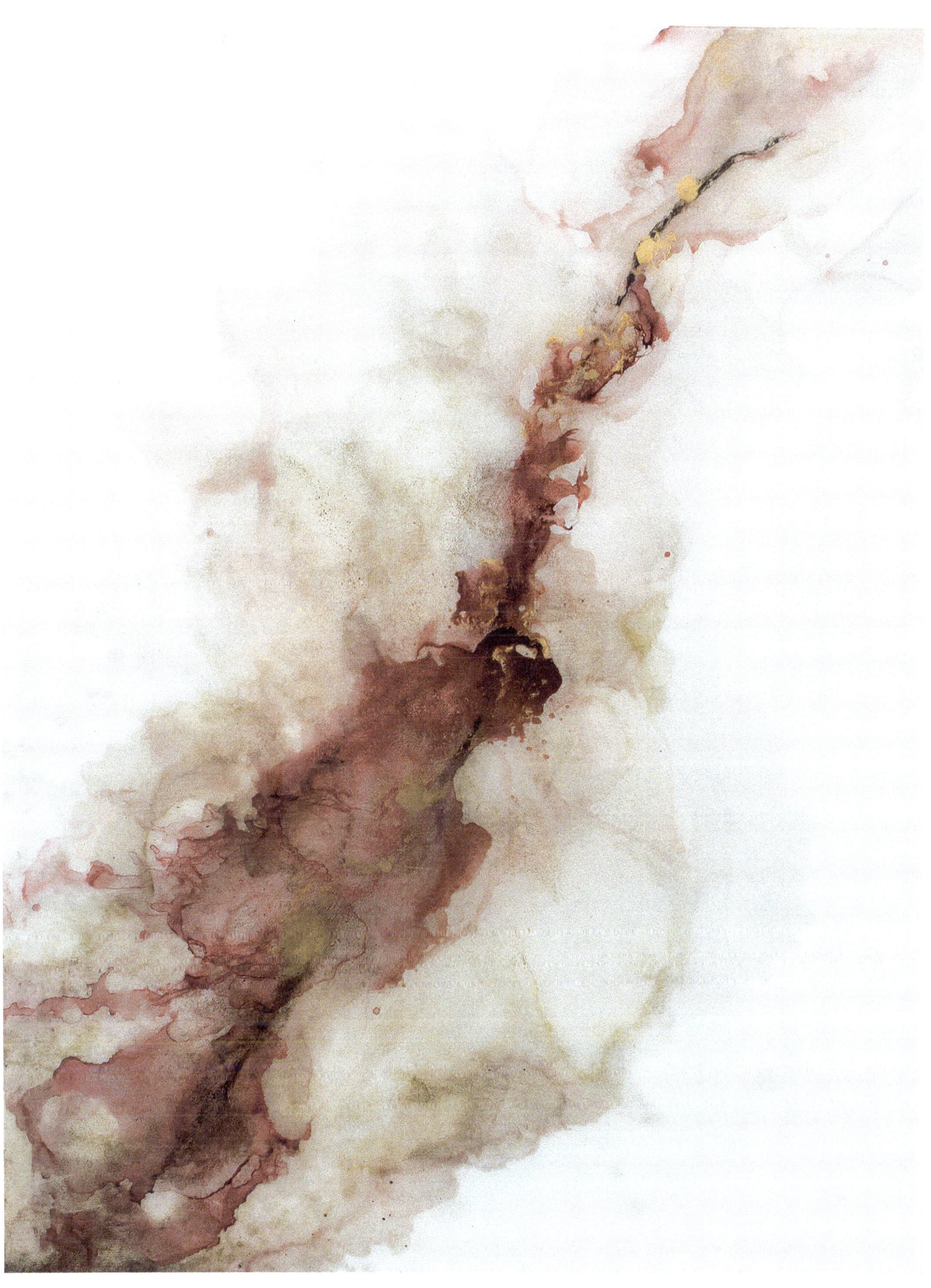

Lively Renaissance, 2020. Ink on mounted canvas, 1200 x 900 mm

FRÉDÉRIC DEMEUSE

Belgium | fredericdemeuse.com

Born in Belgium in 1978, Frédéric Demeuse is a naturalist and ornithologist by training. He lives and works in Brussels. Frédéric Demeuse's work aims to transcribe the vital energy, beauty and poetry of our world, from the most subtle details to the most remote and still primary forests to limitless aesthetics, through visual idealism with both revitalizing and resourcing stylisation purpose. From his explorations in immersion in the most varied and remote environments, he brings us back images whose purpose is to question us on the scale of time, on our relationship to the living community and stirs up our curiosity about what exists beyond our human condition. His images, combinations of living dreams and pure curiosity, give hope that mankind will never forget that our relationship with the biosphere is the most valuable element of our being and of our community of destiny. Author of several books, his work has won awards in the most prestigious international competitions including a first prize at the BBC Wildlife Photographer of the year. His work is regularly exhibited in Belgium, France and abroad. https://www.instagram.com/fredericdemeuse/

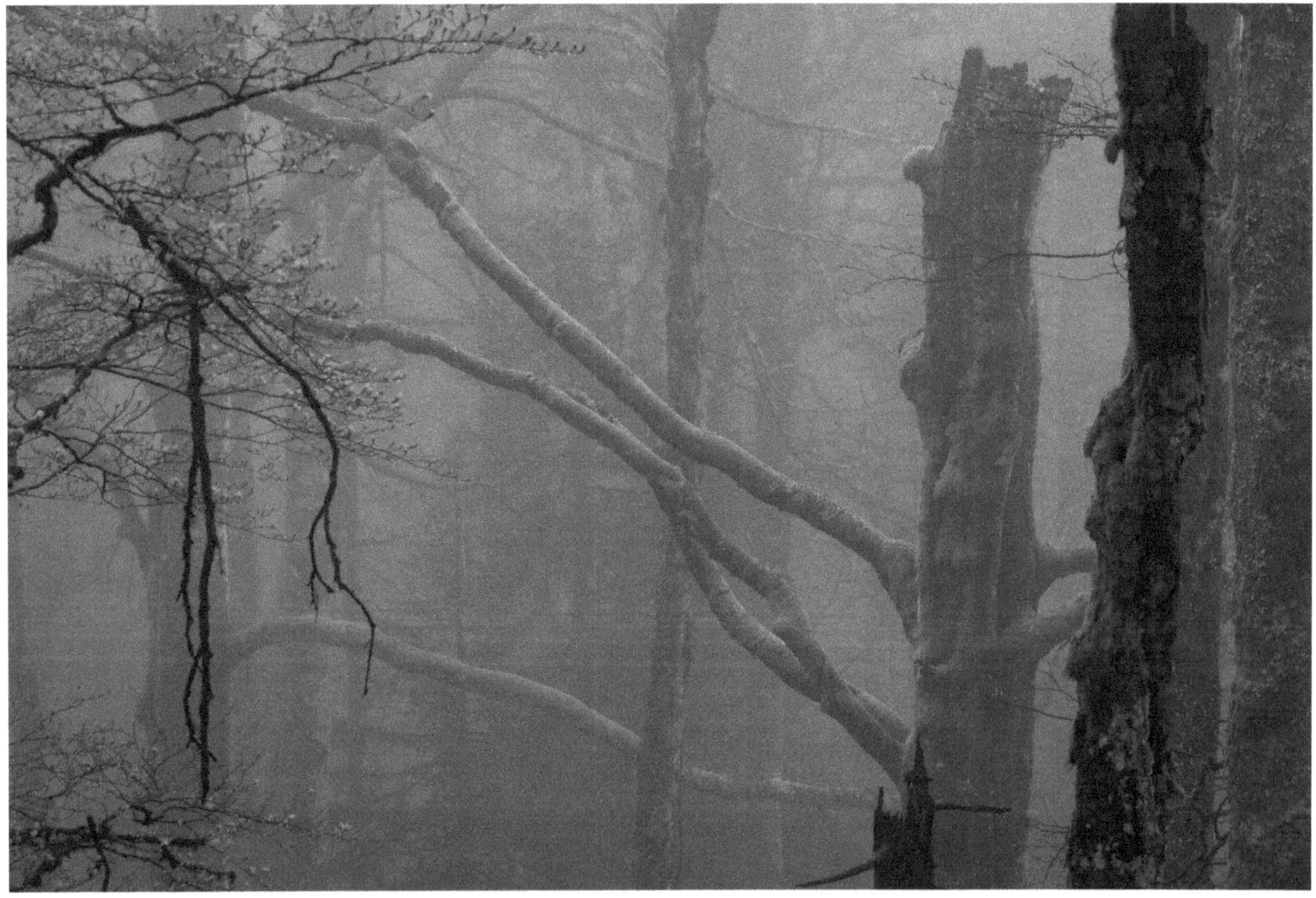

The Conductor, 2022. Impression on Fine-art paper, laminated on dibond, aluminum profiles and wooden frame, 80-120 cm

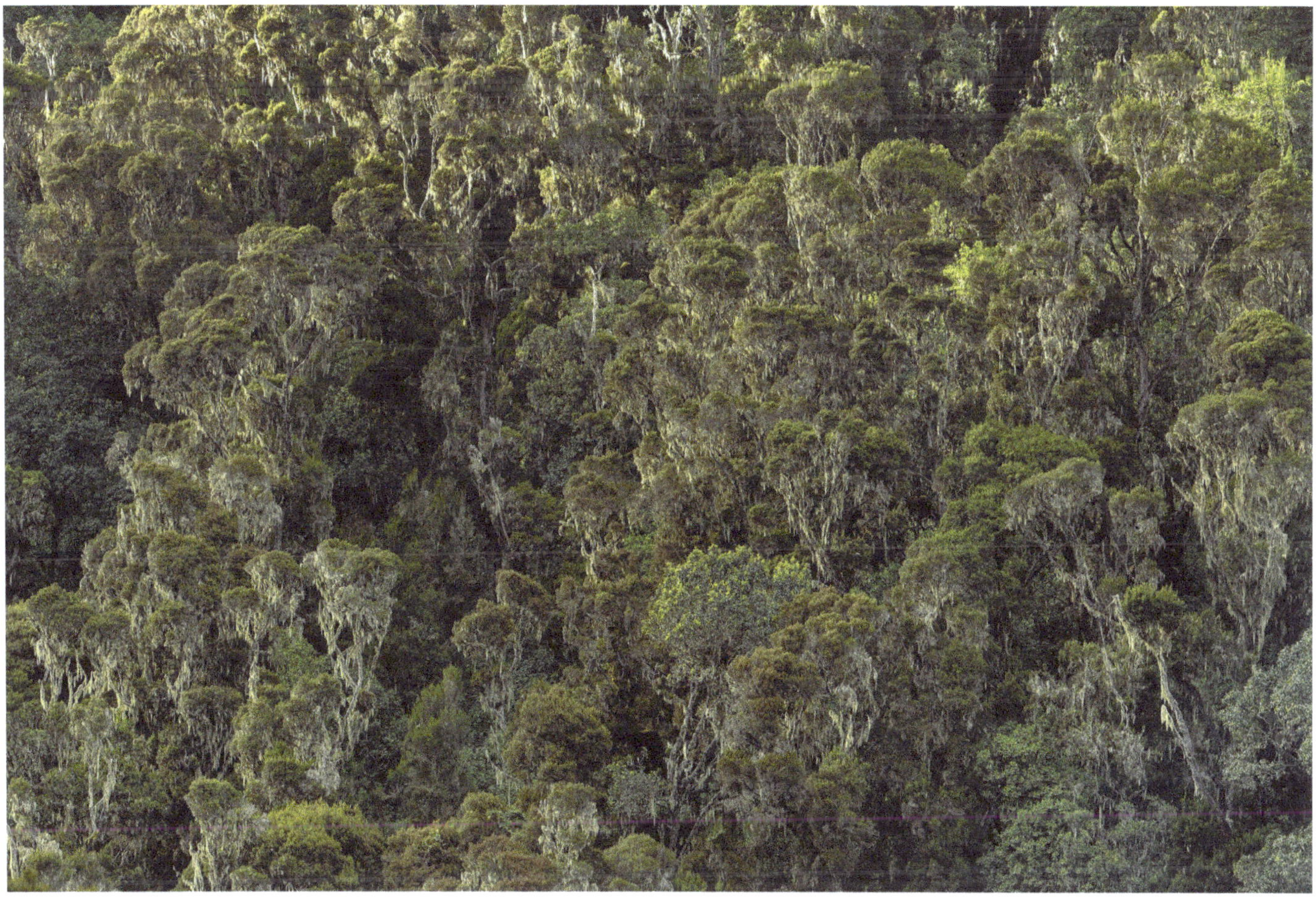

Primeval Eden, 2013. Impression on Fine-art paper, laminated on dibond, aluminum profiles and wooden frame, 80-120 cm

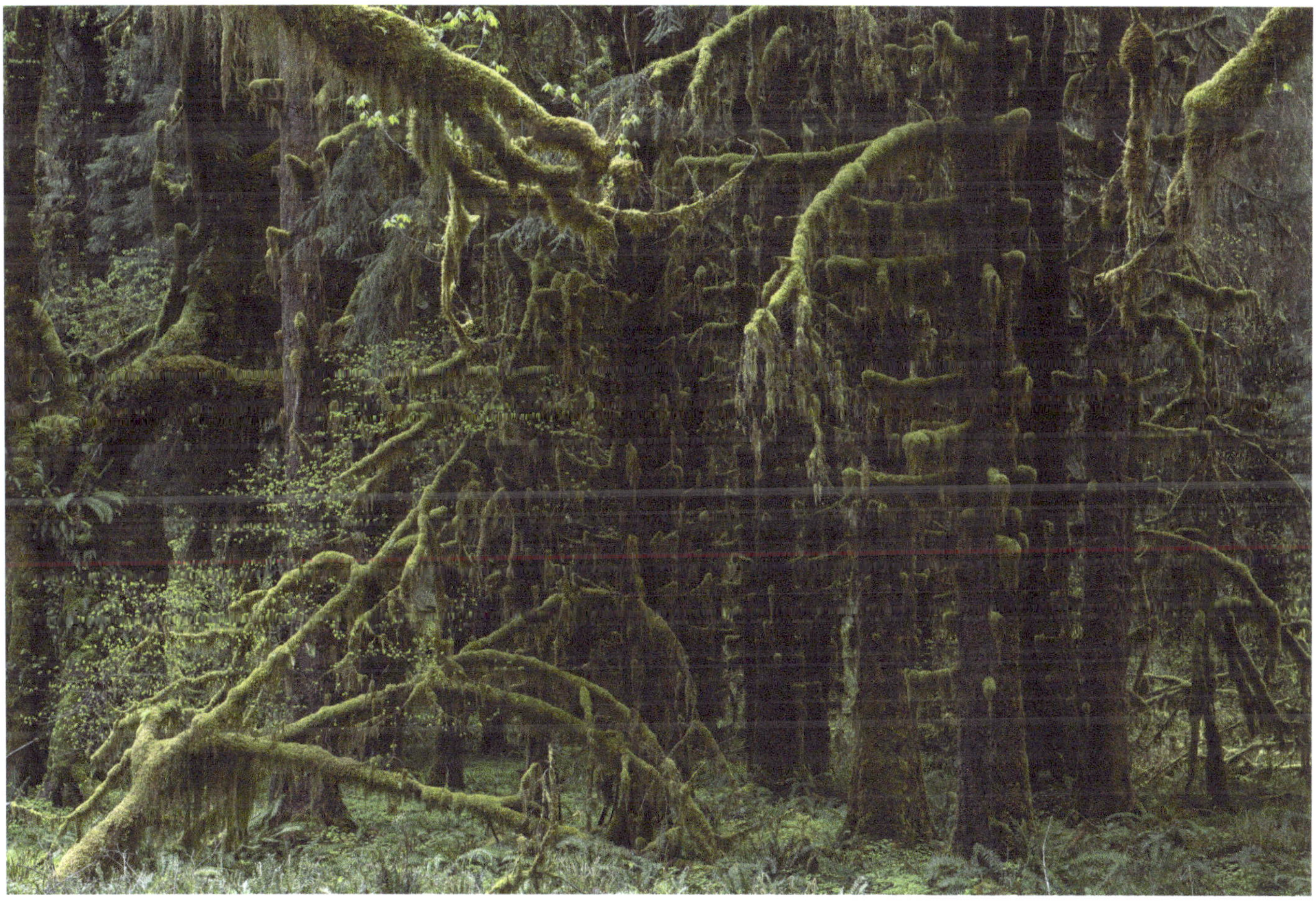

Primeval Green, 2017. Impression on Fine-art paper, laminated on dibond, aluminum profiles and wooden frame, 80-120 cm

MONIKA GLOVICZKI

United States | monikalgloviczki.com

Initially inspired by Impressionist art, Monika Gloviczki modernizes her work by incorporating elements of abstraction and reportage. Her artwork can be described as a form of silent music, a symphony played by pigments to form a harmony of composition and color; a song describing deeper layers and moving beyond the banalities of everyday life to reveal what is extraordinary. Gloviczki was born in Poland, but spent most of her adult life in Paris, where she earned her MD and PhD degrees and worked in the medical field. Gloviczki's artistic education began at an early age with her father, Stanislaw Kazmierczyk, a Polish painter and illustrator, who taught her the basics of drawings, gouache, and oil painting. She also took drawing and painting classes in Warsaw, Paris, at the Ateliers du Carrousel du Louvre, and later in the US. Gloviczki has garnered recognition for her art, exhibiting regularly in the US, but also in France, Italy, and Azerbaijan. Among her shows the most notable are her annual exhibitions at Agora Gallery in New York, NY, from 2016 to present; three exhibitions at M.A.D.S. Art Gallery in Milano, Italy in 2021; the Art 3F Art fair in Paris from 2018 to 2020 and the 19th Salon International d'Art Contemporain in Paris, in 2016. She currently lives and works in Scottsdale, Arizona as a full-time artist. Her works belong to private and public collections in the US and in France.

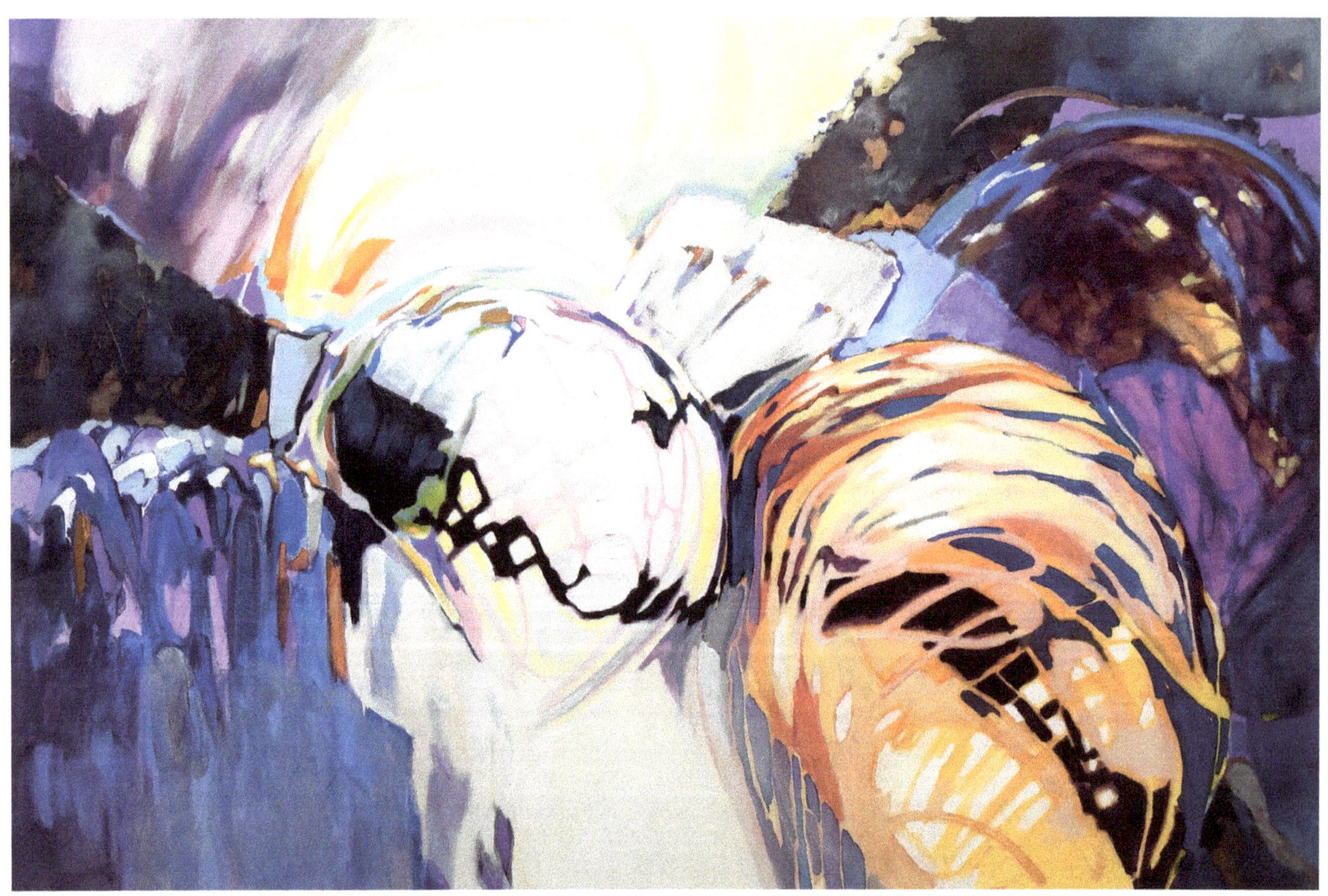

"Interception" 2019, Acrylic on canvas 48x72 inches

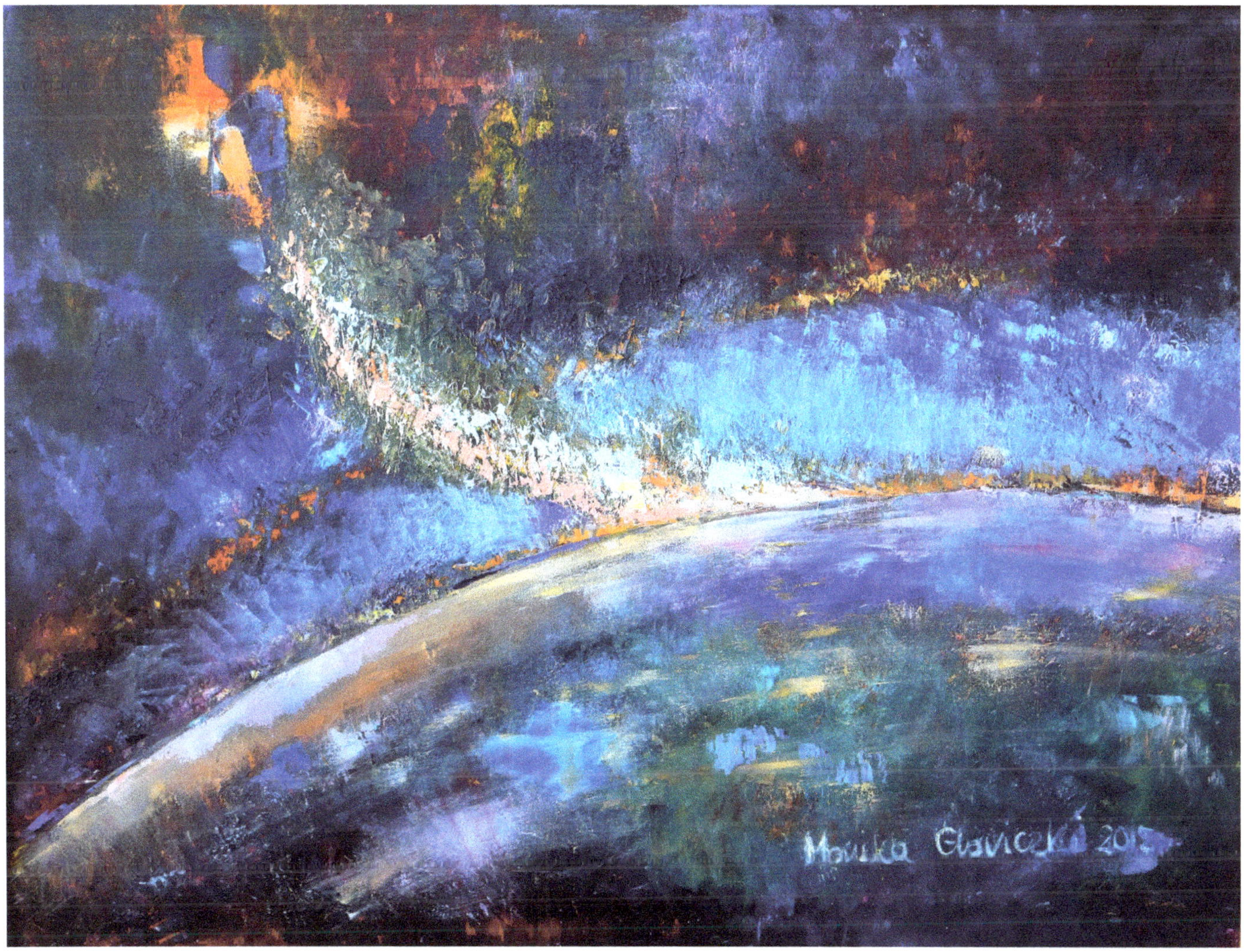

Primeval Eden, 2013. Impression on Fine-art paper, laminated on dibond, aluminum profiles and wooden frame, 80-120 cm

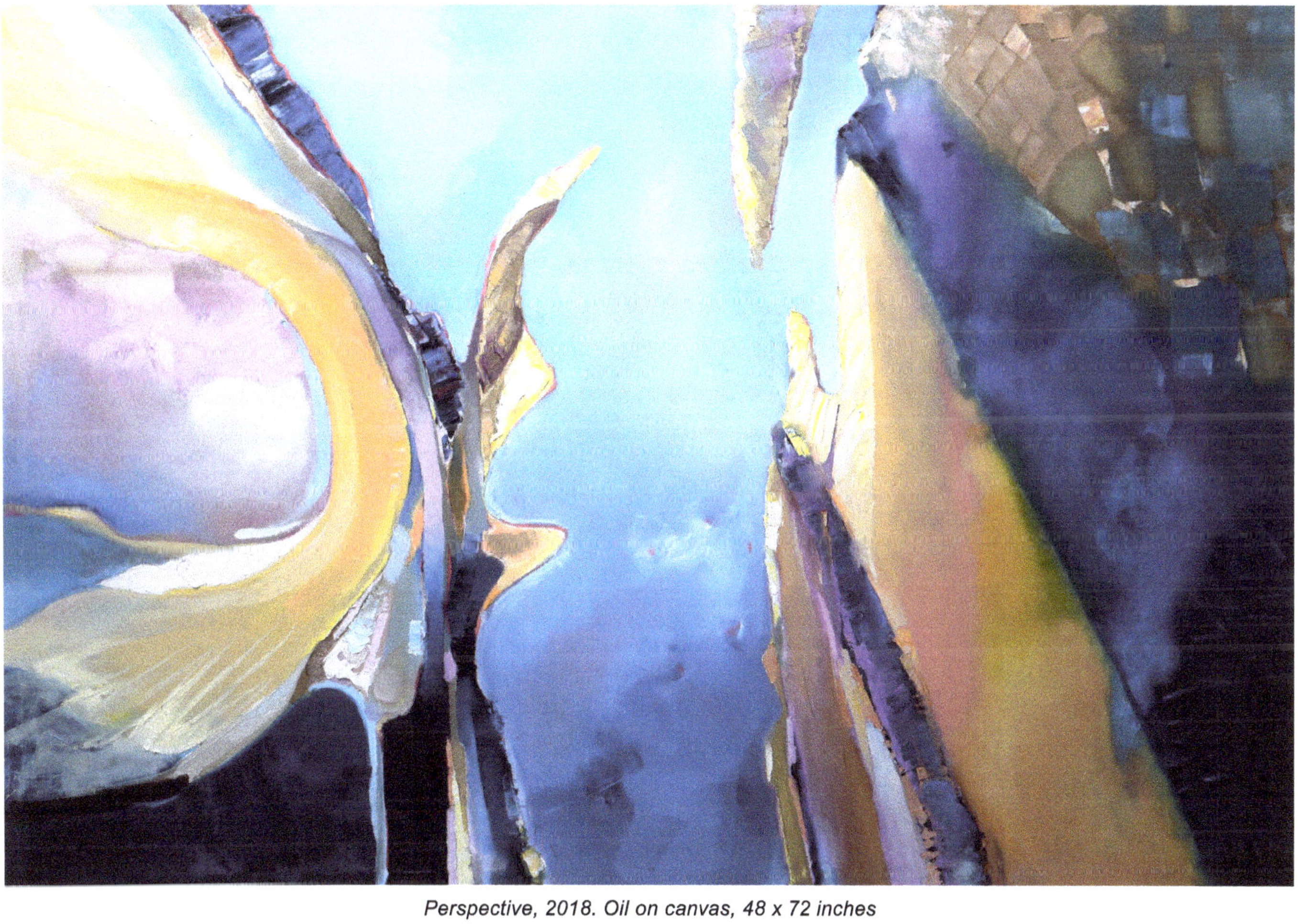

Perspective, 2018. Oil on canvas, 48 x 72 inches

KAT KLEINMAN

United States | katkleinmanart.com

Kat Kleinman is a photo collage artist from the Sacramento, California area. She began her career as an artist in 2016, after she retired as a psychotherapist, working with homeless people for 20 years. Her past work is referenced because it does inform her current work with a focus on positivity and making people feel better, if only for a moment. Kat specializes in floral collages, because the individual flowers combine to create a new and cohesive form, reflective of the healing process. She takes her own photographs, which is important to Kat, because it separates the integrity of her work from those who use more impersonal internet downloads as a source. Each flower is hand cut, a process she calls meditative, and a single collage may require dozens of individual blossoms. Kat is enthusiastic about the potential for color to positively influence emotions, ultimately leading to better relationships between people. Kat's work has been seen in international exhibitions in Tokyo, Barcelona, and Hong Kong, as well as numerous books and magazines, both nationally and internationally.

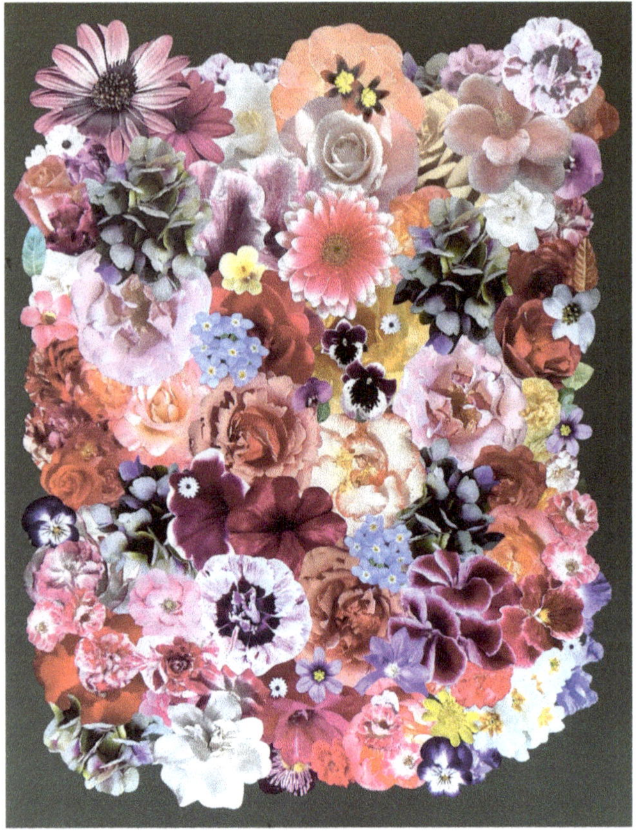

The Happy Garden 2019

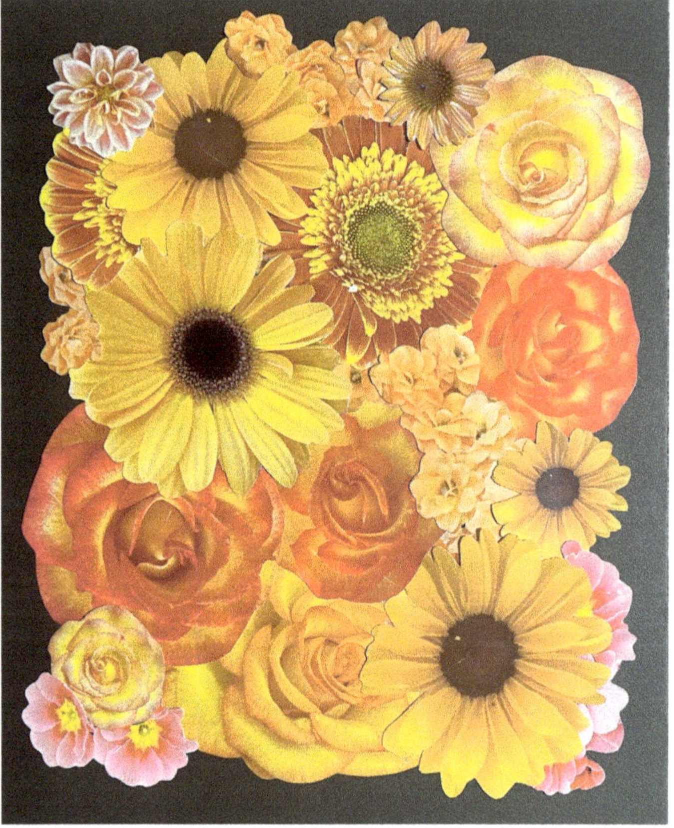

Desert garden, 2021. Oil on canvas, 24 x 20 inches

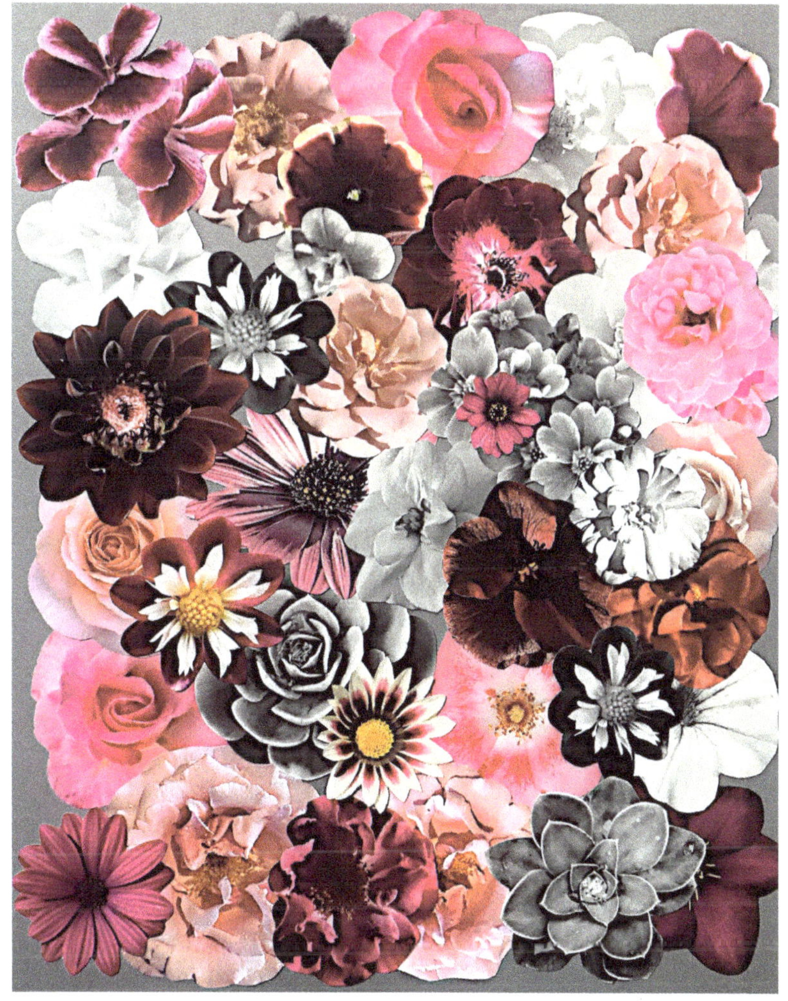

I Prefer Platinum 2019

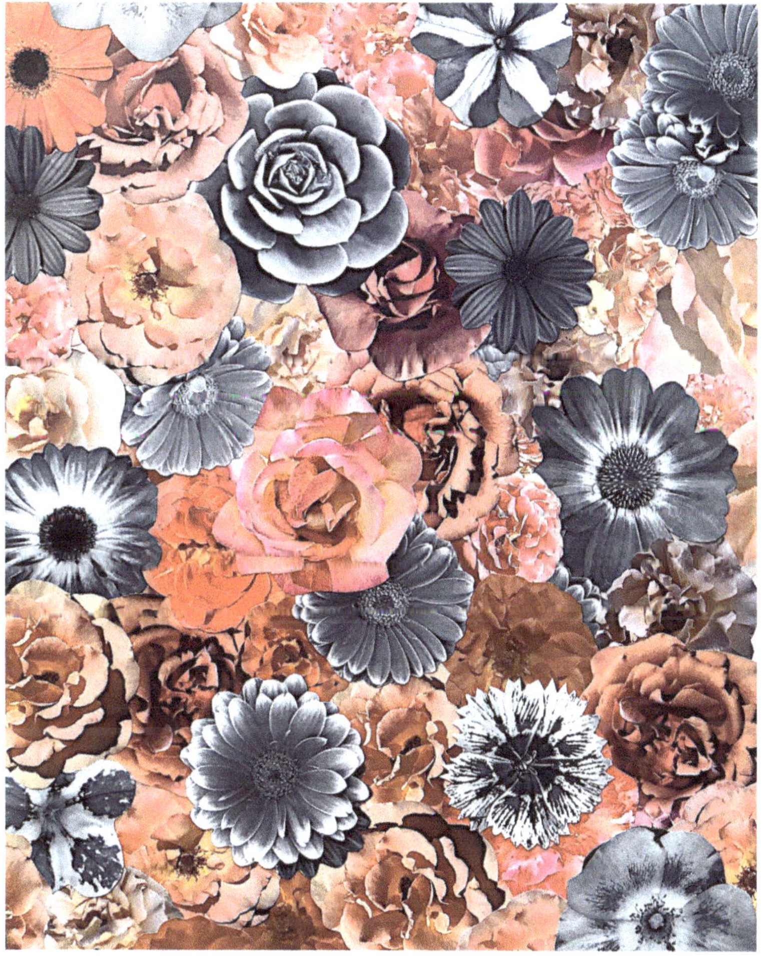

Working Together 2019

IRINA HOWARD

United States | irinahoward.com

Irina Howard is a New York-based artist who explores the complexity of human life experiences. She is internationally recognized for rigorously composed and sublimely musing paintings and sculptures. Her innovative style is inspired by organic forms and textures, bridging reality and imagination and giving a physical form to a conceptual idea. Howard was born and grew up in Ukraine. As a child, she encountered traumatic events that influenced her interaction with the world through her drawings. In her youth, Howard spent time in the elite cultural group committed to arts and literature, where she established her lifelong passion for the arts. By lifting the burden off her shoulders, she emerged with the personal belief that the artist has no right to contribute any more pain to a world full of struggle and despair, which kept her in artistic silence for several years. Her creative reborn happened with a midlife crisis. Howard studied fine arts at the City University of New York and Yale Gordon College of Arts and Sciences. Howard is a recipient of several awards. Her recent recognition is the "Oscar of Visual Arts" as part of the Top 60 Masters of Contemporary Art in 2022 by Art Tour International Magazine. Her work has been widely published in magazines and art books worldwide, including "Important World Artists" by Worldwide Artbooks. Her recent exhibitions are at Museu Marítim de Barcelona in Spain, Art San Diego in California, and Hamptons Fine Art Fair in New York, USA. Her work highlights multiple private collections internationally.

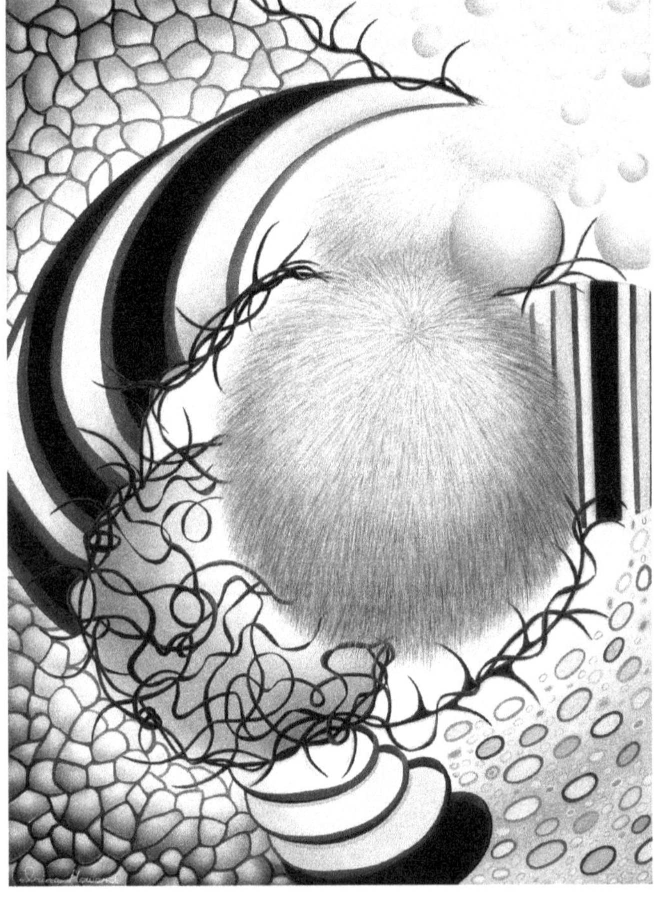

Hope, 2020. Oil on canvas, 102 x 76 cm

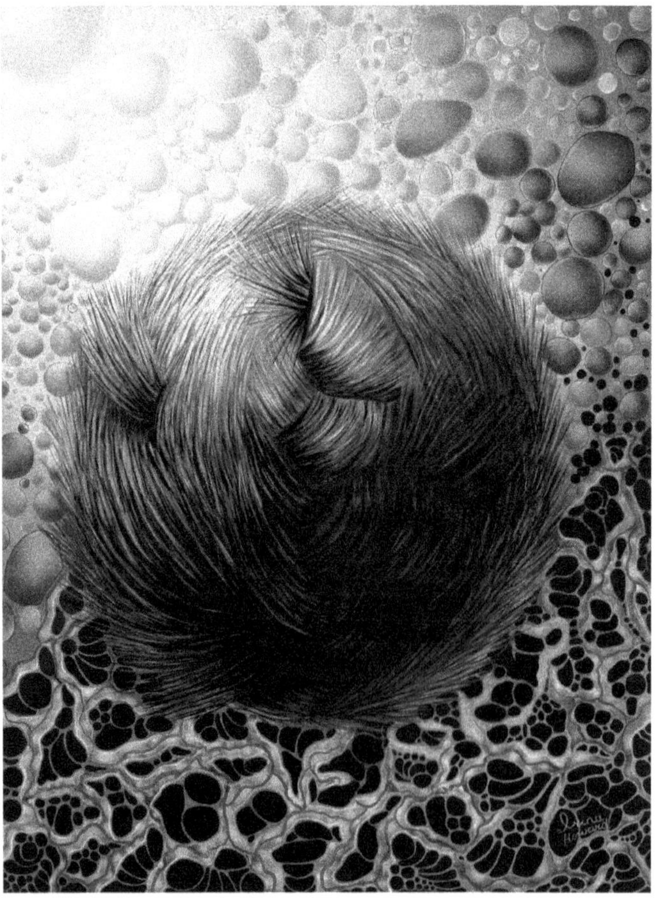

Addiction, 2021. Oil on canvas, 102 x 76 cm

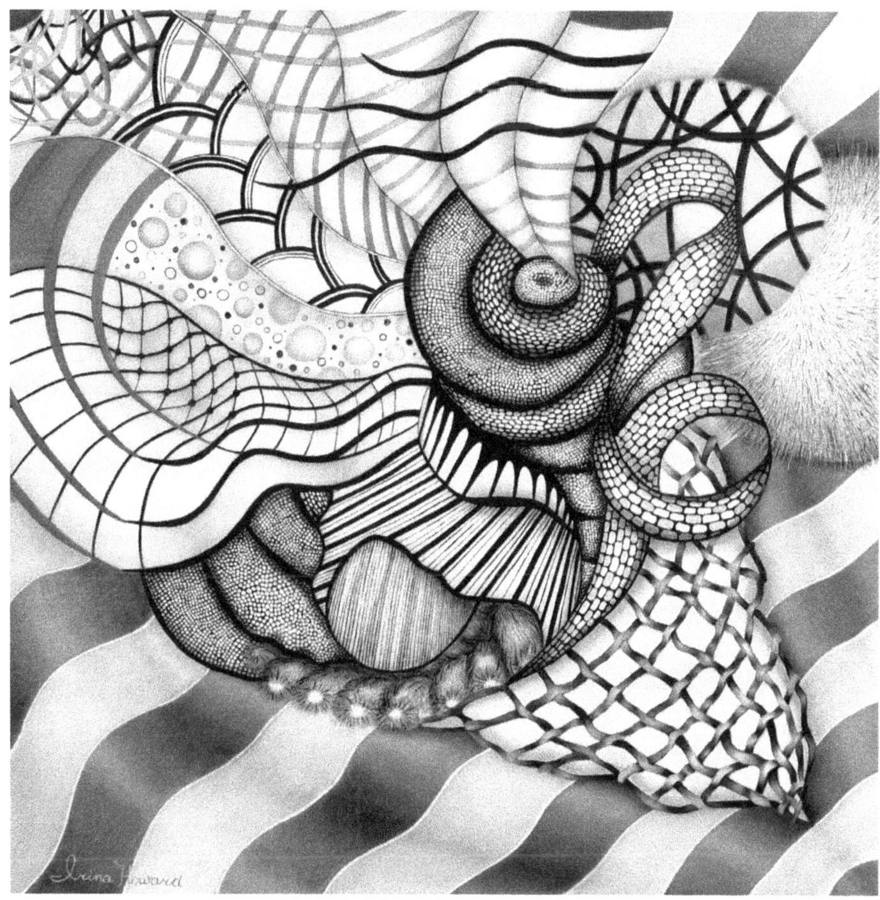

Patterns of Life, 2019. Oil on canvas, 61 x 61 cm

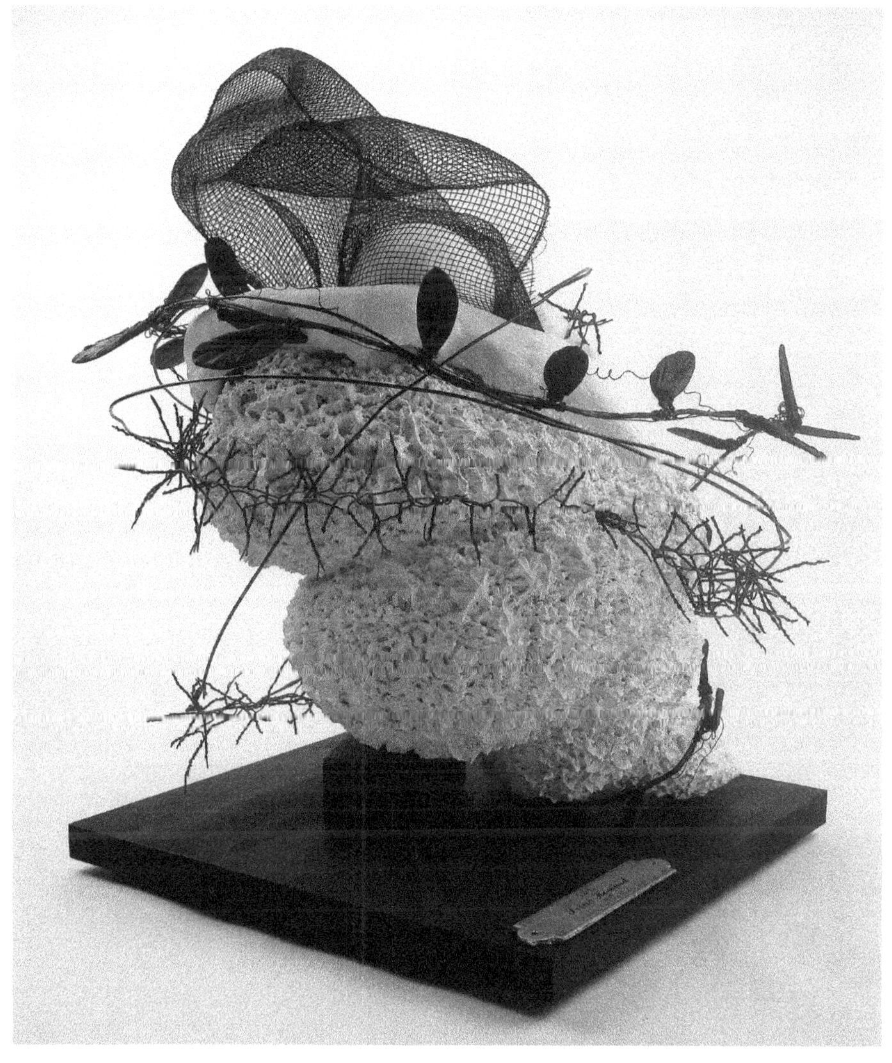

Representation of Life, 2020. Sculpting wires, mesh wire sheet, modeling compound, paper-mashe, spray paint, 41 x 41 x 38 cm

RAMÓN RIVAS

Spain - rivismo.com | ramonrivas-rivismo.blogspot.com

Born in the novelized Land of Don Quixote, Ciudad Real (La Mancha / Spain). His family environment and the multidisciplinary influence of his professional activities; in sports, music, engineering, inventions and art, in Castilla-La Mancha and Madrid, was decisive for artistic creation, of a very personal and different style, called Rivismo, based on the application of Experiential Brushstrokes and , with the aim of bringing novelty and freshness to the world of art. He has made exhibitions; Individual and collective, in; Spain, China, South Korea, Italy, Denmark, United States, among others. Present in several Art Fairs in the United States, there are also his works in the Museum collection, in; Spain, Denmark and South Korea. He has participated in many books, art magazines and social networks, having received prestigious international awards. The work he does defines his personal hallmark. He uses his creativity to be different and look for artistic proposals that surprise, excite and motivate. He applies his imagination to develop creative, innovative works that interact with the viewer. His work is orderly and methodical. He supervises the good execution and composition. He also incorporates scientific and current issues. He makes the painting a walkable space for the viewer. He creates images of precision, with surprising density and such depth that they are visually captivating. His works aim to provoke and catch the viewer, turning him into a creative artist during his visual journey and while the images recorded on his retina last.

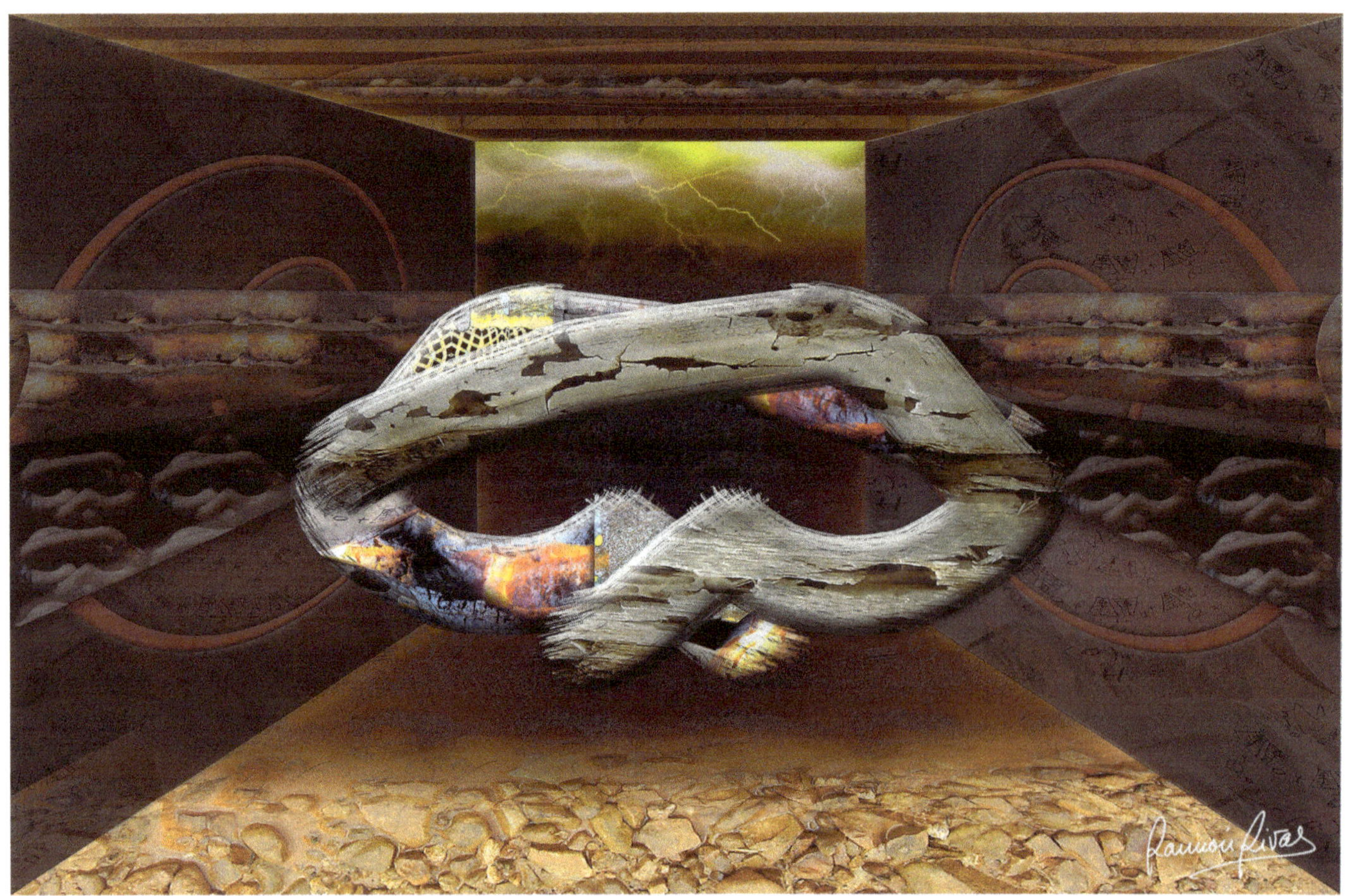

Whims of Balance 2015 Mixed media-Rivismo 130x200 cm

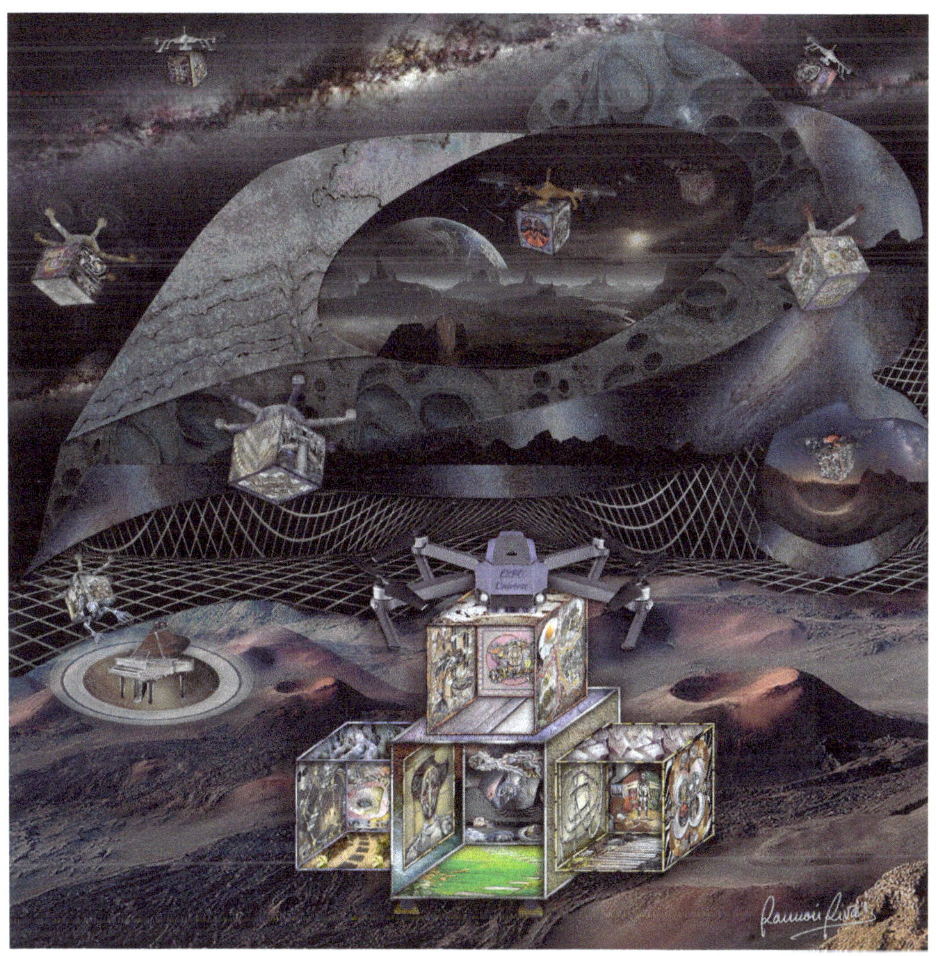

Art Drones in the Universe II 2022 Mixed media-Rivismo 195x195 cm

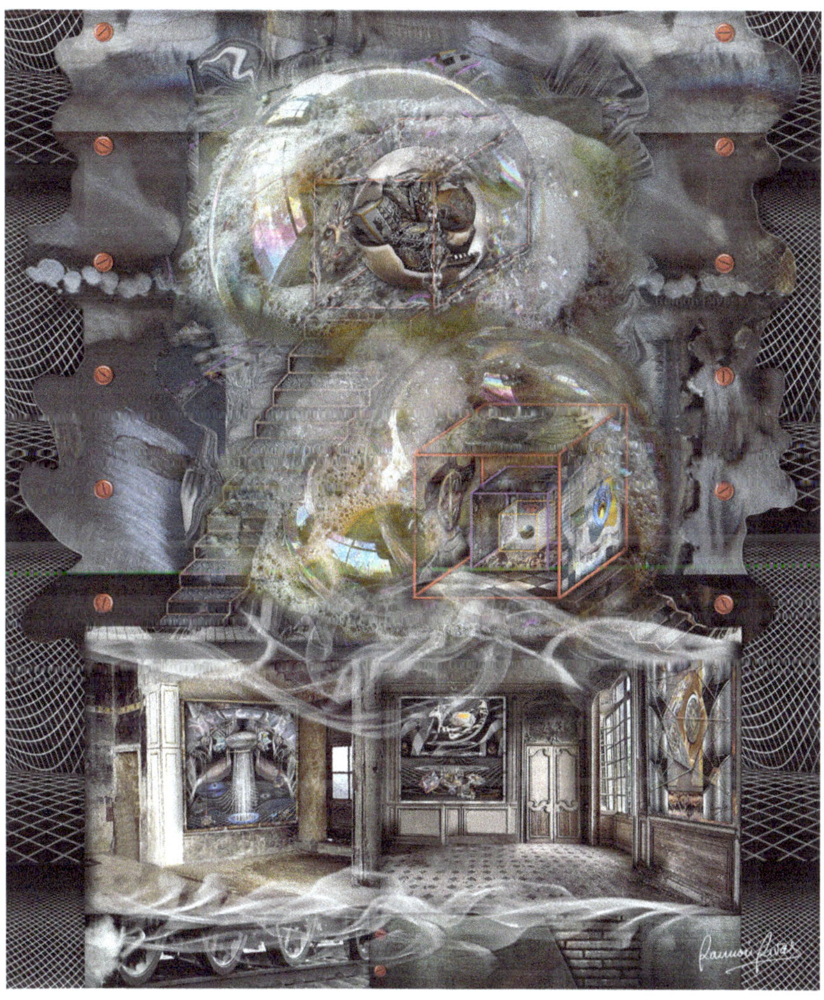

Art Explosion in the Station II 2021 Mixed media-Rivismo 170x200 cm

STEFFI RODIGAS

Germany | steffi-rodigas-artist.com

After a life in various professions and raising three children, Steffi Rodigas broke with all conventions and left her secure job. Since then, she has been creatively expressing her feelings, thoughts and ideas through art and music and has been working as a freelance artist since 2018. In her artistic works you can feel and see her deep connection to nature, animals and the love for detail. She works with acrylics and oils, and watercolors. Her specially developed art form "ART in ART", combines realistic painting and with abstraction. With her passion for three-dimensionality, she often incorporates 3D elements into her paintings and has created numerous sculptures out of building insulation material. It is particularly important to the artist to articulate her emotions and opinions on world events, such as climate change, pollution of the oceans.... to articulate her emotions and opinions. In Germany, she has had 7 solo exhibitions and numerous collective exhibitions. Internationally, works by Steffi Rodigas have been shown in Venice, Rome, London, Madrid, Milano, Paris, New York and Tokyo. In New York, she was involved in "Mother- Earth- Day 2022" and received the ATIM`S TOP 60 Masters Award.

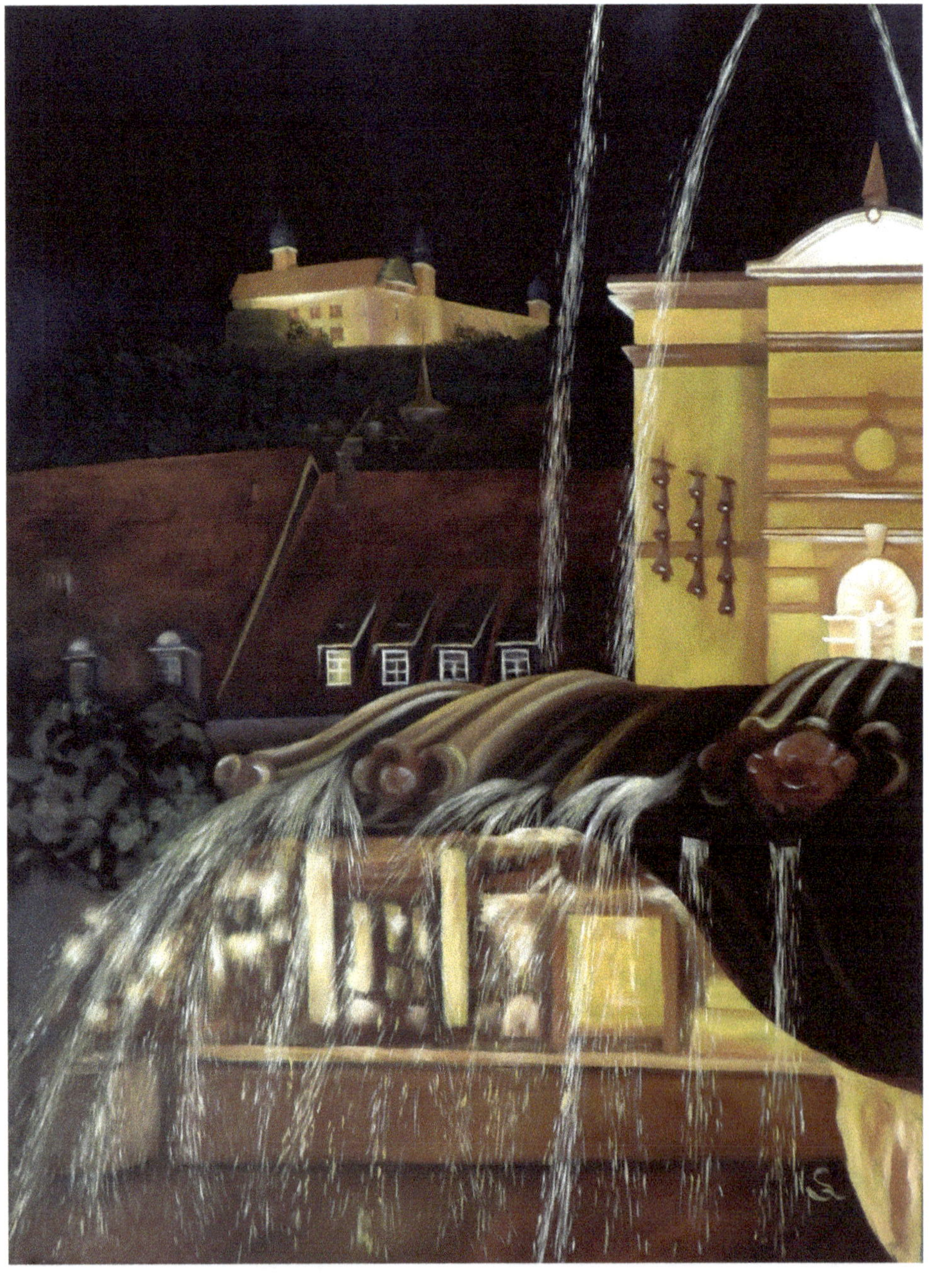

View to the castle, Oil on canvas, 80x60cm

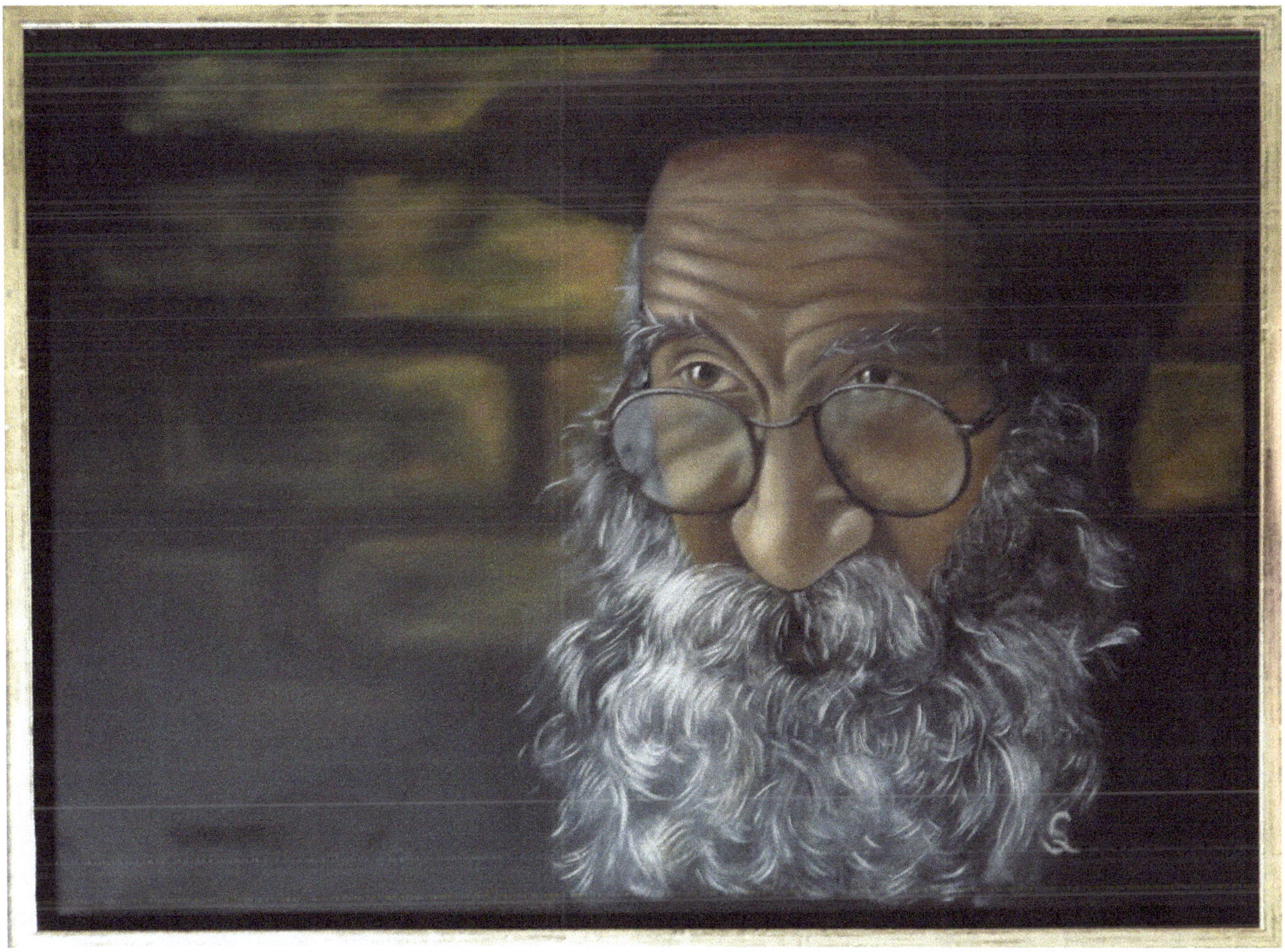

The Wise, Oil on canvas, 55x75cm

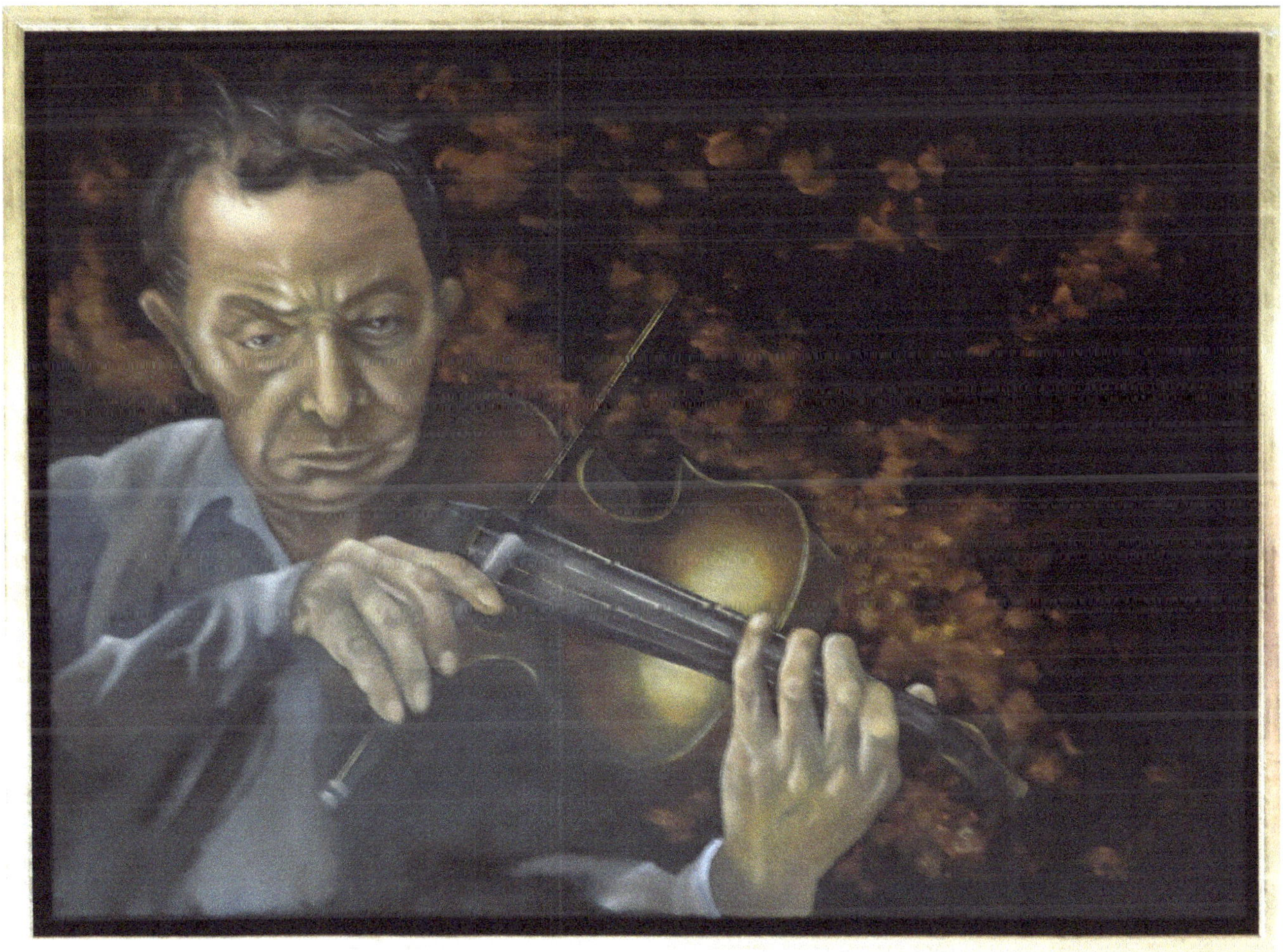

The Passionate, Oil on canvas, 55x75cm

JOJO HUXFORD

United States | nantucketphotos.photography

My creative mind was established very young,from a childhood replete with illness. My imagination was my salvation from these very harsh beginnings 12 to 22. This resource is represented in my art. My art is an immersive experience a sense of independence freedom flight. JKH art flows to the realm the senses. I take you there: without aim presently or subjectively. I fly with color, certain undertones of reality: joy death sorrow sensuality 'the stuff of life. Some have called it creative genius I call it survival 101 from tough beginnings.

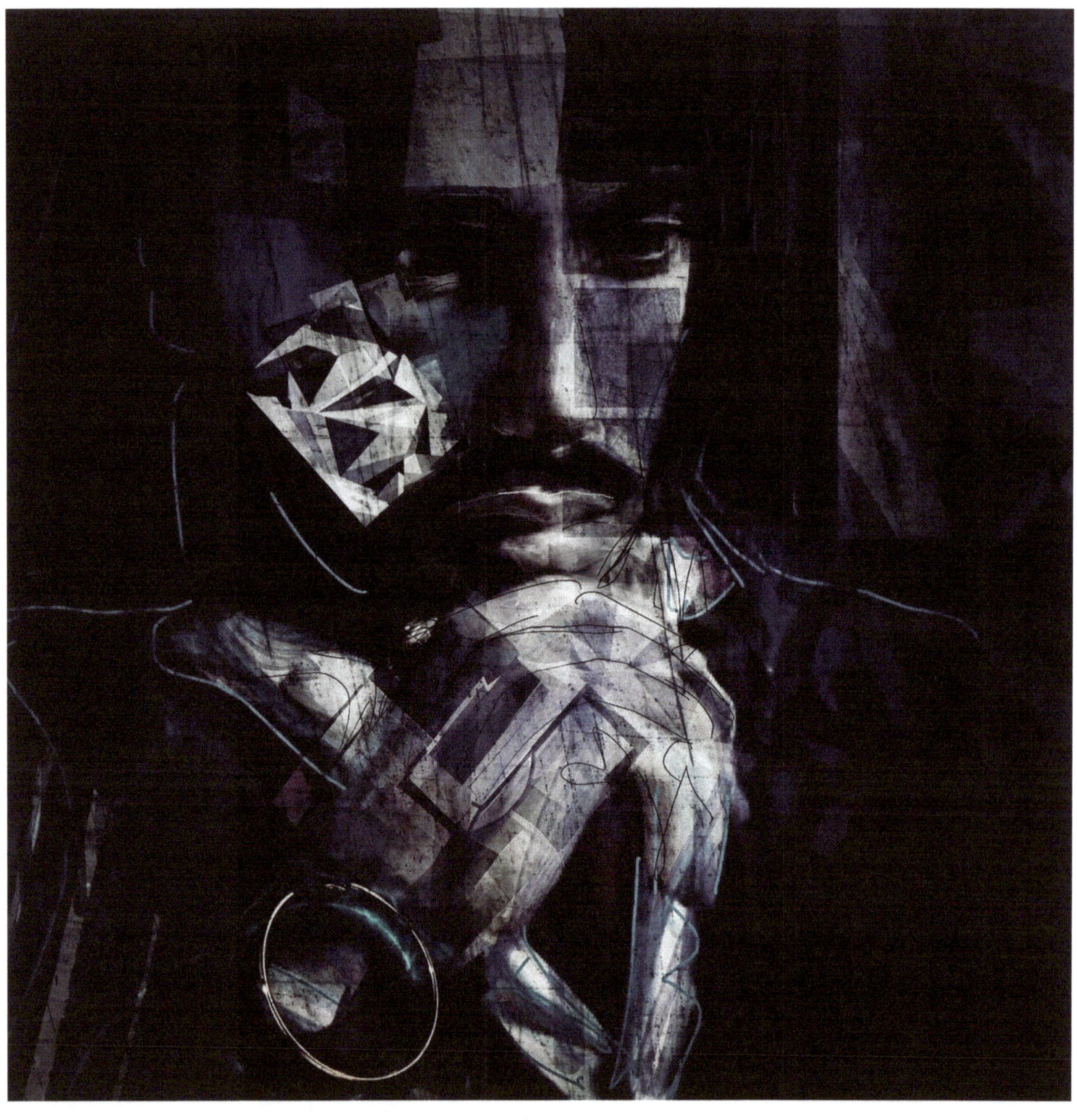

Domino 2021 digital acrylic on Fabriano paper 27.94"by 35.56 cm

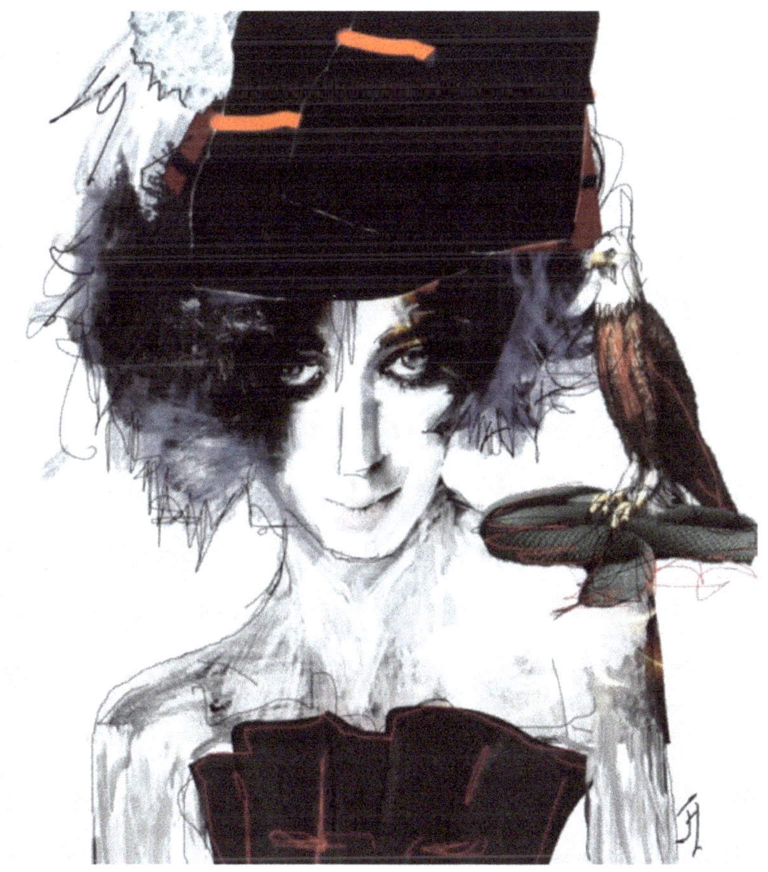

Paris 2021 acrylic ink on Fabriano paper 27.94cm by 35.56cm

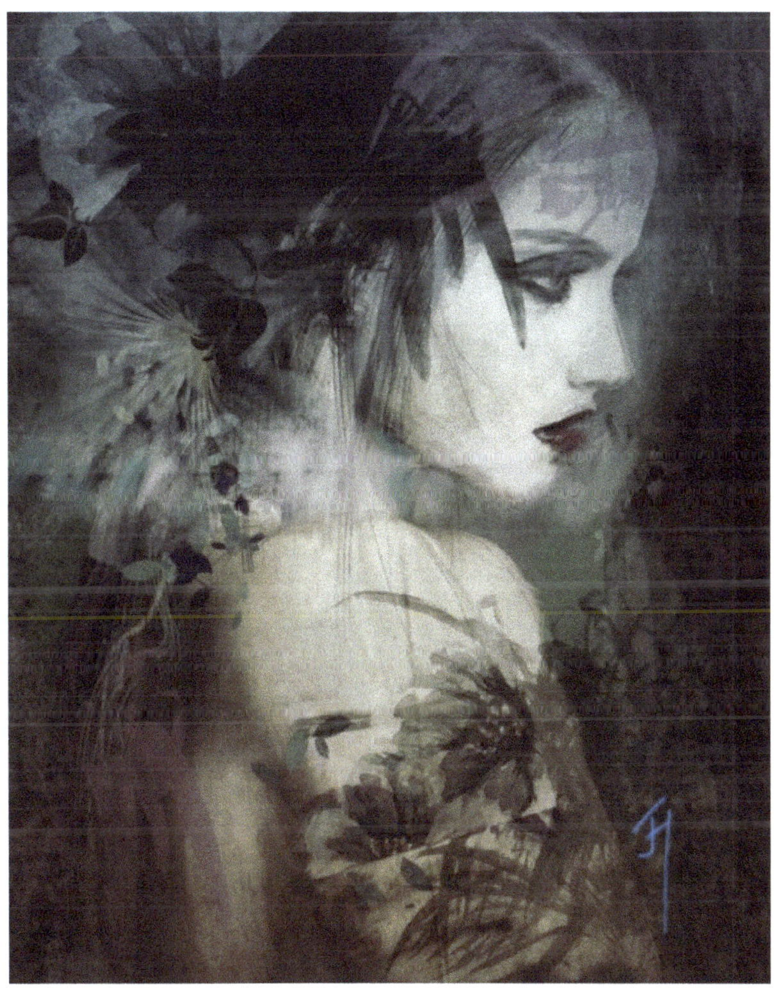

Eve 2021 digital acrylic on Fabriano paper 27.94cm by 35.56cm

BARBARA PALKA WINEK

Poland | palkawinek.pl

Studies at the Academy of Fine Arts in Krakow at the Faculty of Painting. Diploma in 1983. Lives and works in Krakow, Poland. She exhibited several times in Paris, London and New York, in Manhattan (Agora Gallery, Ward-Nasse Gallery, Brodway Gallery, NY Art Fair). She took part in the Florence Biennale, London Biennale, and Tokyo Biennale.

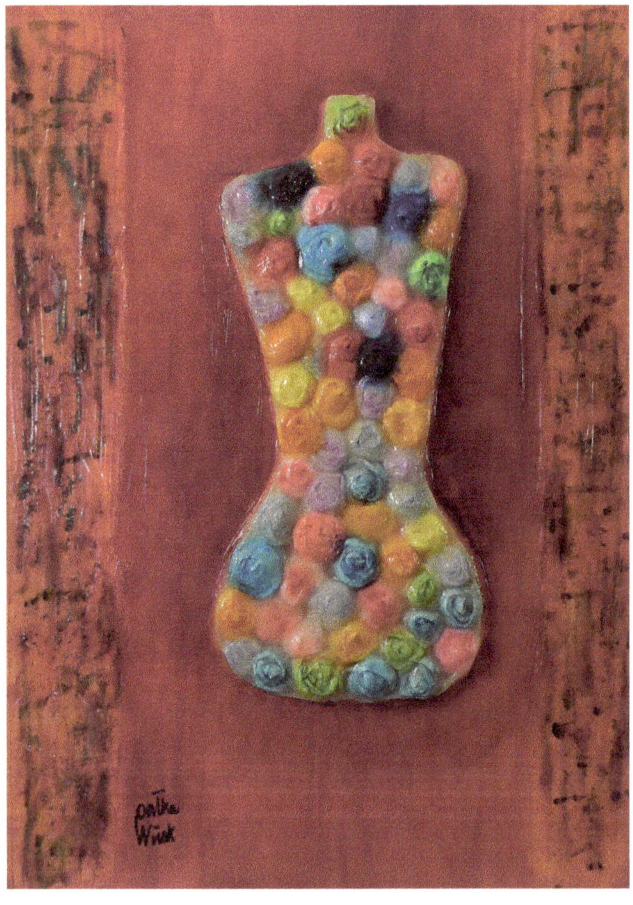

Love, 2022, oil and own tech. on canvas, 140 x 100 cm

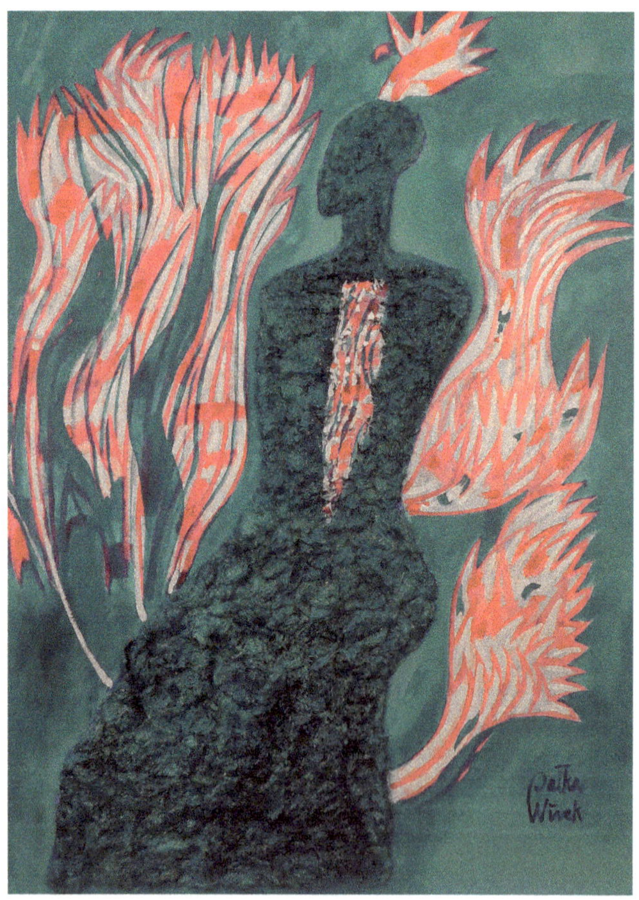

Love, 2022, oil and own tech. on canvas, 140 x 100 cm

LUCIE BOSWELL

United States | lucieboswell.com

Lucie Boswell was born in 1968 in San Francisco and from an early age knew she wanted to communicate to the world as an artist. After studying art at UC Santa Barbara and photography at the renowned Santa Fe Photo Workshop she moved to Los Angeles in 1996 where she has built an impressive resume in photography, painting and mixed media. "I find it an advantage to work in multiple mediums because it allows me the opportunity to explore each and to go beyond their individual boundaries to invent new ways of creating art using color, design and experimental technique. Each piece is a new discovery for the audience and for me as there is no single way of seeing it. My goal is to elicit feelings of intensity and intrigue while evoking both mystery and meaning." Lucie's work has been shown in galleries both nationally and internationally and has been featured in numerous books and publications. Boswell is also an avid patron of the arts supporting individual artists, museums and programs around the world.

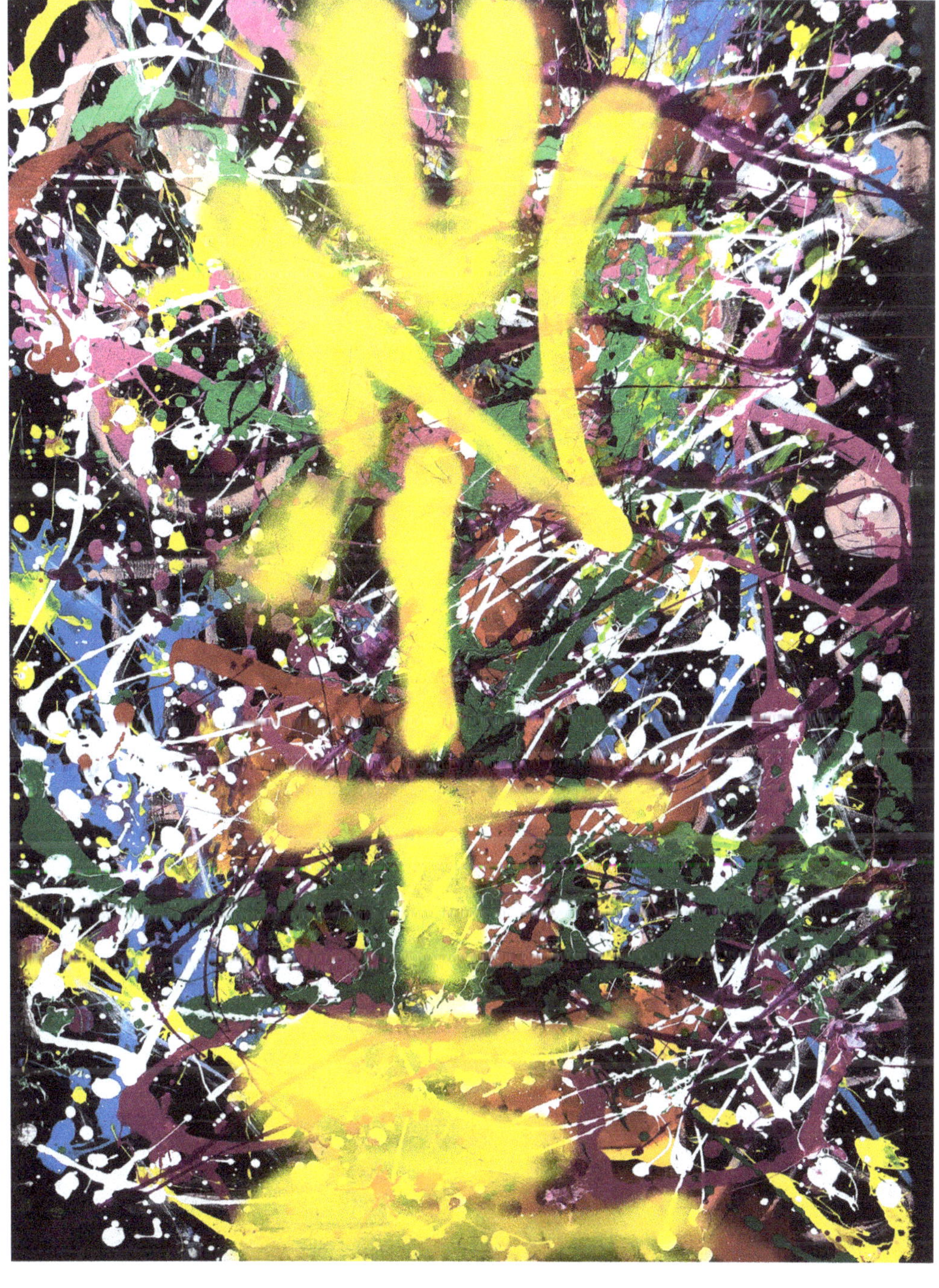

Unite, 2021. Acrylic on canvas, 92 x 122 cm

FRANCO SMITH

Italy | francosmithart.com

Born in Antwerp in 1983 and raised in Milan, Franco Smith is an italian-english photographer interested in travel photography, landscape architecture and life stories. He started to approach photography when he was ten years old using his parents Canon AT-1 and he found this media so fascinating he decided to involve it in his life. At the high school he entered the magic door of the darkroom where the childhood play started to comes to life until he get to La Scala Theatre Academy where he took part in a Stage Photography Master. After studies he started to work as a photographer assistant and then as a freelance photographer. Traveling have contributed to the idea of developing a language to recounting links between places and people, to create a photographic storytelling. A sort of narration through images, without dialogue, based on compositions with a strong visual impact. His works is based on digital collages of original photographs shot by him mixed with wallpaper scraps. The artist purpose is to illustrate his view on locations he visited and to propose you to get in touch with them creating your own perception of the storytelling. You will see iconic objects, monuments, people and nature connected to each other by Franco's imagination.

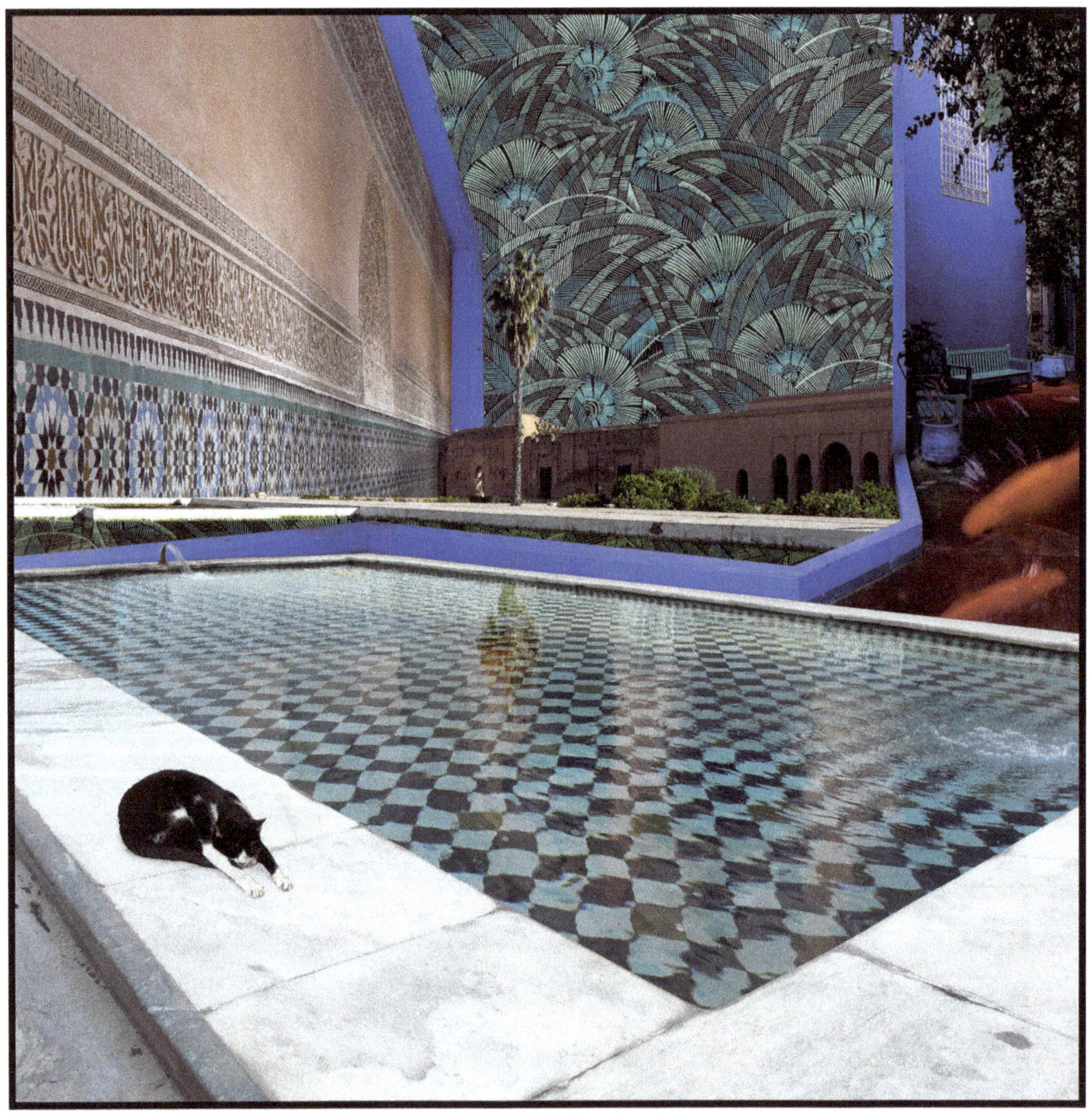

Room n. 2 – LA PISCINE (Marrakech 2011) - Photographic digital collage of original pictures by the author - 60x60 cm - Year 2020

SHIR ZALCMAN

Israel | shirzalcmanart.com

With intention and sincerity, Shir Zalcman's artwork is a piece of herself. The thirty-seven year old Israeli artist paints to reflect the present moment of her everyday, emotional experience. A self-taught artist, she currently lives in central Israel with her family. Her studio is a space to escape, to reflect and confront parts of herself through the process of painting. Mainly using acrylic paint and charcoal mediums, she uses palette knives and brushes to create depth through texture, layering and linework. Choosing a bold colour palette, she intuitively composes these textural patterns by layering them together to explore the visceral nature of feelings. She works in harmony with the fast drying process of acrylic paint, building layers to be completed as a whole rather than in parts. Her paintings have been shown at a variety of exhibitions. Her most recent showing was at the Chianciano 2022 BIENNALE and in 2021 Depths and Layers, a solo exhibition at Tel Aviv. Zalcman has been published in issues of APERO Magazine , COLLECT ART Magazine, ARTMAZINEIUM Magazine, AL-TIBA9 Magazine, ARToday Magazine, LAISHA Magazine And also been shown in ITZUV, Israel's top magazine for house decor.

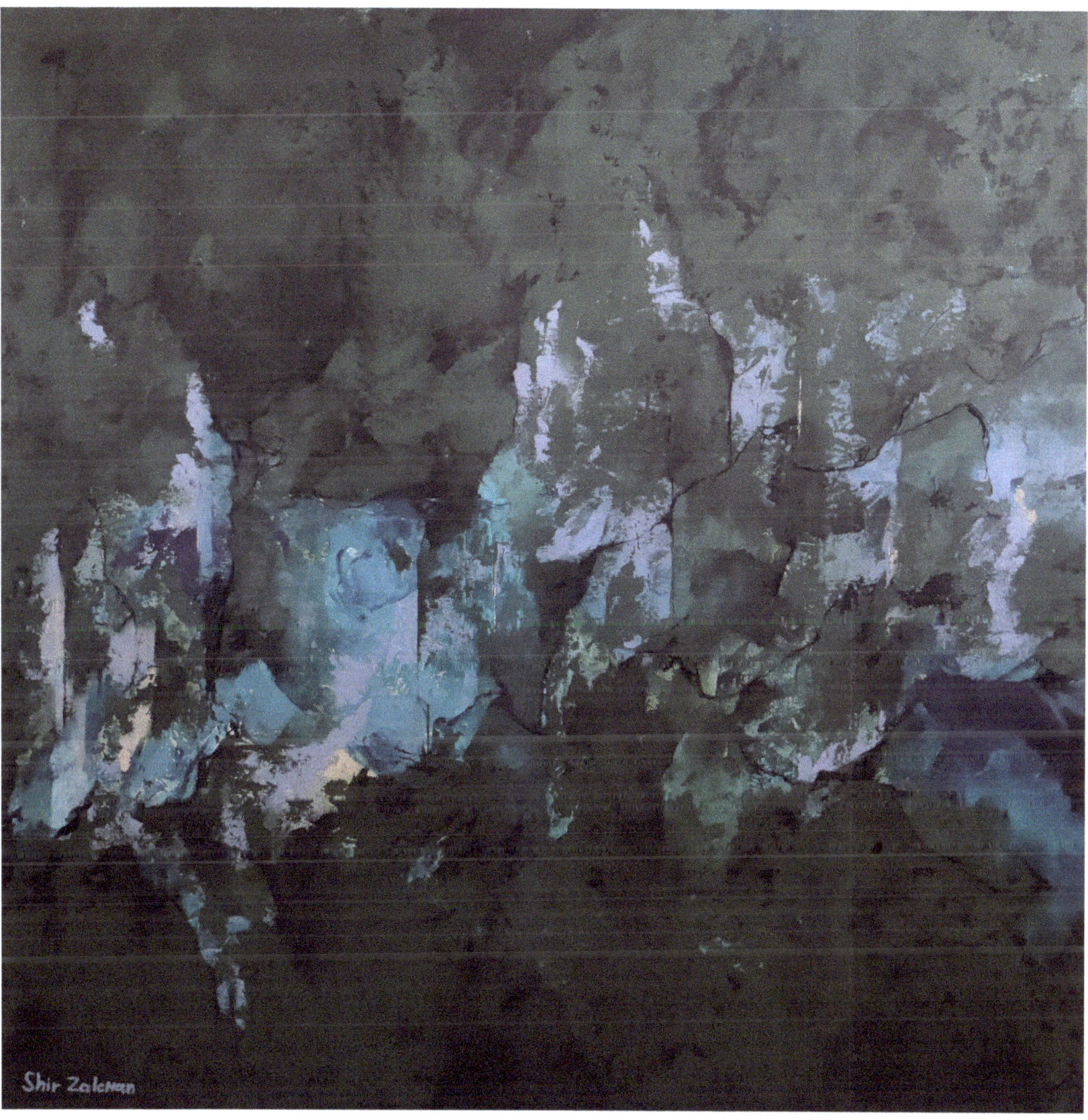

The Unimaginable. Acrylic and charcoal on canvas 120/120

HANNA RHEINZ (HRZ)

Germany | hanna-rheinz.com

Following the ideals of art, I want to spread my wings inside and outside the classical rules of academic art and not be reduced to the laws of markets or trends. Instead I try to follow my curiosity and ambition to connect past and present, and bridge the gaps leading to present and future. I prefer playful experiments and irony in times of change, uncertainty and fluctuation. The gaps and ruptures can be bridged or left as they are: what I see is without limits, without identification, nor the promise to be seen at all. No promises made.

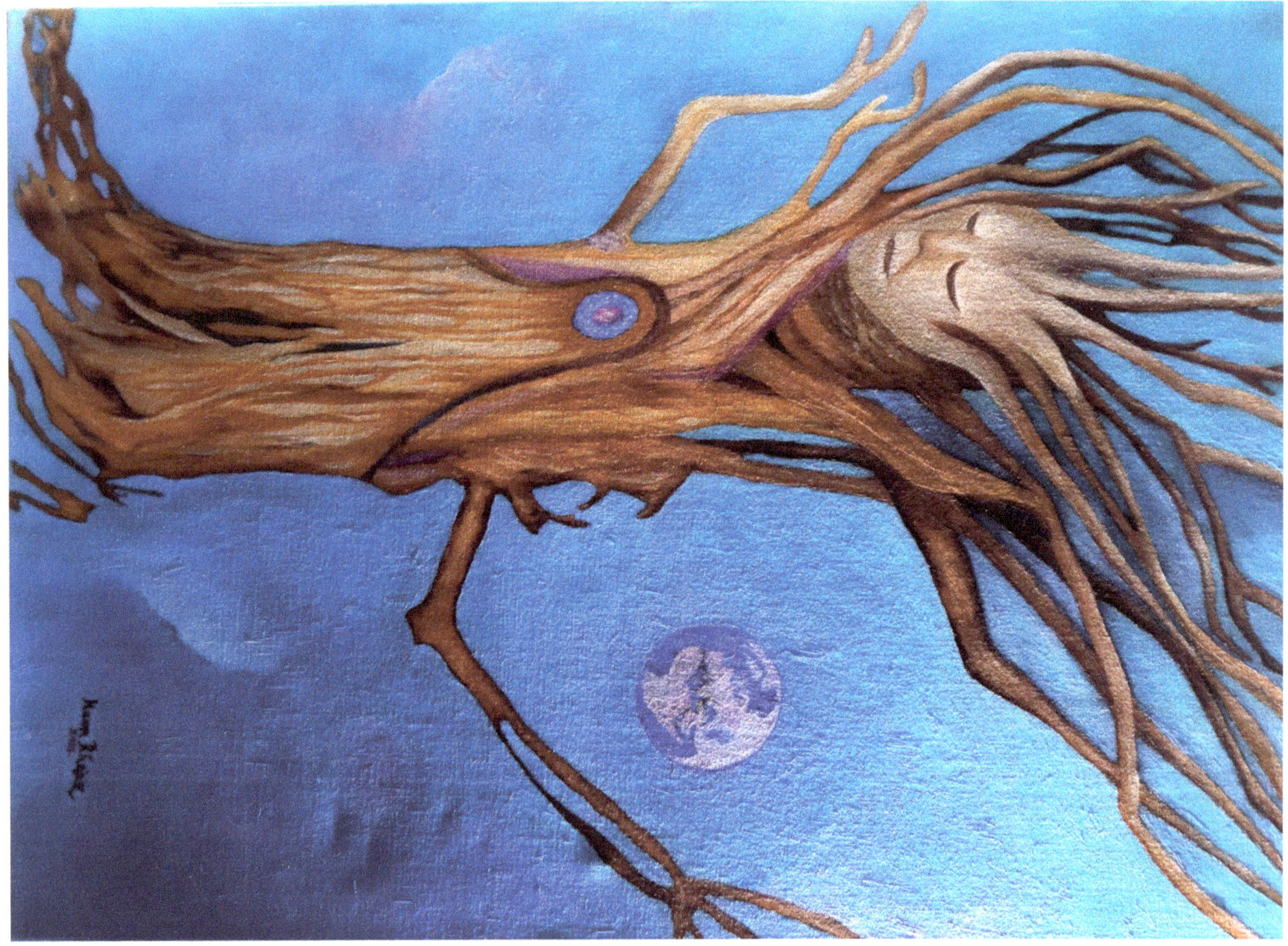

Un-Titled 2022 70 x 100 cm Oil on Canvas

MARINA CHISTY

United States | marinachisty.com

Marina Chisty is a Russian-American artist who currently lives and works in NYC. Her abstract and figurative paintings embody the dynamism and multiple faces of the city, trying to grasp their distinctive differences and substantial equality as human beings. Marina approached art from a very young age, fostering her talent in children's art school in Russia. Her Russian roots are relevant in the development of her creative identity, bringing her closer to abstraction and the symbolic use of color. Throughout her studies, Marina reflected that art was her true purpose and continued to hone her expertise. Marina strives to make an aesthetic but also concrete impact, giving humanitarian support especially to women in need. Marina Chisty's interest in painting women, regardless of ethnicity or physical features, derives from her special connection with the feminine world and concern for women's rights. As an artist, she wants to create opportunities to support women who are underrepresented not only in the art system but also in the broader sphere of business. One of her most important goals is to reach young women who reside in geographic areas with socioeconomic disadvantages, engaging them in art projects. Her portraits represent very different women, characterized by peculiar backgrounds and varied circumstances. However, Marina Chisty's art practice challenges racial, socio-economic, and physical barriers, emphasizing the common need for equal perspective and mutual support.

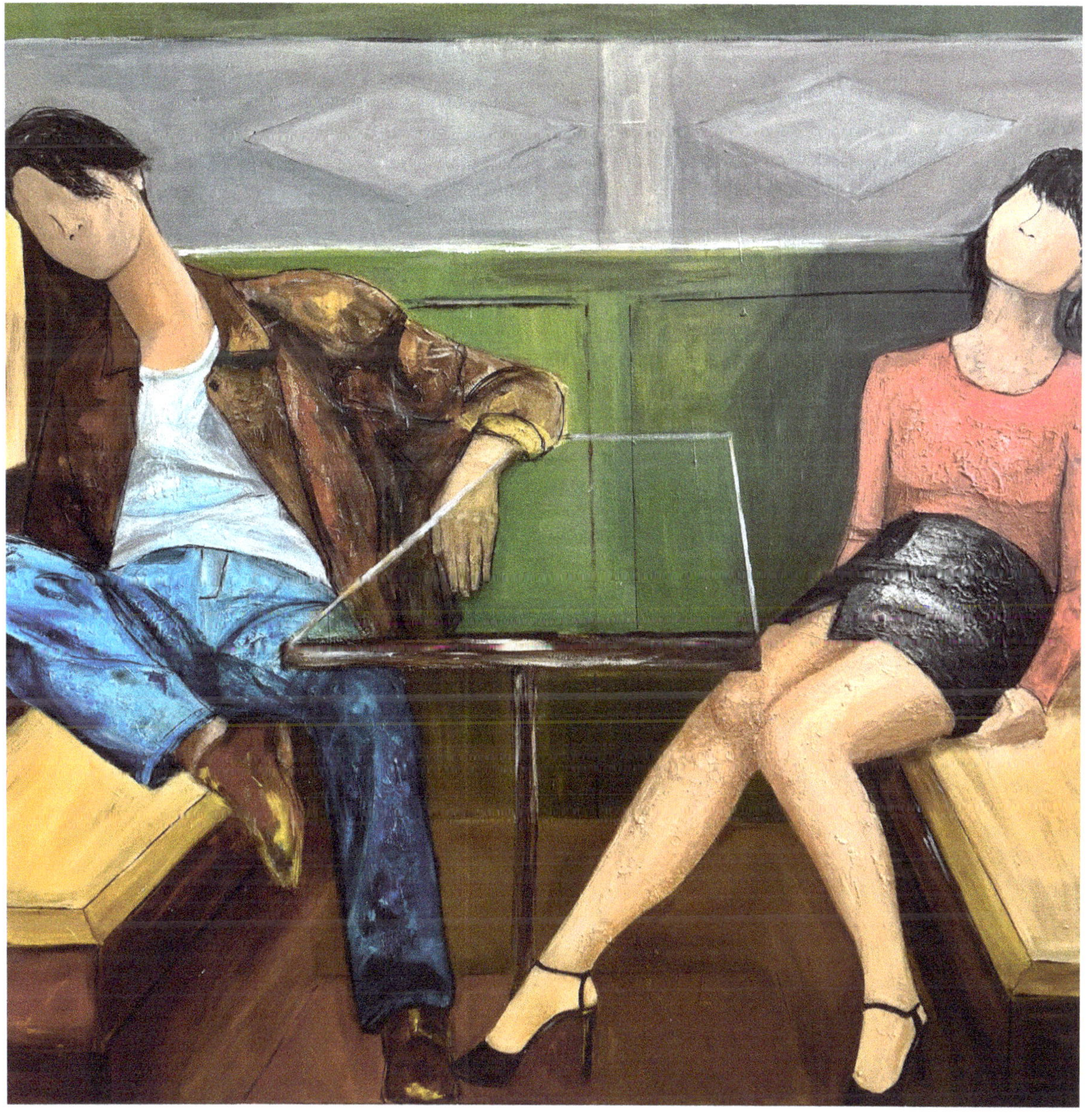

Under my thumb, 2022. Acrylic on canvas, 48 x48 in

MAGDALENA FASCHING

Austria | magdalenafasching.com

Magdalena Fasching was born in Vienna in 1985. When she was 12 years old, she got her first painting material so she started with oil paintings. After school, where she always took part in creative projects, she studied at Wiener Kunstschule with focus on multidisciplinary art. She became more fascinated with illustration and children books art. She also studied recreational/leisure pedagogue for combinating the work with children and art. Now she's working on her children books which she started to illustrate as preparation for publishing. She loves playing with colors and figures in which the viewer can decide by himself what he sees in it. She also loves to let the color flow. Here she is fascinated by the game with the coincidence. She mostly doesn't know at the beginning what the result at the end will be. Magdalena Fasching took part in several exhibitions; most of them in Vienna and Salzburg but also in Venice in summer 2022.

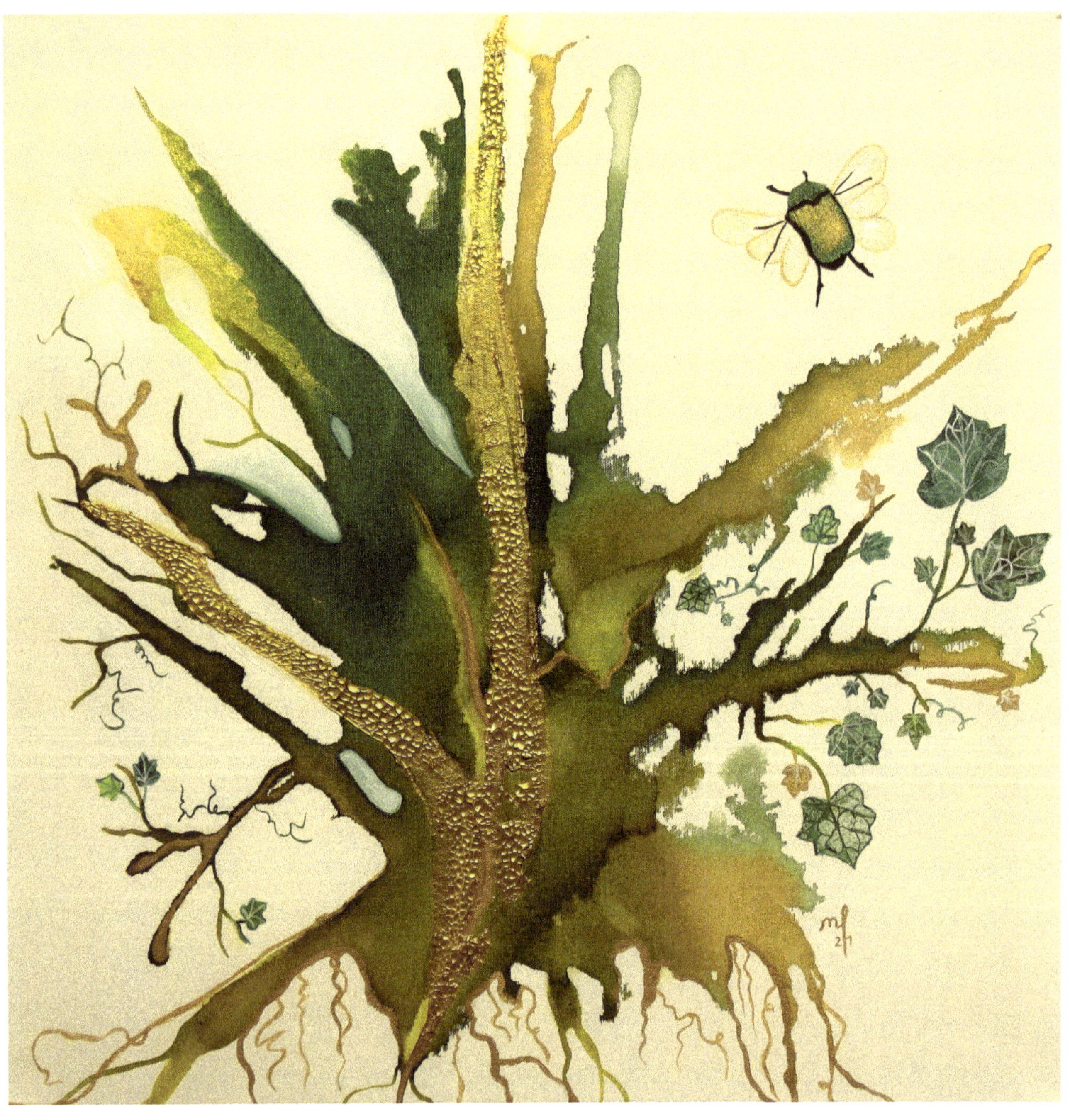

Rosebug, 2021. Mixed Media on canvas, 60x60 cm

MIRO FREI

Switzerland | miro-frei.org

He was born 1974 in the small town Aarau in Switzerland where he also grew up. He studied history and geography at the University of Zurich. He had been working as an artist since 2004 as a balance to the top-heavy studies. In 2007 he exhibited his pastel and acrylic paintings in a solo show at the Kraftwerk gallery in Berlin. In 2009 he was asked to participate in the Florence Biennale. There he met Marina Abramovic. He was deeply shocked by her radical language. 2013 he participated again in the Florence Biennale. He was supported by several foundations: the Zumsteg-Stiftung, the Casinelli-Vogel-Stiftung, the Ernst Göhner Stiftung. 2014 he organized an international group exhibit at the Kapfsteig gallery in Zurich. That exposition was so successful that it was continued in Innsbruck. Frei's installation „Dada is growing up" in 2014 at the artclub in Cologne irritaded and received attention beyond the art scene. Then he was contacted by several galleries from New York City. He decided to go to the Artifact gallery. Further expositions in Zurich and Berlin. In Dezember 2021 he exhibited at the Kunsthalle Bern. In a Show of the art school F+F. In that state museum the incomparable Harald Szeemann has organized "When Attitudes Become Form". The works of Miro Frei are represented in collections in Berlin, Cologne, Berne, Zurich, Feldmeilen and Lausanne. He works and lives in Zurich and Berlin.

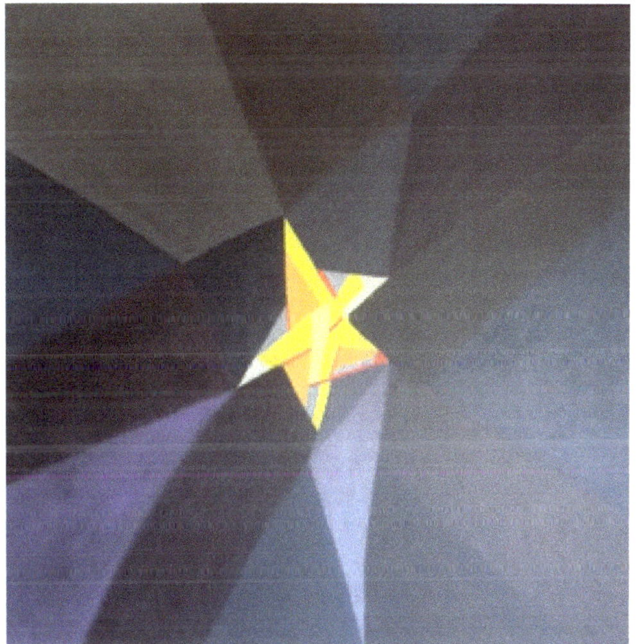

Missed the entrance. 2020, acryl on canvas, 100x100 cm

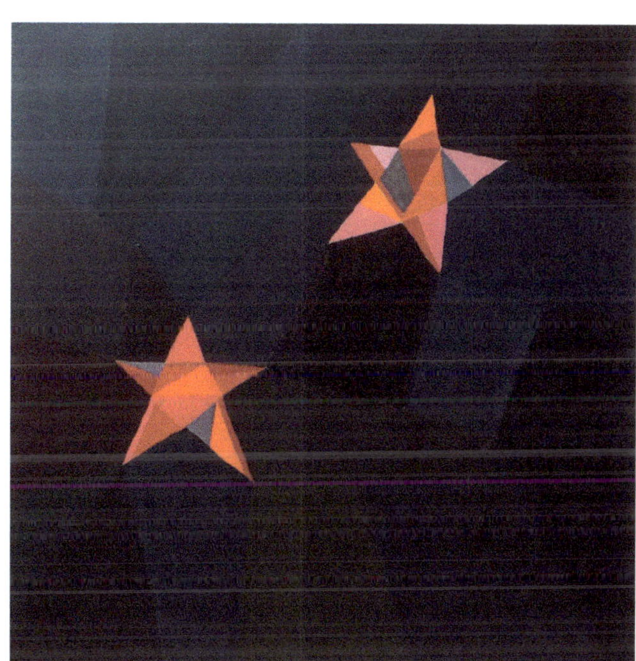

Red star doped. 2021, acryl on canvas, 80x80 cm

HILARY THURSFIELD

Canada | hilarythursfieldart.com

The trends in art reflect the society we live in. Presently art says that absolutely anything you like, glue, glass, string or paint and anything else in between passes for art. The days of spending hours molding something into creativity, be it canvas, clay, or wood are gone for the foreseeable future. Forget art classes and simple perseverance. Those days are gone! We want instant art, like instant gratification. We care little of its content, or how its made. If it fits the purpose and is instant and spontaneous it likely will adorn a wall! Its value is also instantaneous and irrelevant. New voices in art are essential, but just as there is no one method, there is zero formula, or specification to creativity. A continuous trend in art is impossible to predict, just as it is equally impossible to determine the art desires of a nation in crisis. Simply put, we like what we like without unnecessary explanation for it. Trends in art are fast and furious and extremely hard to keep up with and maintain. Just as in life, it often feels like we are always playing catch up! The wind blows in many directions and as artists we try to stand our ground with our current work. The trend is always forward looking and we avoid this at our peril, reminding us that change is constant and inevitable in any generation.

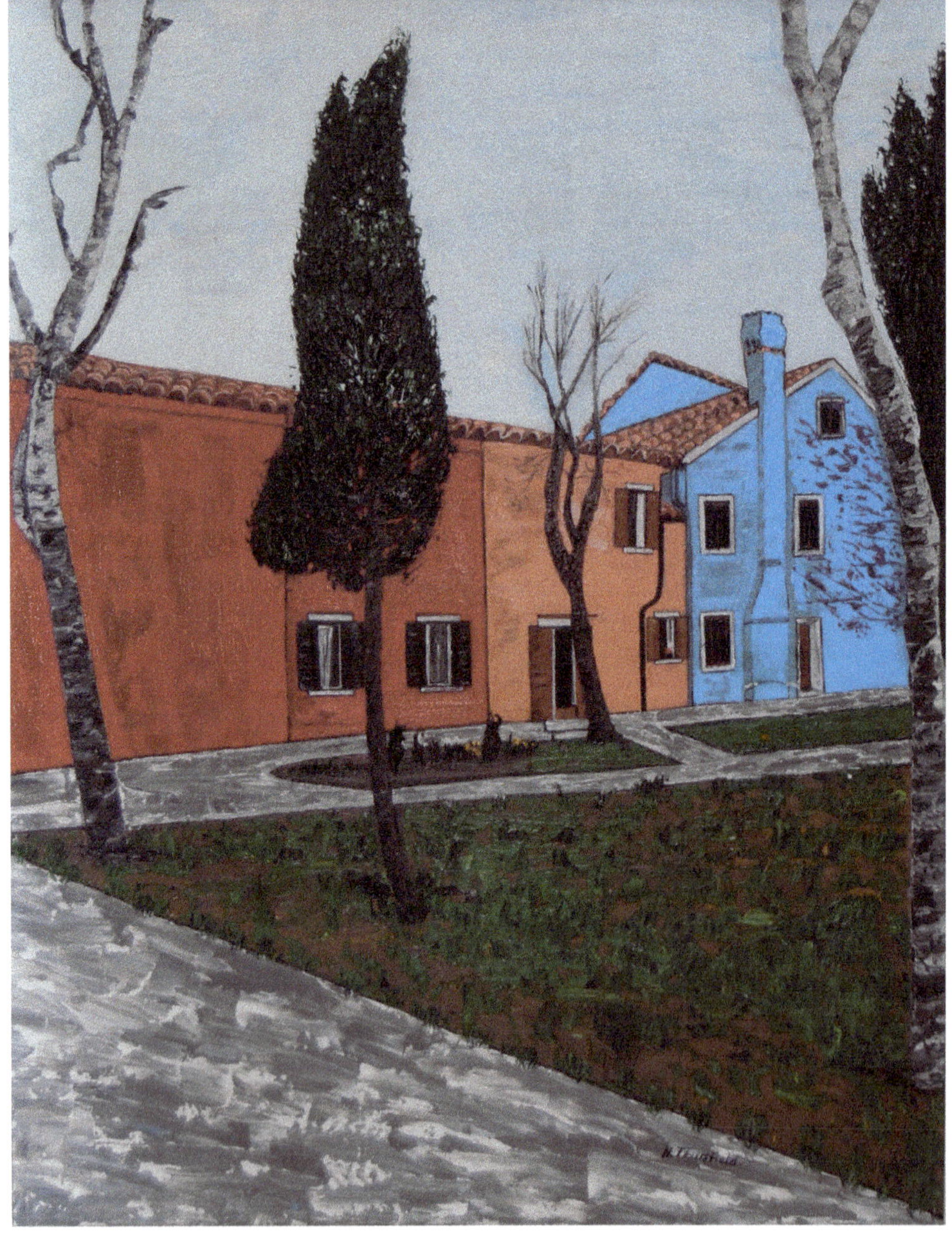

Burano Houses

FATINHA RAMOS

Portugal | fatinha.com

Fatinha Ramos is an Antwerp-based illustrator and visual artist originally from Portugal. After working for twelve years in design and art direction, she took the leap of faith to follow the old dream of becoming a full-time illustrator. With strong conceptual illustrations, she takes you on a journey through a unique universe of rich colors and singular textures. Her destination? To strike an emotional chord with you. She often raises important social issues such as global warming, sexism, racism, giving a voice to those who need to be heard. In addition to editorial illustrations, children's books, cultural and governmental illustrations, advertisement, murals, animation, fashion, theater, ceramics, and personal projects, she also gives talks, lectures and workshops around the world. Clients include: MoMA (The Museum of Modern Art), Google, The New York Times, TIME, The Washington Post, Scientific American, The Smithsonian Magazine, The Boston Globe, Amnesty International, Flemish Government …

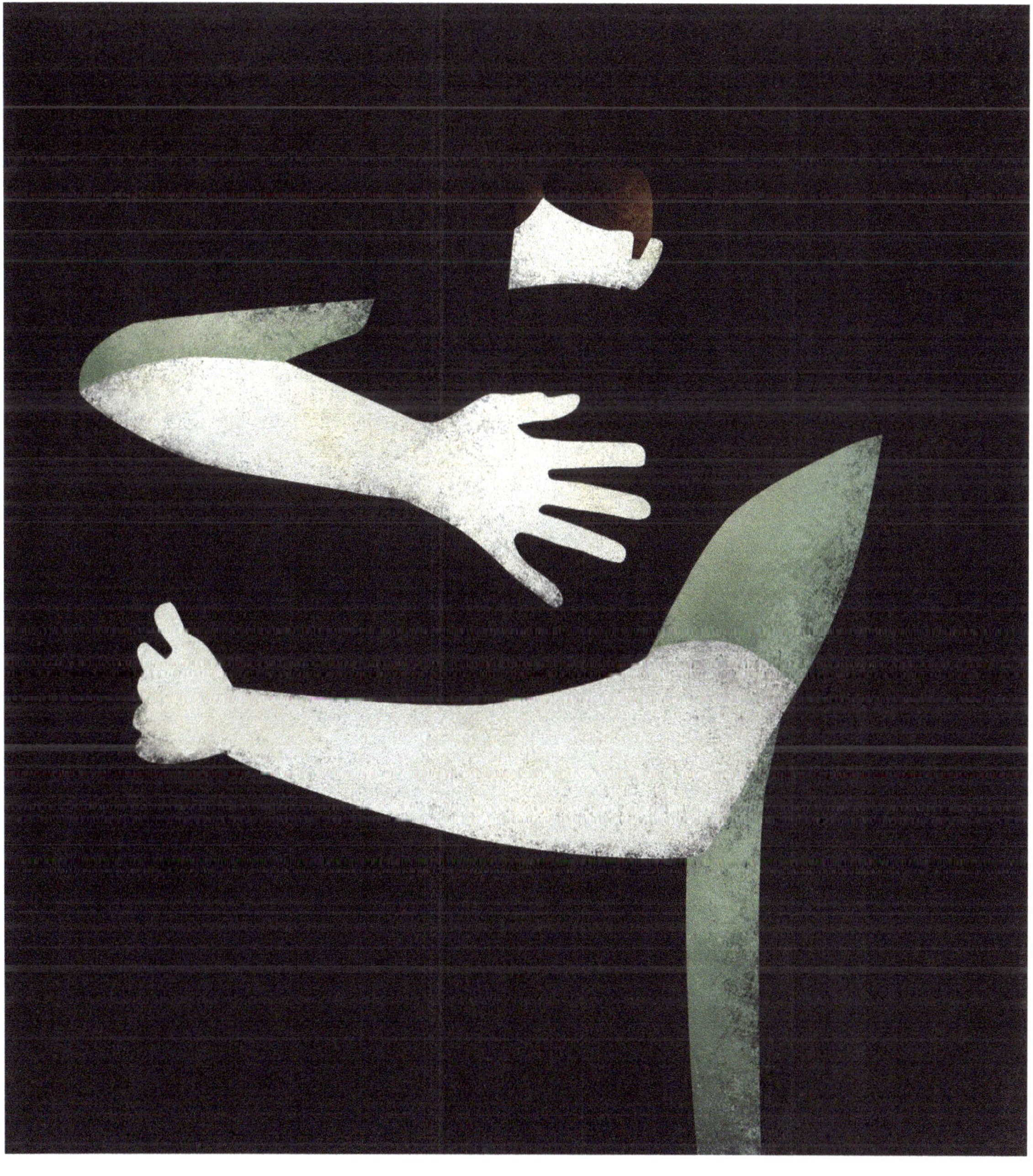

Suicide

KAITLYN WALLACE

United States | kaitlynwallaceart.com

I am interested in making art that facilitates conversations around freedom, autonomy, futility, and suffering. Growing up in Las Vegas and attending Catholic school, my influences surrounding womanhood were polarizing. Whether it was in Church or on a billboard, representations of women were an overwhelming object of my environment. By appropriating Christian iconography and combining it with the hyper-sexual aesthetics of Las Vegas, I paint images that reflect and further complicate ideologies related to the body, social conditioning, and self-realization. Under the established patriarchy, navigating the boundaries between objectification and subjectivity can be muddy and confusing. I want to expand this conflict between who we are and who we are conditioned to be, and shamelessly transcend these binaries. My position on this has been informed by the writings of feminist philosophers and research about the way art history has dictated representations gender, sexuality, and the intersections between them. It feels empowering to recontextualize iconic representations of women by articulating the performativity of womanhood. I choose to stylize my portraits and figures to play with objectification and the elusiveness of idealized beauty. I combine non-natural color palettes that demand attention, with traditional Baroque techniques, such as diagonal compositions and chiaroscuro, to push and pull sensations of familiarity, history and modernity, and to examine how the objectification of women has pervaded art history and continues today. I want my art to question how we exist in spaces that aren't designed for us, and to consider the dynamics between agency and environment.

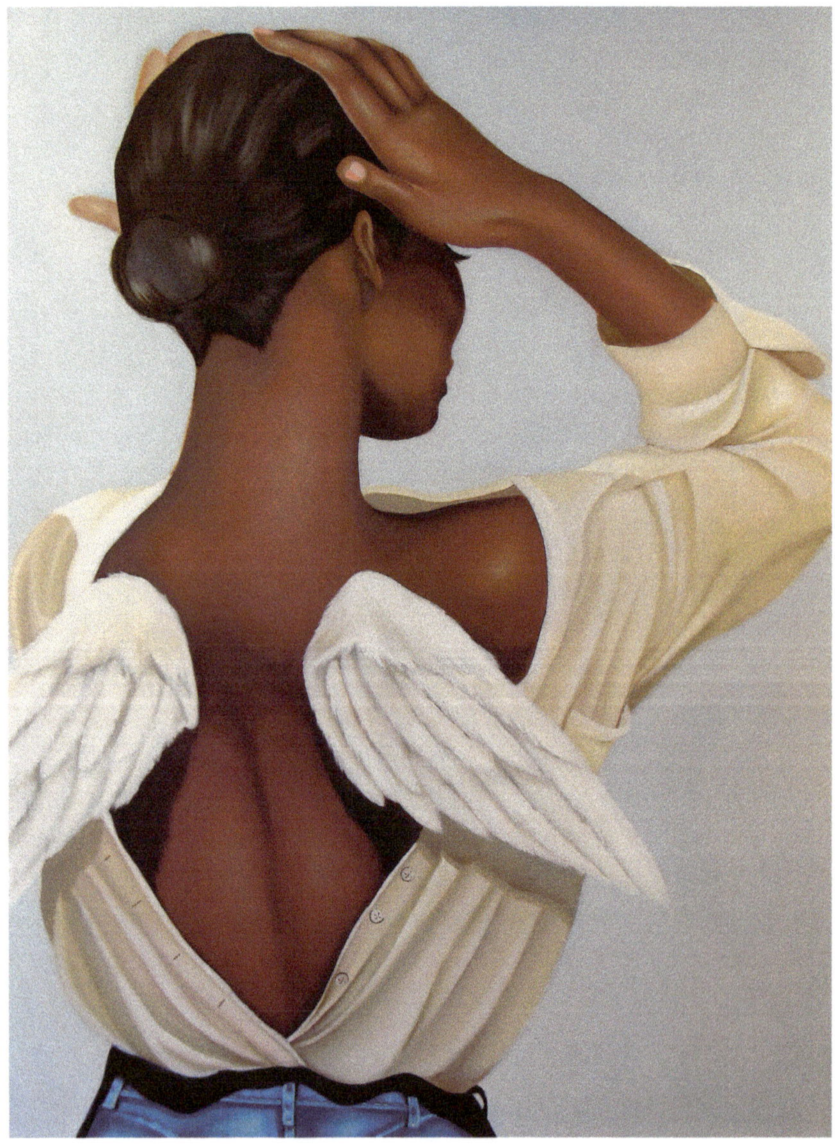

Paradiso

BRITTA ORTIZ

Denmark | britta-ortiz.dk

I have been making art all my life, but only started showing my art to the outside world in 2010. I make art because it is necessary for me to use both the right and left hemispheres of my brain in a busy everyday life. Art is my free space. I am a self-taught artist who has, however, been taught on various courses and by various artists. From them I have learned some of the techniques I use, but I have developed the artistic expression myself when I freed myself from their training. I work in various art forms, the most prominent of which are: Graphics, oil painting, drawing, watercolor and ceramics. I love to learn new things and I continuously incorporate new art forms into my artistic world. Since 2010 I have exhibited in many places in Denmark and in countries such as the USA, England, Italy, Austria and Germany. I have helped found several artists' associations, and my art can be seen in many art books and art magazines. I also have an education as a doctor and have studied psychology and health anthropology and still work full-time in a very hectic everyday life, where I apply my book-based educations.

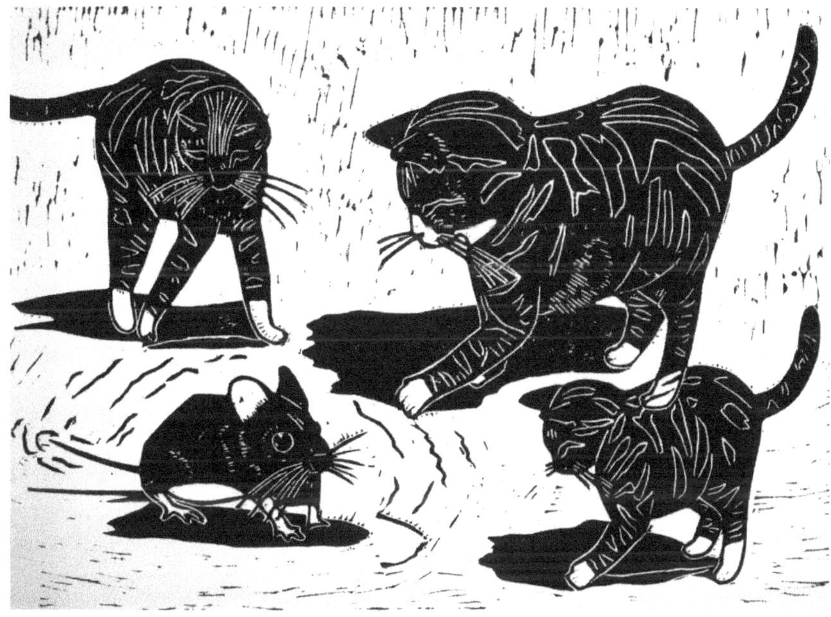

Kattens leg med musen, 2022, linocut printed on paper, 30 x 42 cm without frame and passepartout

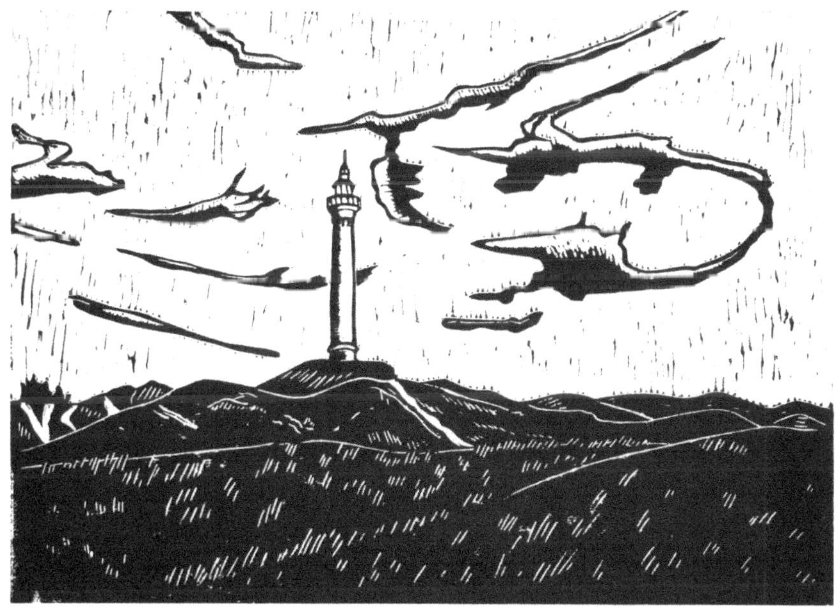

Lyngvig Lighthouse, linocut printed on paper, 30 x 42 cm without frame and passepartout.

WENDY COHEN

Australia | wendycohen.net.au

Wendy Cohen is a Sydney-based artist who has earned BFA and MFA degrees. Her art practice depicts energy and movement that rotates with an interplay of various shapes, tones of color, and light. The viewer is invited to participate in the depth and mystery of the 3D effects created with diverse shapes, lines, and forms. As a result, her works are imbued with a sense of curiosity, wonderment, and intrigue that is open to the viewer's interpretation. Her aim is to create a whimsical vibrant abstracted language that brings to life collaged recycled materials that interact with the shapes, lines, and forms of each composition. However, the primary focus of her practice is to transform the static space of each painting with synchronized contrasting colours highlighting its chemistry and resonance.

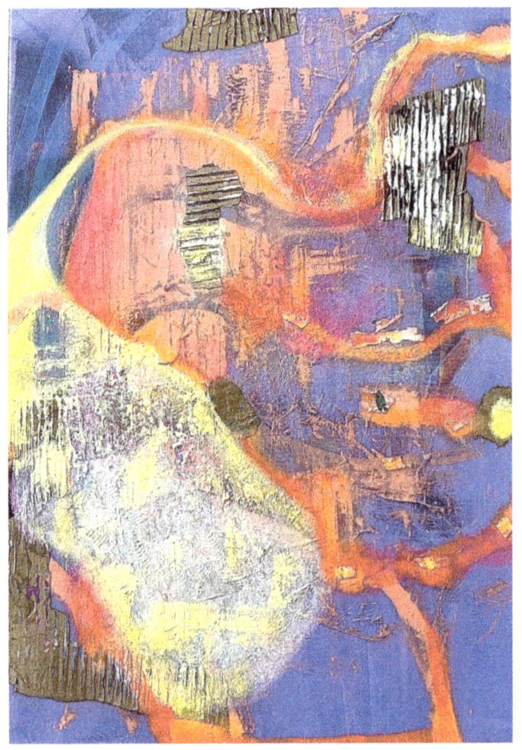

Silky Cocoon Emergence, 2022, 50cm x 70cm

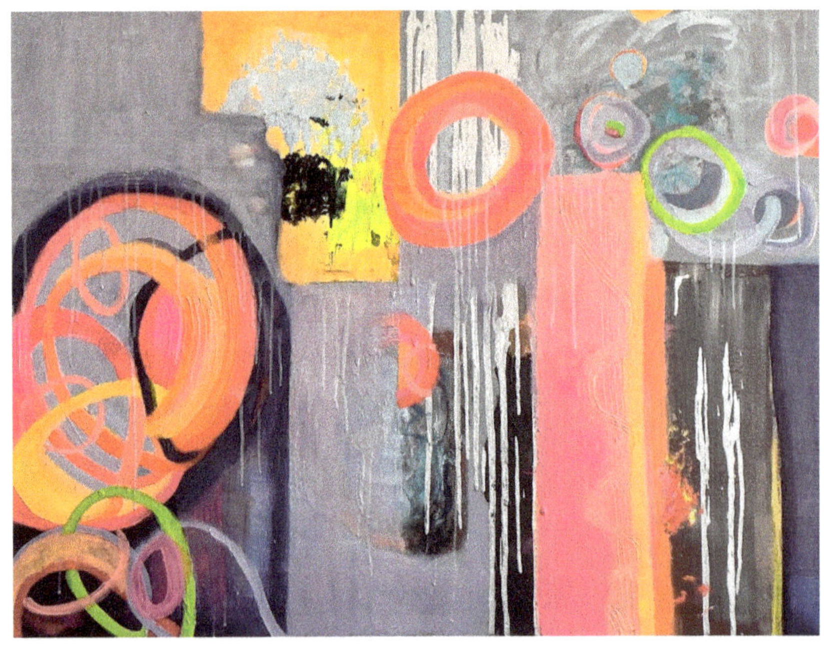

Doesnt Rain It Storms, 2022, acrylic on linen canvas, 92cm x 122cm

HOWARD HARRIS

United States | h-harris@live.com

Howard Harris has long been fascinated by both visual perception and design. The Denver, Colorado, USA native earned a BFA from Kansas City Art Institute, MID (Masters Industrial Design) from Pratt Institute in New York, studying with internationally renowned design theorist Rowena Reed Kostellow. Harris has spent more than 35 years combining design and technology, where he has won many prestigious professional awards. Now his creative energy has turned to his lifelong passion, photography. With an iconoclastic streak that had seen him consistently forging new directions in design, he was bound to approach the photographic image unconventionally. In 2017 Harris was granted a United States Patent for a Layered Artwork, proving his photographic work's uniqueness and inventiveness. Since then, his work has appeared in many books and publications, such as The Great Masters of Contemporary Art, ARTtour International Artists of the Decade, Art Collectors Choice Japan, International Contemporary Masters, and Top 10 Contemporary Artists, to mention a few. He has also been awarded Artists for a Green Planet Artist of the Decade, International Prize Raffaello, International Prize Giulio Cesare, International Prize Leonardo Da Vinci, International Prize Caravaggio, Contemporary Art Curator Magazines Artist of the Future, and more. He serves as a Trustee of The Kansas City Art Institute and has won the Who's Who Worldwide Lifetime Achievement and the USA Small Businessperson of the Year. His work is shown internationally and represented by galleries in the United States, the U.K., and Europe.

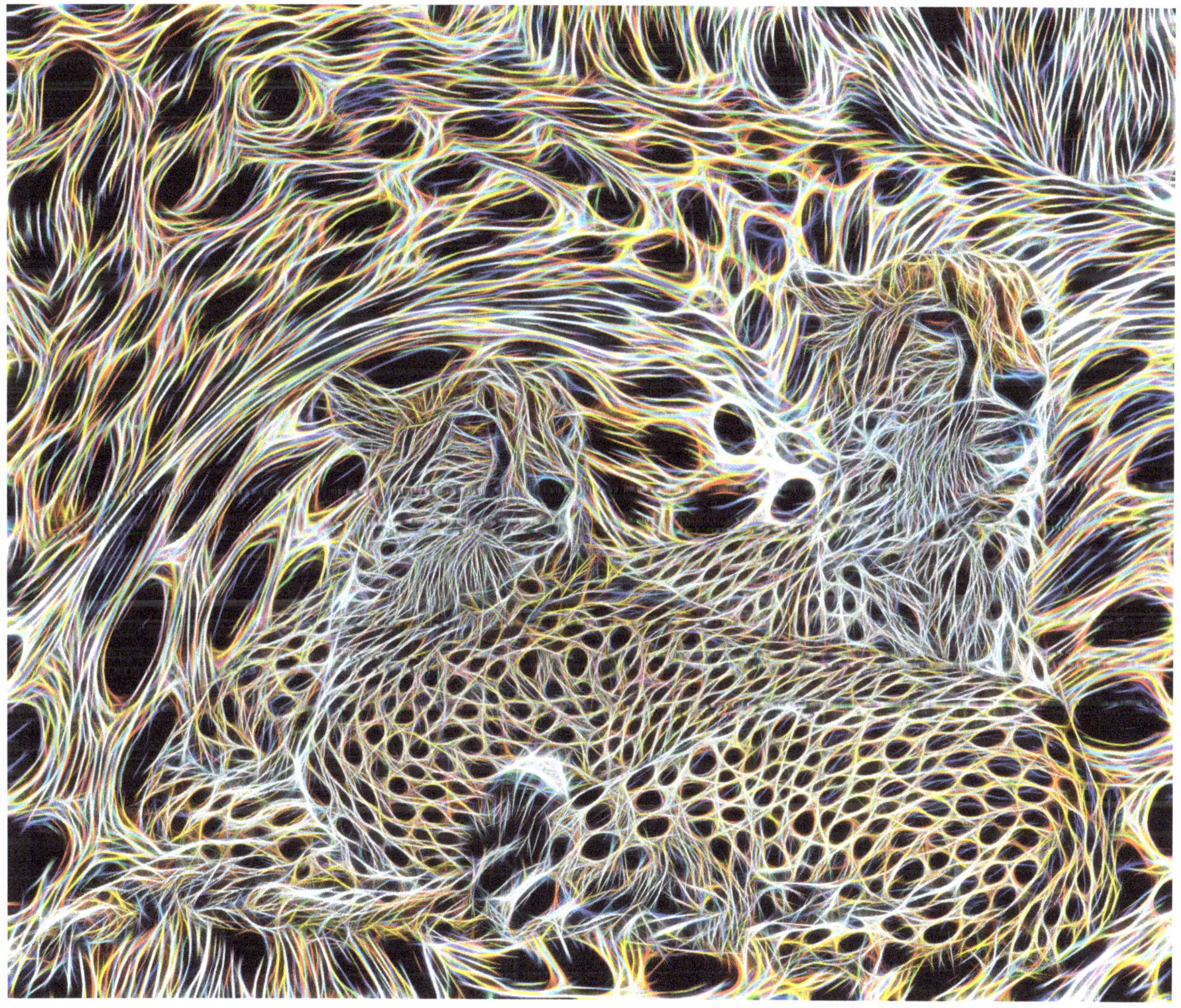

Cheetah, Sublimation on aluminum with an acrylic overlay, 91.44 x 76.2 cm

EVELINE GÖLDI

Switzerland | eveline-goeldi.ch

Eveline Göldi won the art prize of the Historical Museum of Bern in 2018. In 2022 she was awarded as voice of tomorrow by contemporary art curator magazine. The fascination for colors find reflection in her works, powerful, energetic, moving, imposing and colorful brushwork with a touch of sensual, cheerful und touching segments. She is presented in national and international galleries and art fairs. Please find more information on her website.

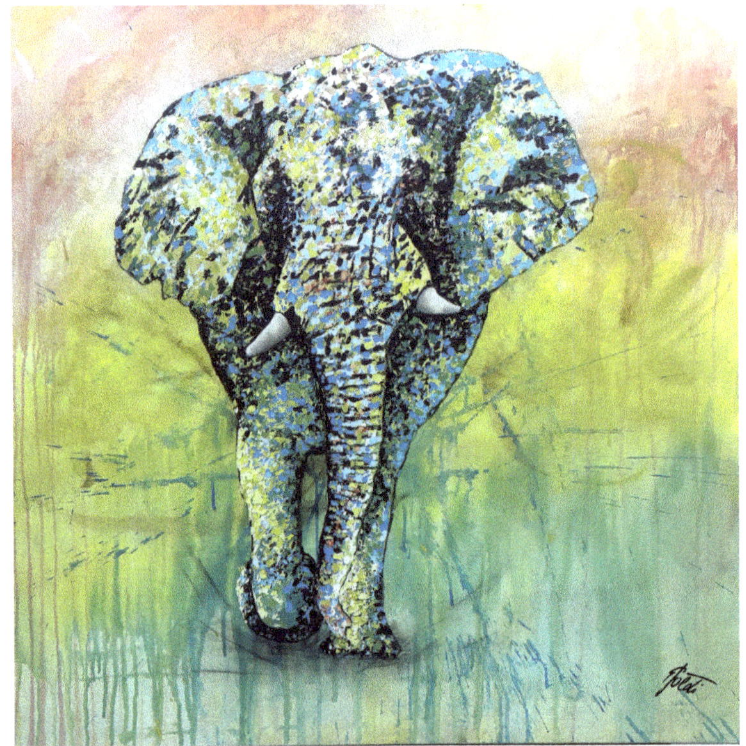

Elephant at the Sea. 2022. Acrylic & Oil on canvas. 100 x 100 cm

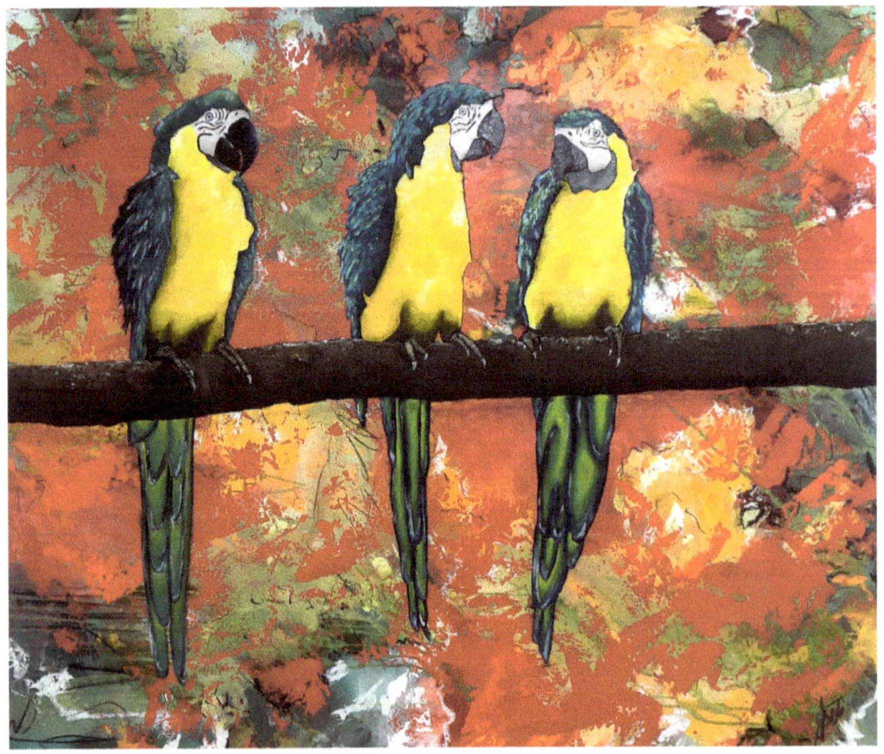

Parrots in the Jungle, 2022. Acrylic & Oil on canvas. 120 x 100 cm

ANDREW BINDER

United States | andrewbinder.com

Andrew Binder is a contemporary visual artist from the United States. In his work he strives to create imagery that invites the viewer to have their own subjective experience and interpretation. Despite much of his work being figurative, he is more concerned with self-expression rather than representation. Through an experimental and improvisational process that combines new and traditional media, he uses his art as an expressive outlet to convey a sense of feeling, atmosphere, transitory memory, and the existential experience of the individual.

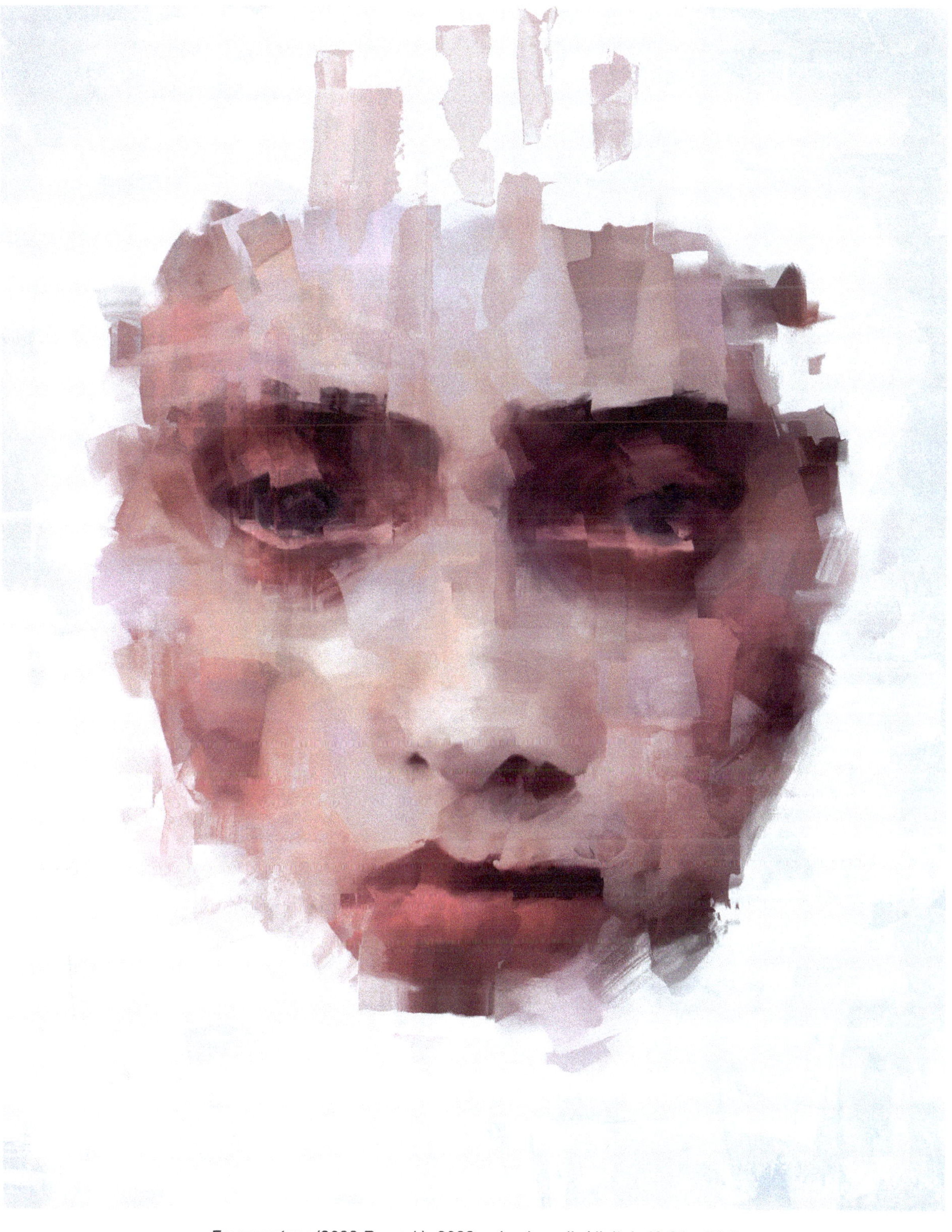

Fragmentary (2022 Rework), 2022, mixed-media/digital, 40.64 x 50.8

PATRICIA SPOON

United States | spoonpatricia2@gamil.com

My name is Patricia Spoon. I am an abstract and modern artist from Virginia, USA. Early in my educational career, I developed a strong interest in the arts. This has continued with me into my adulthood studies. Visiting museums, taking nature trips, and learning about world culture, has contributed to my passion to the field of art. My practice in the field of art ,is modern and abstract art . My influences include self individuality,lines,geometric patterns, angles, colors, movement and nature . For my creative process, I begin to absorb self individuality and nature. I express nature with lines and geometric patterns. Colors are a huge influence in my art. I use both bold and soft colors to express self individuality and nature. Lines ,angles and geometric patterns, are used in my art to show the beauty of nature.These factors,make my paintings come alive. Motion and tone is incorporated into my art . These components are vital to my art . My art composition becomes symphony on canvas. It displays my creativity and is what makes my art unique ..

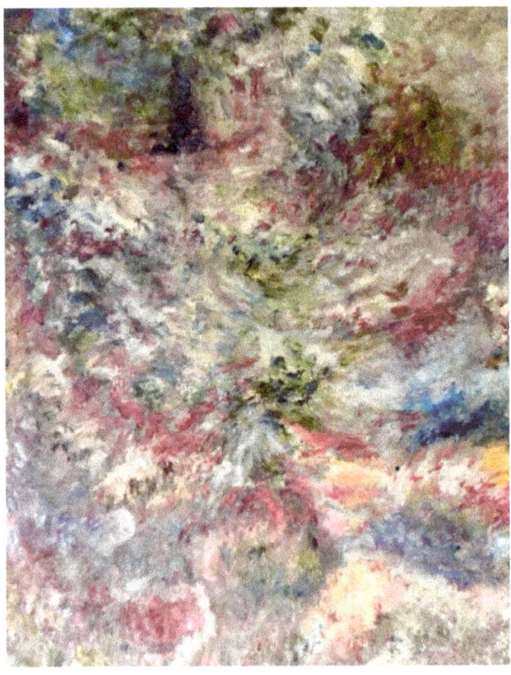

Colors,18x24, 2021

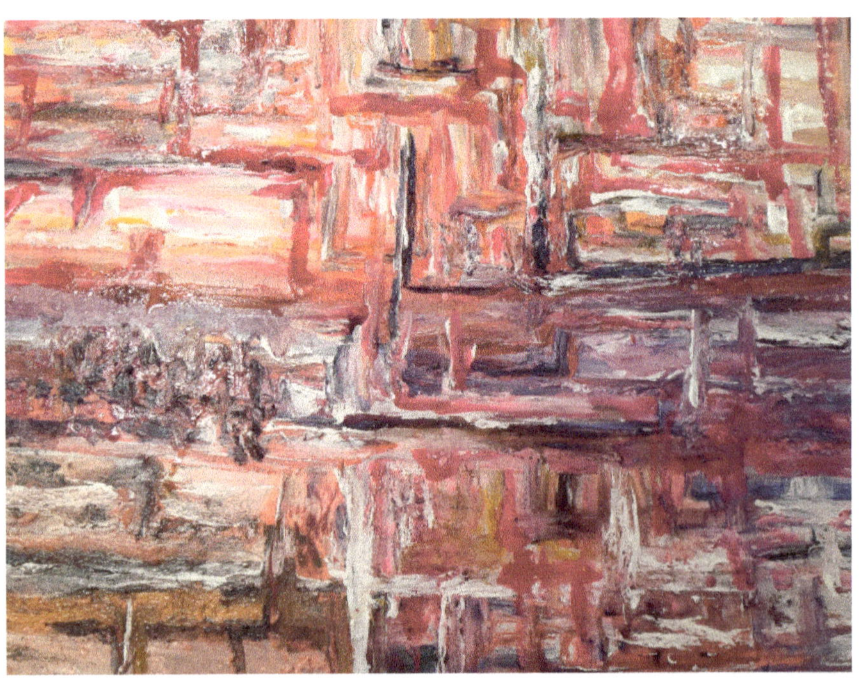

Elemental,18x24,2021

DAVID TANNER

Switzerland | davidtannerart.ch

David Tanner lives and works in switzerland. His metal workshop is located underneath a carpentry in the center of St.Gallen. He has always been creative but has only been actively a metalartist since 2015. His apprenticeship in the metal industry gave him the neccessary knowledge, skills and thus the foundation for his career as an artist. Art out of metal. Why metal? For him, metal has something enduring about it. It stays solid and isn't easily damaged. That is exactly what he wants for his projects. He would like his artwork to be preserved. It is important to him that they can be found, viewed, and enjoyed long into future. His goal as an artist is to create large pieces of work to show them in public spaces. Tanner is eager to take the viewer back in time ,so that they can feel the pure joy of nostalgia.
He works `almost` exclusively with metal.
His love of grinding and welding metal allows him to really let the sparks fly.
His workshop hoards many different metal-work machines. Some of which have been acquired out of pure enthusiasm for metalworking, but not necessarily needed at this present time.
He eagerly presents his work down to the smallest detail and invests time improving and perfecting his processes.
This passion for detail shows that David is quite possibly a perfectionist.
 Subject for his art, is often taken from the influences of his childhood or from music.
Being a former DJ is clearly reflected in his work.
The general public has often referred to his art as old school.

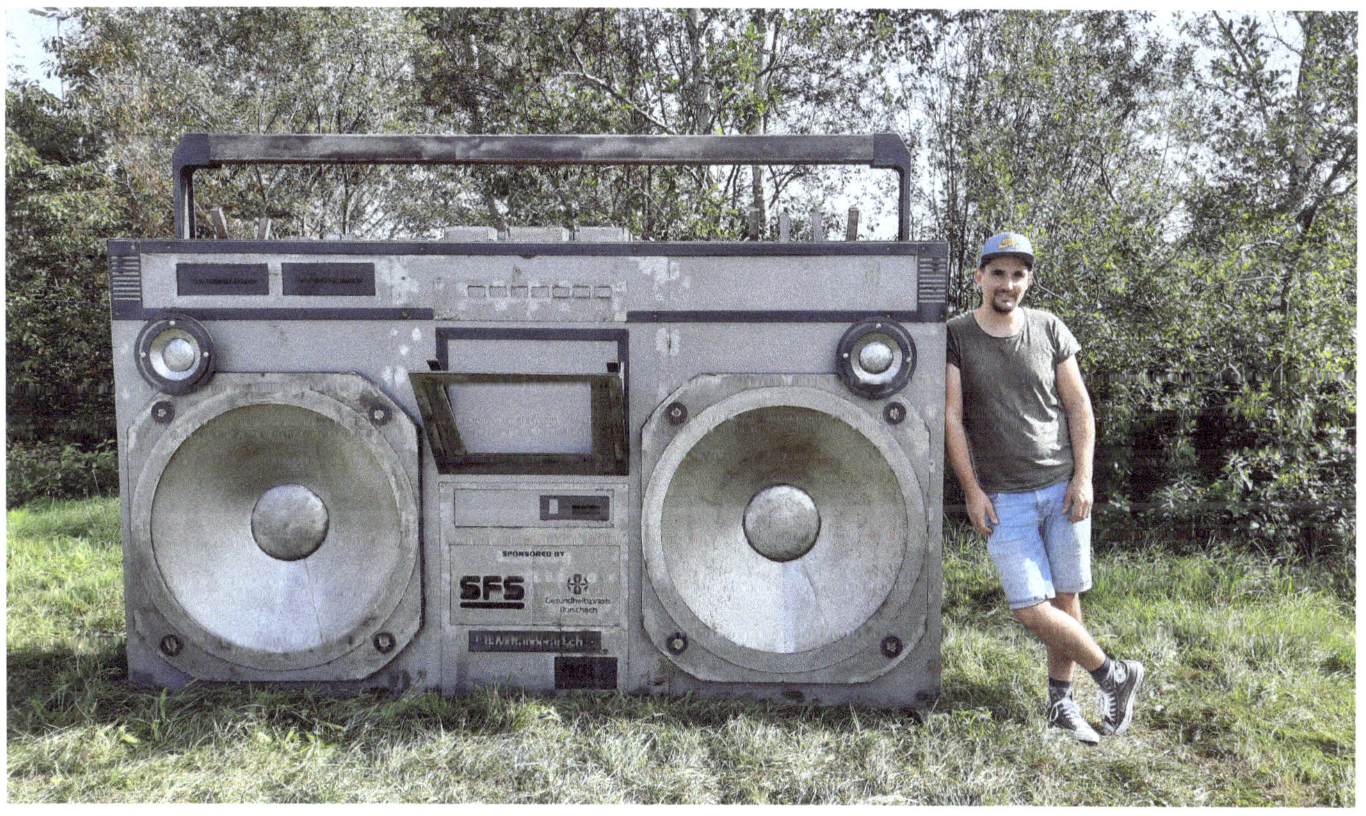

Radiomania, 2021. sheetmetal welded, 3m x 2m x 0.7m

KATHY STANLEY

United States | sacredartjourneys.com

Kathy Stanley, M.A. is a Jamaican-born artist living on the US West Coast. An intuitive artist and ecopsychology educator, her visionary art acrylic paintings reflect meditative inner journeys of exploring the ecological self, centering around images that celebrate earth, the rising feminine spirit and invoke wholeness, joy and aliveness. Kathy holds a Master's degree in Women's Spirituality with Specializations in Spiritual Guidance and Creative Expression. She is currently a Senior Adjunct Lecturer in the School of Undergraduate Studies at the California Institute of Integral Studies in San Francisco. Her various eco-literacy classes are designed to inspire confident and engaged participation in the global effort towards an ecologically sustainable society. Her article "The Land That Owns Us: Identity and Place of Birth" was published in the September 2022 issue of the Ecopsychology Journal. She is currently working on a Ph.D. in East-West Psychology. She also holds professional certification in Luminous Healing and Shamanic Energy Medicine from the Light Body School of Dr. Alberto Villoldo's Four Winds Society. She is represented by MONAT Art Gallery and Van Gogh Art Gallery in Madrid, Spain. Her art has been seen at the Luxembourg Art Fair in September 2022 & 2021, at Monaco Art Fair in June 2022 and in solo and group exhibits in Madrid, Spain, Portland and Seattle, in international virtual exhibitions hosted by galleries in Milan, Bologna, Madrid and London, as well as in House and Garden Magazine, The World of Interiors Magazine, Condé Nast Traveller Magazine and Vanity Fair UK edition.

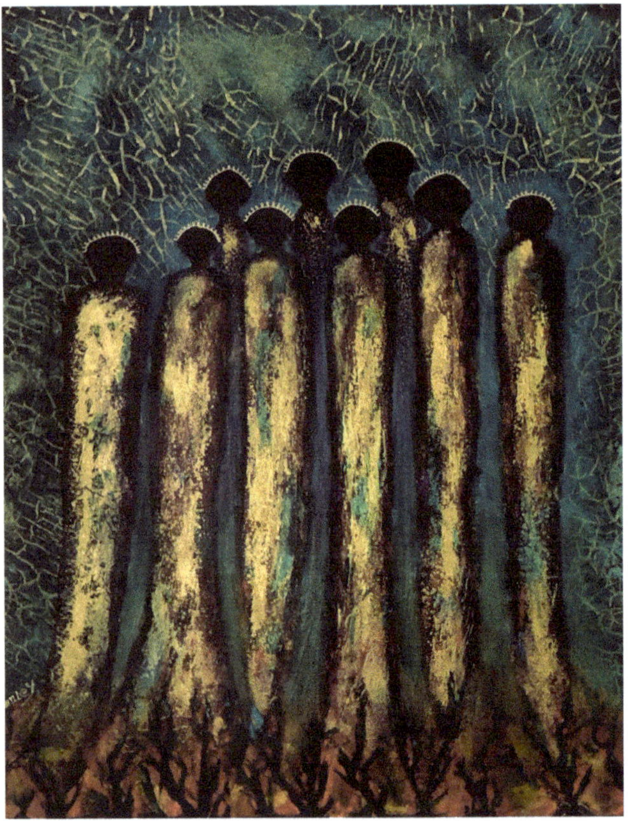

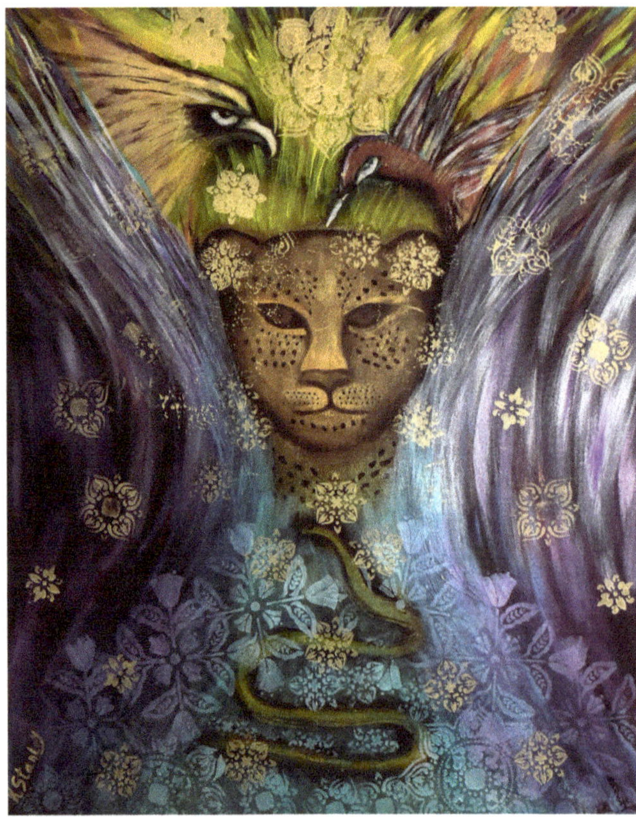

Queendom Come, 2019. Acrylic on Canvas, 60.96 cm x 76.2 cm
(24 x 30 inches)

Rainbow Jaguar, 2020, Acrylic on Canvas, 60.96 cm x 76.2 cm
(24 x30 inches)

EDDA GYLFADÓTTIR

Iceland | eddagylfa.is

Edda Jóna Gylfadóttir was born 1967 and raised in Reykjavík Iceland. Like most people tend to do when they grow up, she thought it's best to learn something practical. After finishing a BA degree in Psychology she worked for many years with handicapped people. But always being creative she decided to take an u turn and go back to school. After finishing some foundation studies in Ceramics and as well as in Art and Design she applied for the Iceland University of the Art where she graduated in BA Product design 2009. After a journey through life, working and studying and graduating from different schools, she found her place and today she paints and designs ceramics in her studio inspired by everything that goes by in her daily life. She likes to create different things depending on how she feels. All kinds of things inspire her like emotions, people, weather, colors and Icelandic nature which is a real candy box. The days are never the same. One day she is completely hooked on designing ceramics and the next on painting. She even walks with muddy hands and picks up the brushes and starts painting. Sounds a little hyperactive but she is a very calm person.

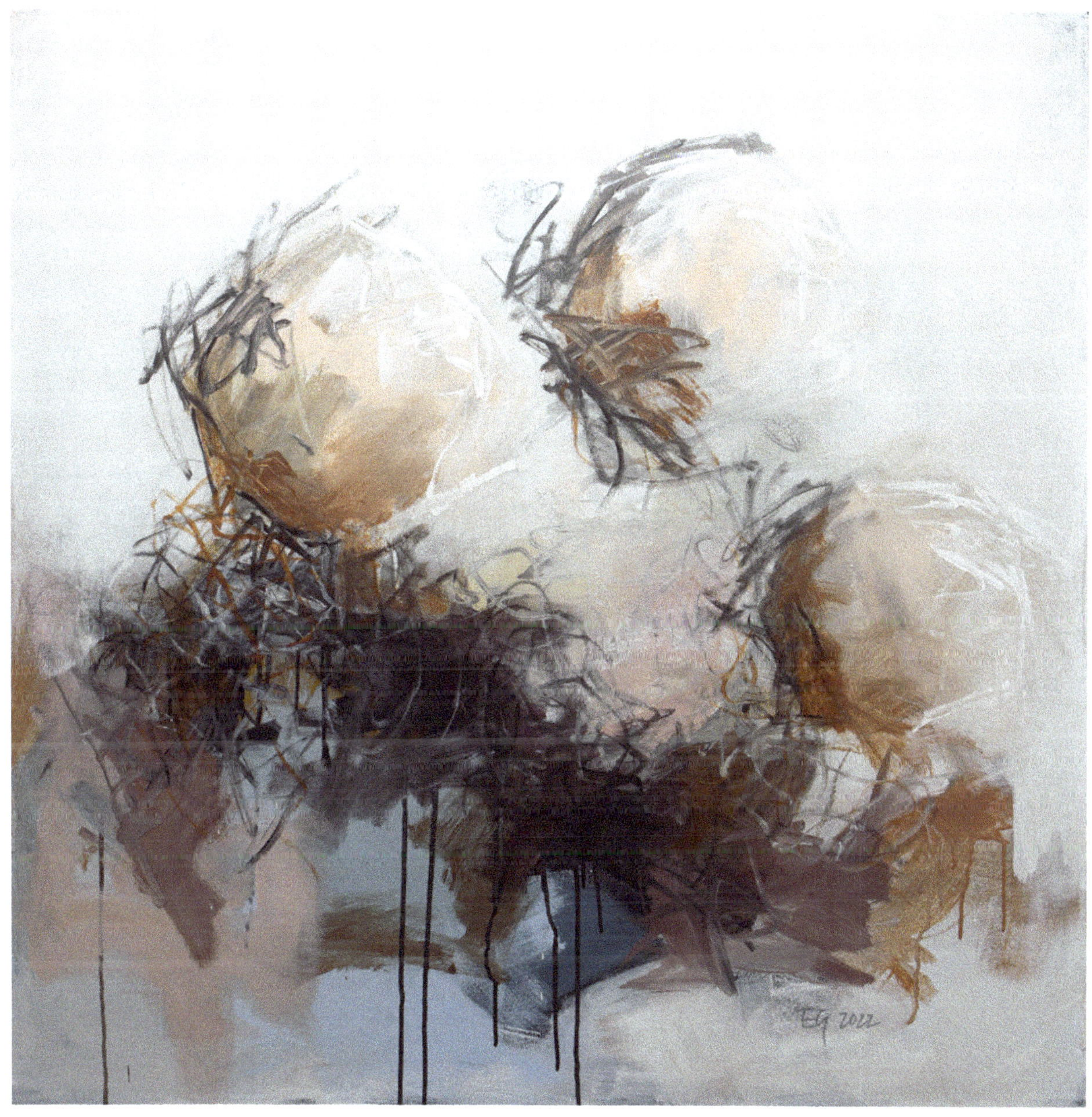

Brothers 2022. Acrylic on canvas, 100x100 cm

KOQUI HANDAL

Bolivia | galeria.arte@koquihandal.com

José Luis "Koqui" Handal was born in La Paz, Bolivia in 1961. His passion for art was evident from an early age and it was in 1997 that he assembled his firts workshop where he gave life to clay, accomplishing extraordinary works in ceramics. Entirely self –taught, in 2005 he ventured into paiting, and since then has participated in national and international expositions. His constant drive and curiosity took him to sculpting in ceramics, bronze, and steel. Today his art is on permanent display in La Paz and Santa Cruz, Bolivia; Buenos Aires, Argentina; and the United States. His visión as an artist reflects his way of seeing the world through a powerful and striking prism, evidenced by the euphoric colors and enormity of some of his pieces. "In art, I find spiritual balance. I focus on the impasto technique in my paintings, infusing a variety of vibrant colors. I am a versatile and passionate artist, and what I hope to achieve through my art is a transmission of sensations and emotions. I pour all the strength I have into my work so that by looking at it, a viewer may understand me through colors and content; antlers compete with waning moons and manes reflect the sun's rays. Through my work I want to reignite a lost respect for the beauty and majesty of the natural world."

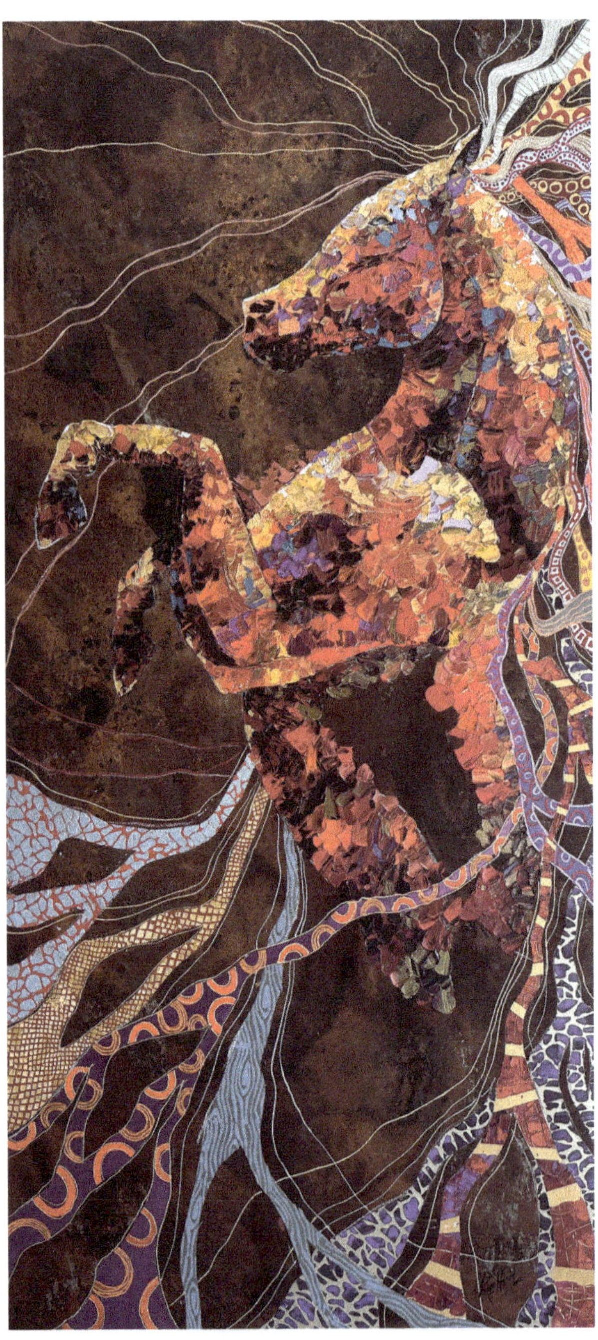

Simon, acrylic on metal. 1.90m x 1m, year 2022

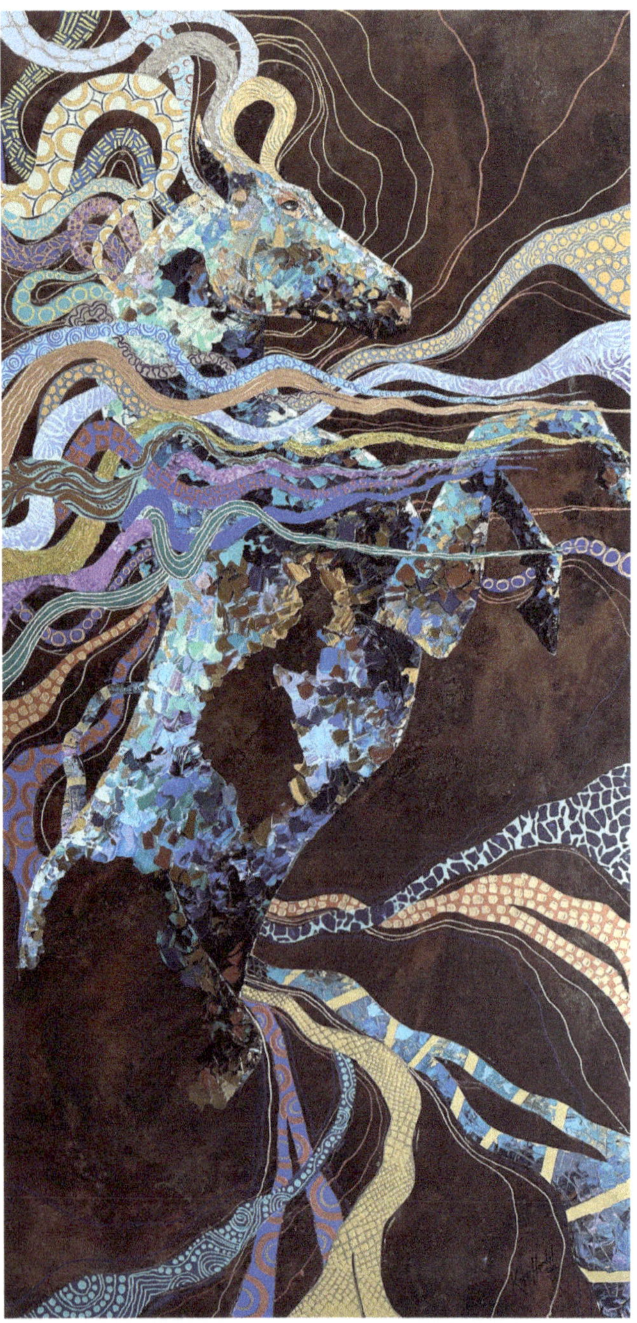

Coral, acrylic on metal, 1.90m x 1m. year 2022

MARCELLE MANSOUR

Australia | marcellemansour.com.au

Marcelle Mansour is a multi-award-winning Australian multidisciplinary visual artist, bilingual writer, poet, journalist contributor and Peace Ambassador. She received both Masters of Fine Arts (MFA) and Studio Arts (MSA) from the University of Sydney and previously a Bachelor of Arts (B.A.) in English Language & Literature from Egypt. She has exhibited nationally and internationally in Biennales and major international exhibitions in Sydney, New York, Paris (Louvre), Venice, London, Florence, Amsterdam and Barcelona. Her work spans from representational art to abstract, digital and light art in a variety of mediums and styles that balance classical insight with contemporary formulation. Originally of Palestinian Christian Heritage who experienced wars before migrating to Australia. Inspired by her Western-Eastern cultural backgrounds, her artistic voice is shaped by the impact of war affecting women and civilians. Her work of illuminating light was painted with light itself as a material to impinge the medium of perception. The shifting colors of changeable light highlights the theme of universal human experiences in a phenomenological manner. Her art aspires to influence viewers to rethink human issues with a purpose of gaining self-knowledge of human consciousness, transformation and healing, reflecting on global challenges facing humanity towards reshaping reality. Marcelle Mansour received numerous international art prizes including an Honorary Presidential Award, The Medal of the Order of Australia (OAM) in the 2017 Queen's Birthday Honours, ATIM's Top 60 Masters Award, ATIM's Collector's Choice Award, International Art Prize Paris, International Prize Barcelona, and The Best Modern and Contemporary Artists London Prize.

Transformation, 2014. Light Art, 44 x 33 cm.

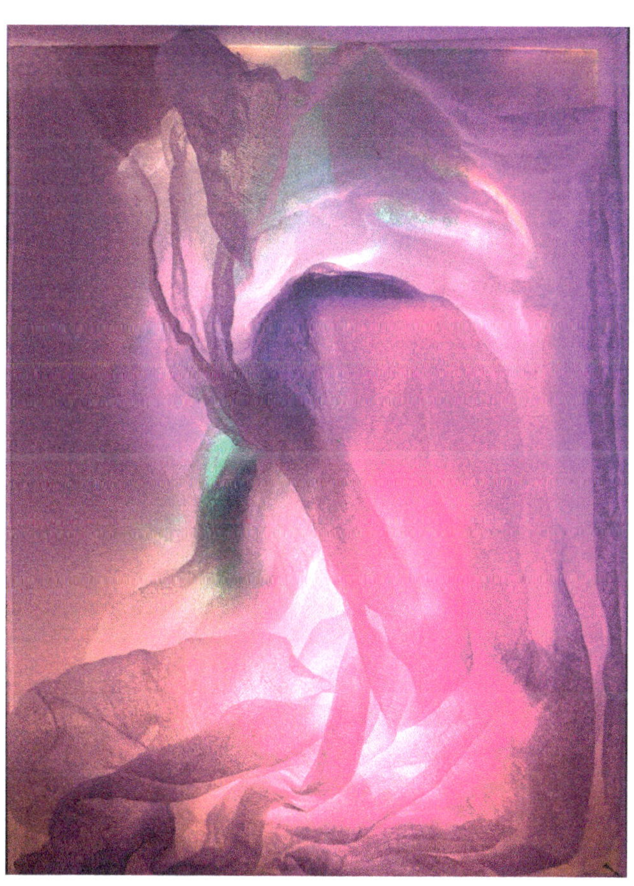

Healing, 2014. Light Art, 44 x 33 cm.

LENE KLOVBORG

Denmark | leneklovborg.com

Lene Klovborg has always loved colours. As a child she used to pick wild flowers and arrange them. Later photography became her passion and she discovered an instinct for motives, light and shade, and contrast. It was a surprise to her when she began to paint. During a cup of coffee she suddenly had to buy canvasses, brushes and colours, and by nightfall she had created her first painting. She has taught herself everything. She is curious and follows her intuition when she develops new techniques. She works with acrylic on canvas and uses bright, intense, warm nuances that suit the way she paints, which is abstract modern impressionism. Her inspiration is nature. It possesses an amazing ability to touch and comfort - pure happiness. She has travelled in Rome, along the Danish shores of the North Sea, and in Yorkshire, and she uses emotions of these places in her art. She had an accident some years back, and it was on the exact date two years later - that she began to paint. To her it is a reminder that something amazing can blossom the most unexpected places. She truly believes that art can change your life. Like nature it has the power to touch, heal, excite, inspire, and bring you joy. Her greatest achievement is when someone finds that in her paintings. This winter she will work on a series of smaller, simpler paintings to encourage and inspire people that are unfamiliar with art.

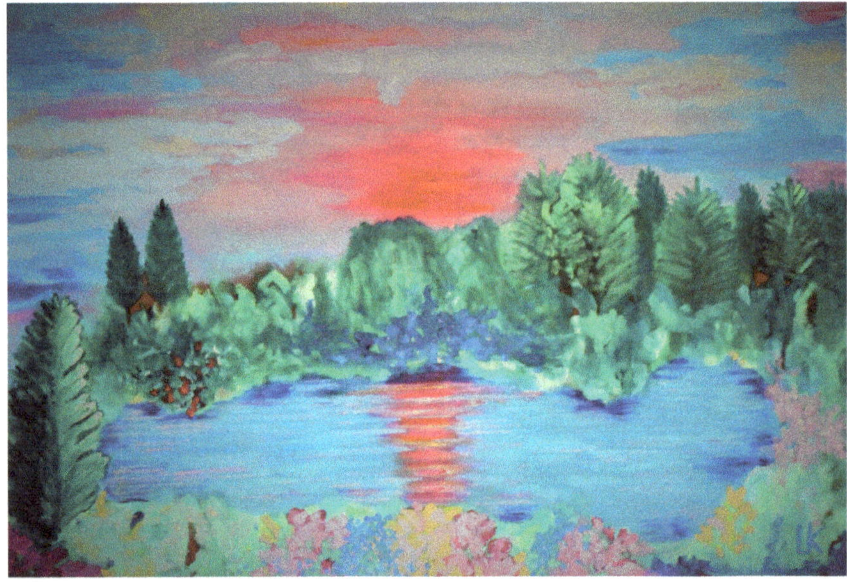

Summer Sunset, 2022. Acrylic on canvas, 65 x 90 cm

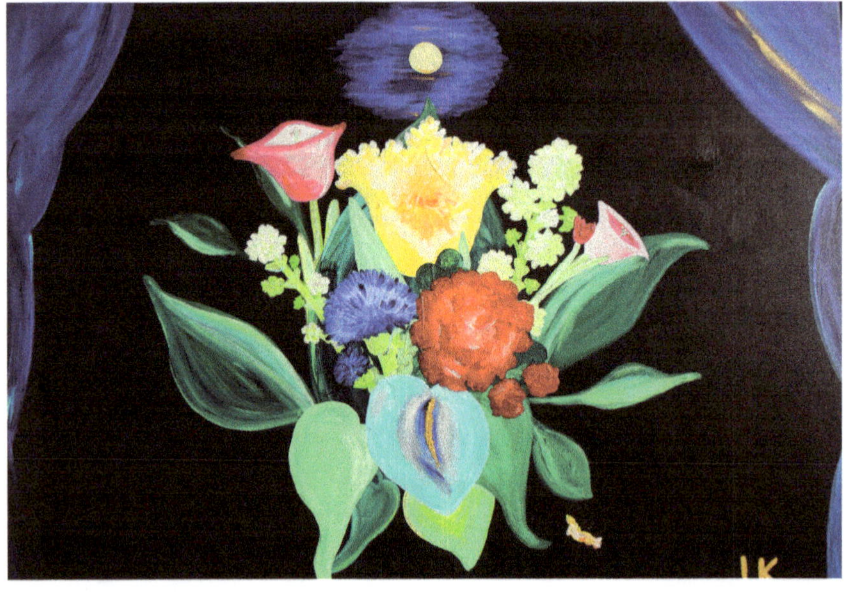

Summer Night, 2022. Acrylic on canvas, 65 x 90 cm

GM SACCO

Italy | gmsacco.com

GM Sacco is a university professor of computer science, who resigned to devote himself full-time to his artistic interests. He has been photographing for a long time, first on film, then digitally and finally digitally and on large format film. His interest for art is not limited to photography and he was the publisher of an acclaimed CD-ROM series on painters of the Italian Renaissance, which included the first hypertextual edition of Vasari's Lives of Artists. He likes to think of himself as an image peddler rather than a photographer and believes that painters, from Duccio to contemporaries, have a significant influence in his work. His works span from architecture, to abandoned decaying buildings (factories primarily), to nudes, to still life. He is especially concerned by the impermanence of things and, like Webster, is "much possessed by death". At the same time, his works investigate metaphysics, what exists beyond our limited experience and could tame the horror of death. In the last ten years he has won more than 60 awards in the most important international competitions, such as IPA – International Photo Awards, Tokyo Foto Awards, Fine Art Photo Awards, PX3 – Prix de la Photographie Paris. He also appeared in more than ten exhibitions in places such as Rome, Milan, Venice, Glasgow and Tokyo.

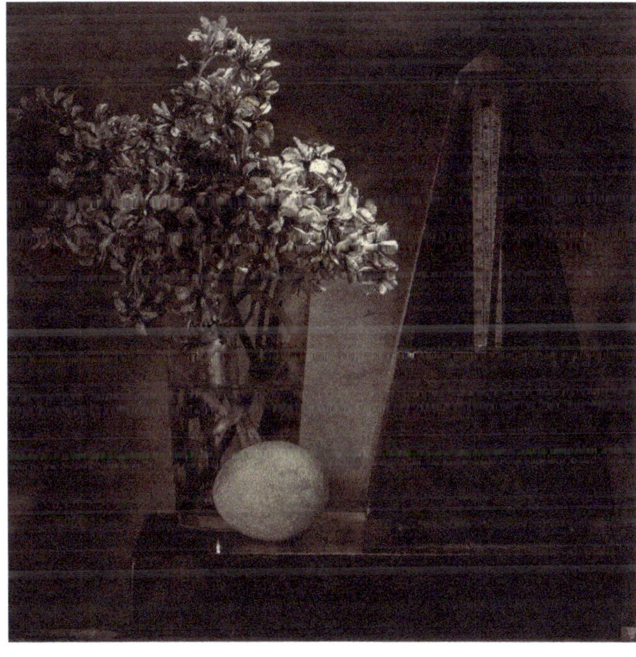

Chronos Kairos Aion - photo - 2021

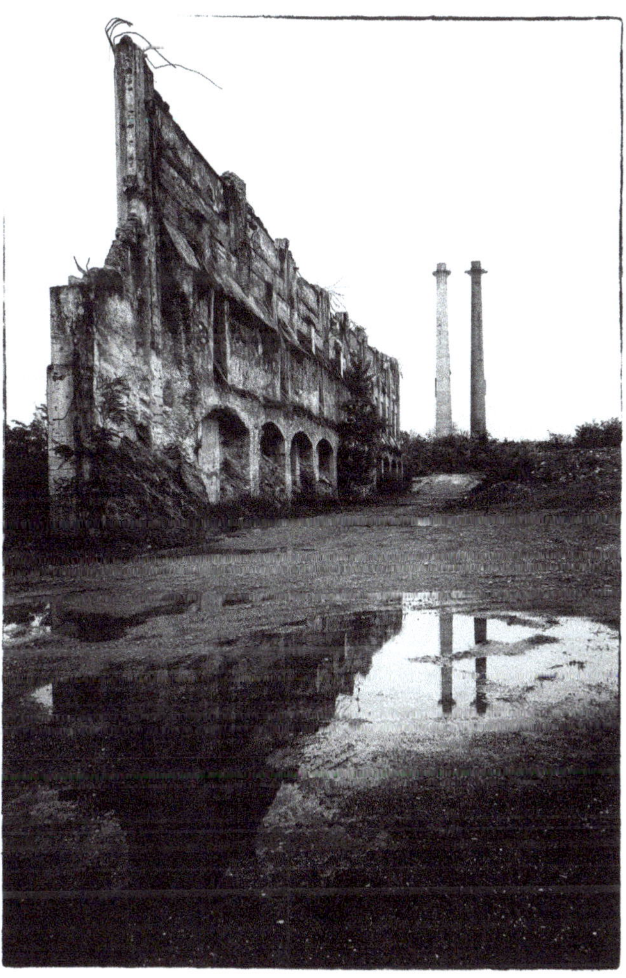

Silent Theaters XXI - photo - 2017

REZAUL HOQUE

Bangladesh | rezaulhoque.com

Rezaul Hoque is a professional artist, having graduated from the Institute of Fine Arts, University of Dhaka, in Bangladesh. Hoque is also a material development consultant, and works with non-profit agencies like OXFAM and CARE, to develop communications materials in sectors like education, gender and women's rights. Since 1993, while still a university student, Reza created and since then has been experimenting and perfecting a unique technique, i.e., painting using heat convection to create a soft illusion and an atypical dimension with a different aesthetic. Hoque was born in and grew up in Kurigram, one the poorest districts of Bangladesh, seeing extreme poverty, hunger and famine. Despite the hardship, he felt the simple people of his district faced these challenges with unfaltering resolve and continued to see dreams of a beautiful life. Reza strives to depict their suffering and strength. The main themes of his work are exploitation, deprivation, rights, inequality, struggle, hope, and the deep-seated perceptions of life people have. Hoque feels passionately about social justice and believes that art plays a role in bringing the plight of deprived people to the fore. He conveys his concerns through both subject matter and technique, as his process also implies the feeling of being burnt by life's struggles. Through his art he aims to spread awareness and advocate for justice. Hoque currently lives and works in Bangladesh, where he is active in the local artist community. He has exhibited in national and international exhibitions, and has even donated his works to various causes for fundraising purposes.

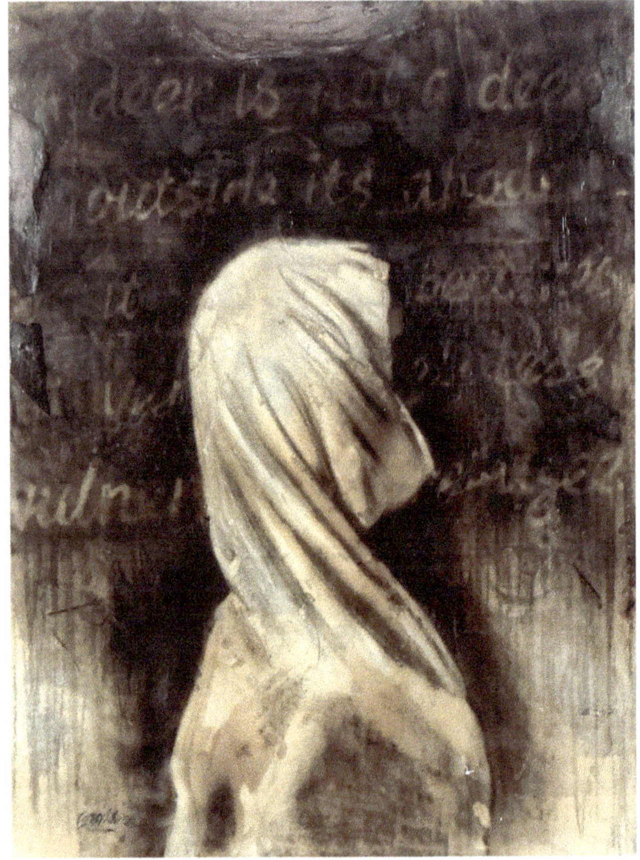

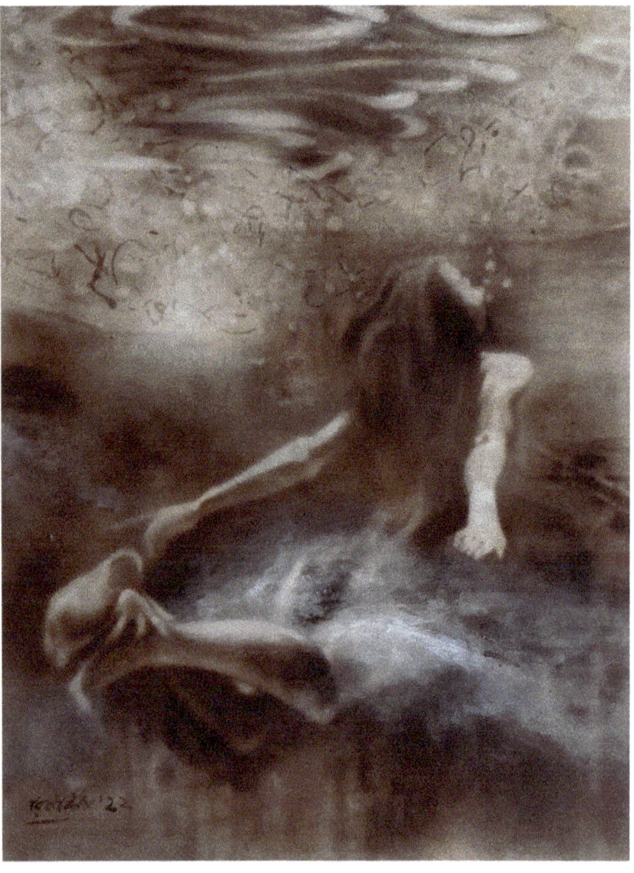

Away 3, 2022, Paper burn & Acrylic, 61 x 46 cm

Freee..., 2022, Paper burn & Acrylic, 60 x 45 cm

CLAUDIA HABRINGER

Austria | claudia-habringer.com

Claudia Habringer presents her new approach to Visual Art. She calls it Art by Resonance. Her striking lines and bright colors are showing her perceptions. In resonance with a targeted energy field her artworks seem to evolve themselves. As a trained actress, creativity trainer and energetic coach she has found her new purpose. Drawing perception. She has never followed a certain art form but aimed to surrender to the flow. Mostly she uses markers and acrylic colors to draw on coated fabric, canvas and canvas board by following her senses. It is above all an act of making the invisible visible. Her abstract approach appears full of symbols and different levels and spaces. The most important thing is to stay in touch with the chosen resonance field during the process. The process begins with the first line, which represents a perceived movement of the target object, and ends when a sense of complete satisfaction is reached. After all, the canvas or paper contains the blueprint of the subject. She is definitely always looking for the big picture, the view from above, and her approach to art is a path with infinite possibilities to the point.

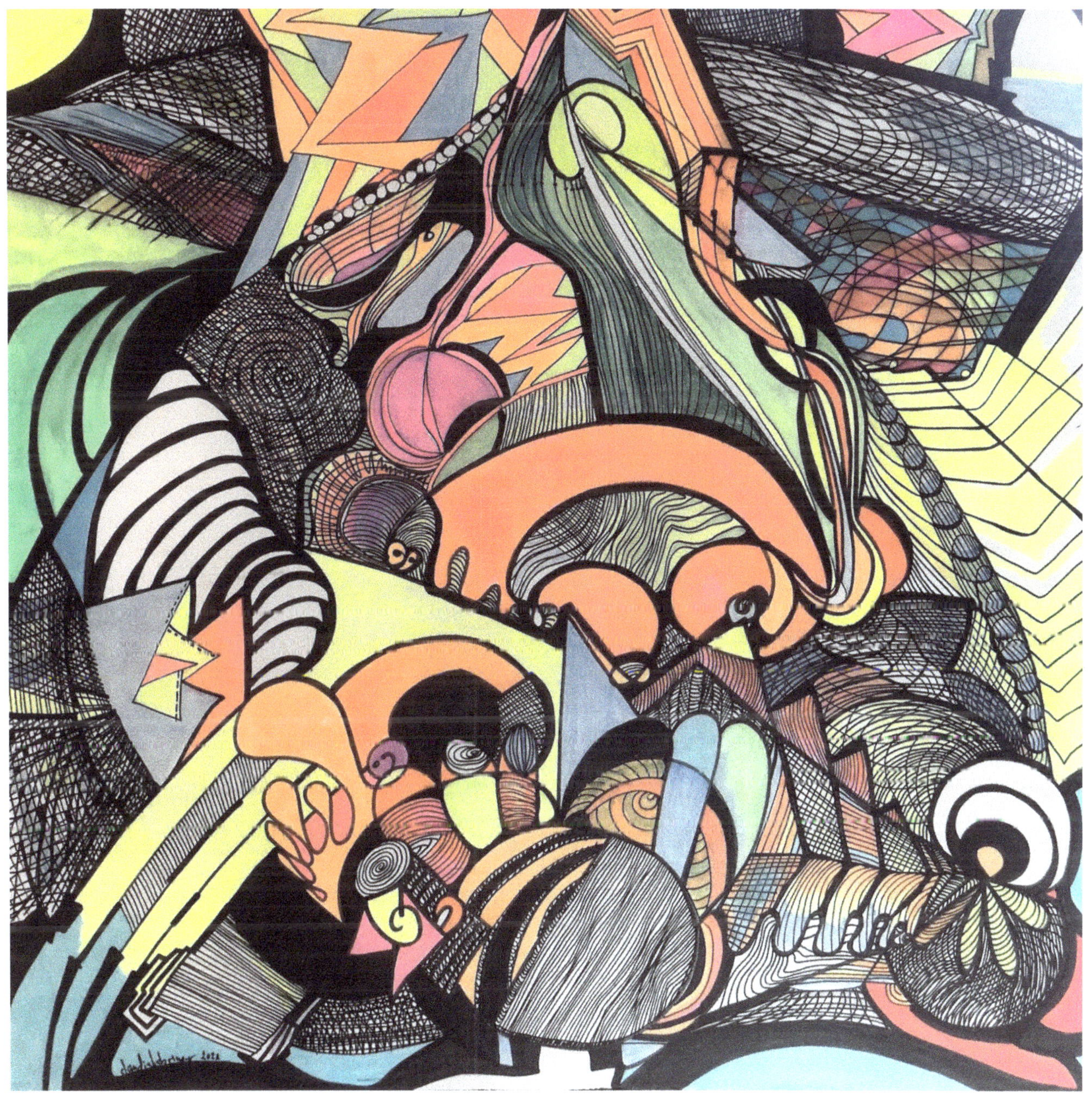

in resonance with LUDOVICO EINAUDI and his music, 2021, Marker and acrylic on canvas, 100 x 100cm

AOMI KIKUCHI

Japan | aomikikuchi.com

Aomi Kikuchi is a textile artist based in Kyoto, Japan. She holds a BFA from Kyoto University of Art & Design (Japan) and an MFA from Pratt Institute (USA). Aomi has exhibited her work throughout the world including at Woman's Essence Show 2022 (Paris),The First Suzhou Craft Biennale 2021(China), Art Laguna 2021(Italy) and Art Laguna at Villa dei Cedri 2022. Her work is based on Japanese aesthetic principles and the teachings of the Buddha. "Wabi-sabi", a well known philosophy that beauty is found in imperfections and "Mono-no-aware", the feeling of sympathy for that which changes or perishes such as the seasons and all living things. The Buddha states that life is impermanent, insubstantial and suffering. People feel suffering when they seek something everlasting yet while existence is not eternal, the activities of matter and life are conceptually infinite. Over 30 years, Aomi has dedicated extensive and immersive practice to various textile materials and techniques including Traditional Yuzen Kimono Dyeing, Japanese Embroidery, and Weaving. Aomi takes inspiration from the fragility and fleetingness found in natural cycles and in textiles such as extremely thin fibers, goose down, and wool fiber. She explores impermanence and infinity through the use of biology and nature with textiles and waste.

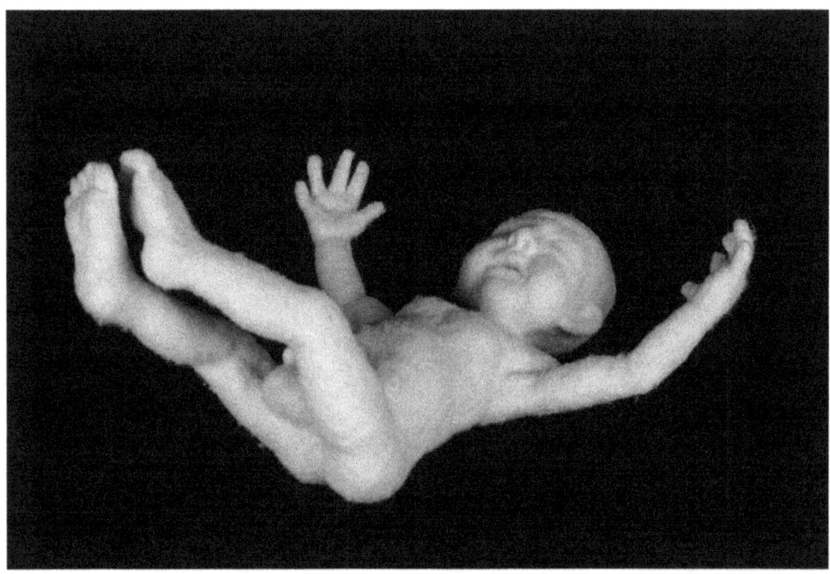

Suffering being Born-1/ 40x30x20 (cm) Wool Fiber

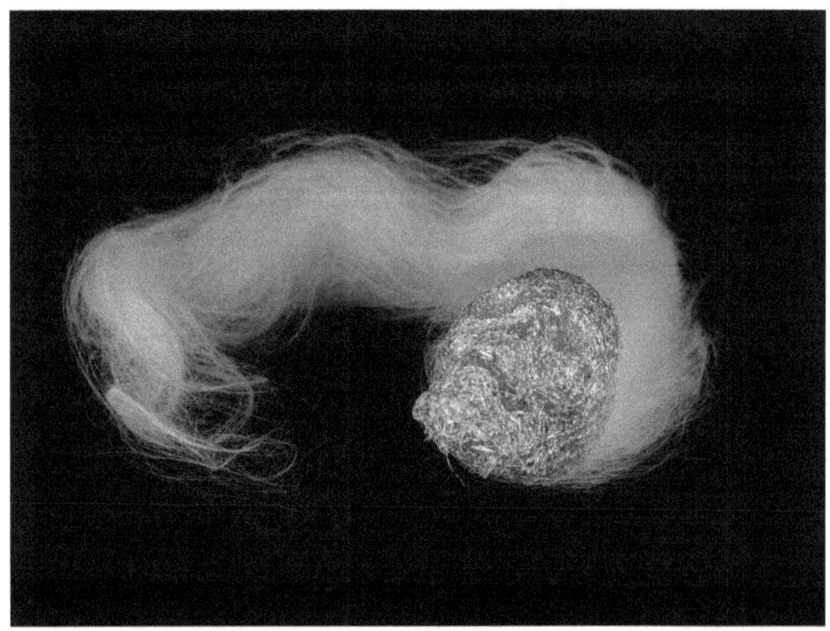

Woman 2022/ Wire, Synthetic Fiber/ 70x12x10 (cm)

WERONIKA RACZYNSKA

Poland | raczynska.net

Weronika Raczynska was born in 1978 in Warsaw, Poland. In the years 1997-2002 studied painting at the European Academy of Arts (EAS) in Warsaw, Poland. In 2002 graduated with a Master of Fine Arts degree in painting (distinction). From 2008-2010 studied painting at The Jan Matejko Academy of Fine Arts (ASP) in Cracow, Poland. In 2010 completed post-graduate studies in painting. She has had 17 solo exhibitions of painting and more than 120 group exhibitions in Warsaw, Poland; Cracow, Poland, as well as in Basel, Switzerland; Kishinev, Moldavia; London, United Kingdom; New York, United States of America; Paris, France; Rome, Italy and Milan, Italy among others. In 2022 received a scholarship from the Creation Support Fund of the ZAIKS Association of Authors. Paintings by Weronika Raczynska can be found in private collections in Poland and other countries of Europe, and also in New Zealand, the Philippines and the United States of America, as well as in public collection of the Office of Artistic Exhibitions (BWA) in Kielce, Poland. The paintings of Weronika Raczynska belong to figurative art but already with the experience of "New Wild" and the movement of New Expression, and also of the New Figuration aesthetic, thus appearing in still expressive but already silenced version. The artist's interest is focused on a man / woman and his / her not easy existence in contemporary realities. She lives and works in Warsaw, Poland.

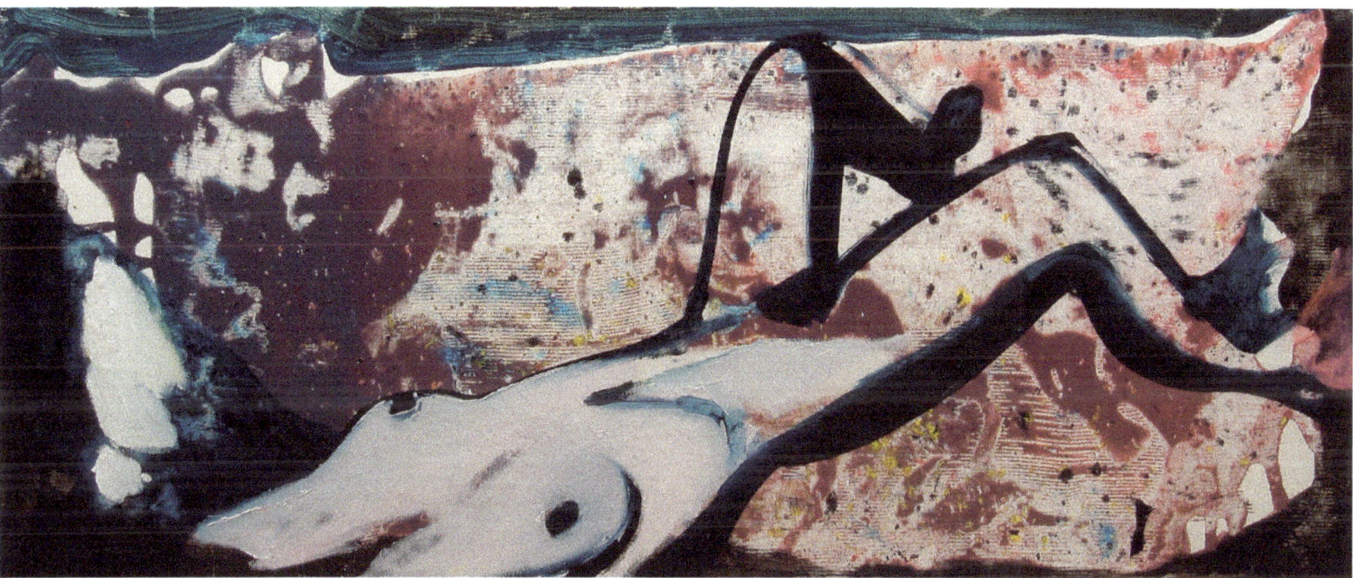

Return From The Stars. Perto, 2021, acrylic & oil on canvas, 40 x 96 cm

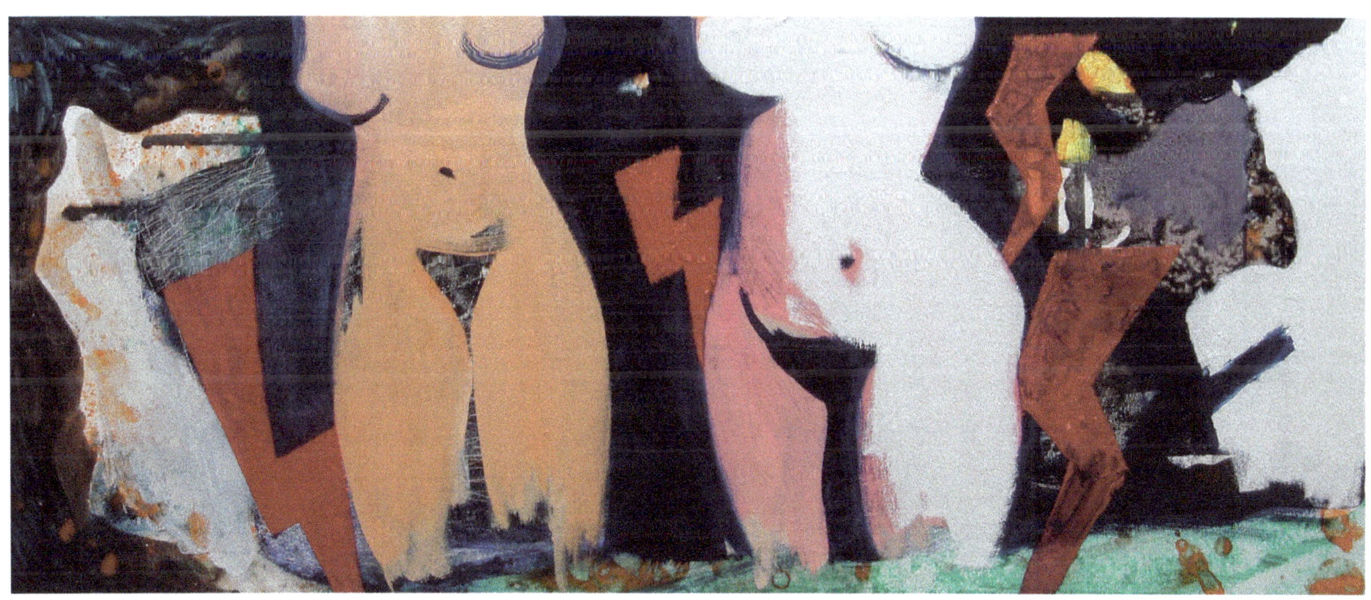

Return From The Stars. Sturm und Drang, 2021, acrylic & oil on canvas, 40 x 95 cm

ROBERT VAN DE GRAAF

The Netherlands | robertvandegraaf.com

Robert van de Graaf (b. 1983, the Netherlands) is interested in the connections and relations between the mystical in this world, the sense and the dimension of the spiritual world and our soul. In his exploration he is seeking the mystical hidden in this world which he translates into metaphorical paintings. The works express a complex interplay of visual impressions combined with emotional and spiritual reflection. Each piece gives substance to his ongoing personal journey to seek meaning in life. The artworks aim to elicit a gaze back at the viewer, a reflection of feelings, crossing the line from observation to introspection. Van de Graaf draws his inspiration from religious and spiritual stories, mythology, mystical places and the philosophy of life. He transforms his inspiration into contemporary interpretations while richly referring to artists through all times of art history such as Caspar David Friedrich, Anselm Kiefer, Joan Mitchell and the old masters. Though primarily working on his oil paintings, he is also using drawings and watercolours during the creation process. The paintings are often large in scale and balance between the figurative and the abstract, giving a certain freedom to the viewer. Van de Graaf received a Master of Science (MSc) degree in Architecture (Technical University Delft) in 2009. At an early age he enjoyed an intense private painting and drawing training (1996 - 2001) by the Dutch artist Erica Meyster (1949 - 2006). His art is held in private collections through the Netherlands, the United States and France.

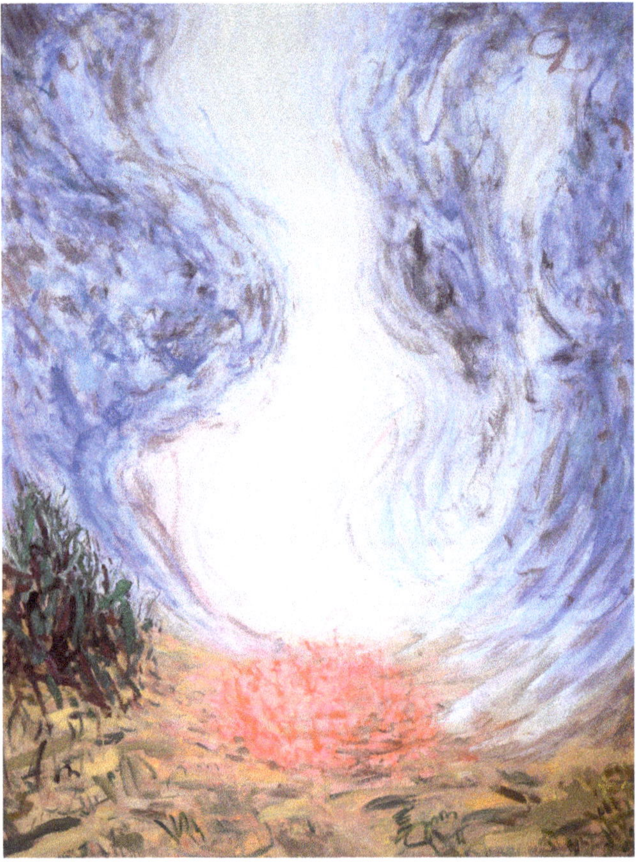

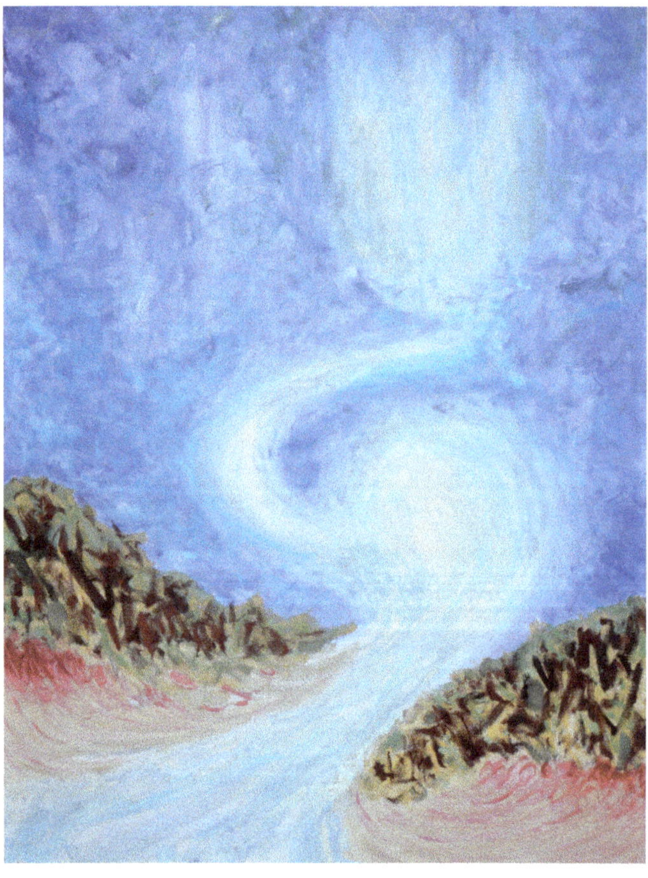

Let the Flowers in Your Heart Bloom / 2022 / Oil on rough linen / 210 x 160 x 2,5 cm

The Birth of Air Castles / 2022 / Oil on rough linen / 210 x 160 x 2,5 cm

NATHA OUT OF THE BLUE

Thailand | nathaoutoftheblue.com

Natha Out of the Blue represent part of her name (Nathakorn) and her spontaneity. Chiangmai, north of Thailand is her origin working studio base. She is a self-taught artist that has been creating her subject matter that blend with her inspiration and design on her canvas with several techniques she inspired. Painting on canvas, she will be preparing her gouache color from the pigment mixing them with the binders. She uses gouache to have some earth tone that she likes. Acrylic colors still take part and being playful on her canvas. The way "OUT OF THE BLUE" action has inspired her most of the time. It is when she feels drawn to establish the creation with a plentiful of energy. She states "The ideas of each artwork sometime are guided through my intuition from the voice within". She tries to convey the message of the artwork to touch upon the viewers. She hopes that her artwork has spoken to the viewers in certain way. These artworks are in the series "transformation". The ideas came during autumn 2021 when she was been in contact with strike changes. It led her emotions to dive deeply into her own darkness. She was sick with diarrhea and a rare fever. Her spirit is not in her good shape. She recognized those wobbly feelings, fear and loneliness. She is connecting with herself to pass through those nights. It is common and not usually serious symptoms. The experiences learned were her inspiration for this series.

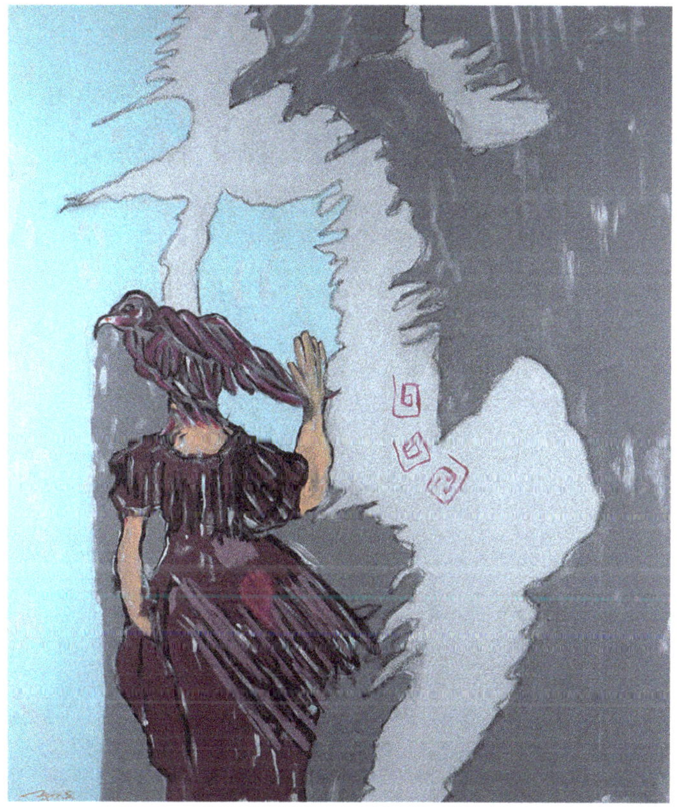

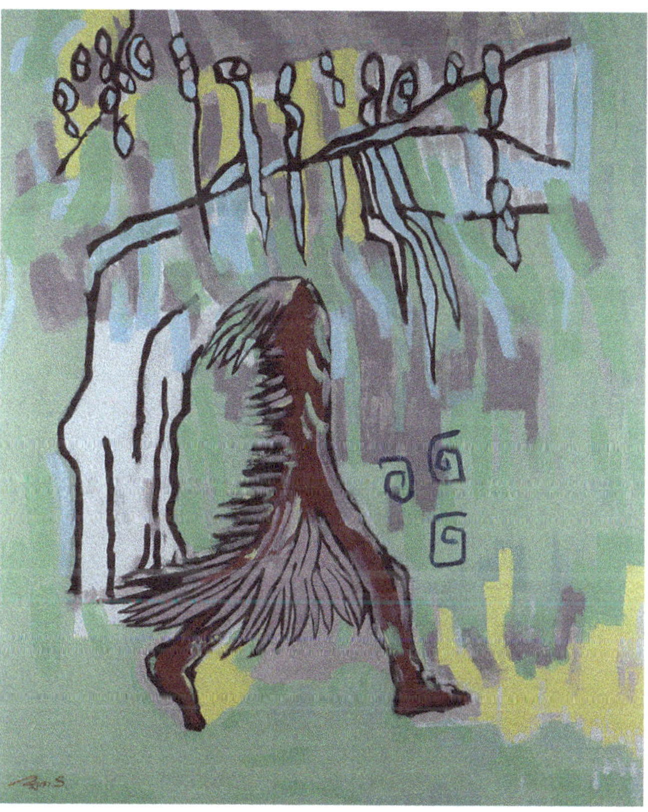

"Walking through the shadow", 2022, Acrylic- gouache colors, 50x60x4cm

"Dancing on her own", 2022, Acrylic- gouache colors, 50x60x4cm

JULIET PETRARULO

Isle of Man | julietpetra@hotmail.co.uk

My name is Juliet Petrarulo. I am an instinctive and semi abstract artist. I paint every day at home in my studio, I have been painting since I can remember. In 2006 I was accepted into the Isle of Man art college on the foundation course which led onto a degree. After four years I gained a 1st honours degree in fine art and design. Whilst I was at college, I had nine art works blown up onto wall sized canvases for a commission to the drug and alcohol rehabilitation centre on the Island. I have also exhibited work on the Island and sold some of my art. In 2020 I put two images in the Art Curator magazine and from this I had responses from galleries all around the world. In 2022 I chose PAKS gallery in Austria and have two paintings in their galleries in Austria, Munich and Vienna all year. On 17th November 2022, I will have two paintings exhibited at Middlethorpe Hall, York which will be promoting placrylic paints which are non-plastic, natural dye pigments. I have used these materials for the two paintings I have submitted. My feelings about my art are positive and focused now about the earth and the way we effect our environment. Being aware of using plastic free and natural dies in pigments is the way forward for me. Nature and the environment and memories from my childhood are connections in my art work.

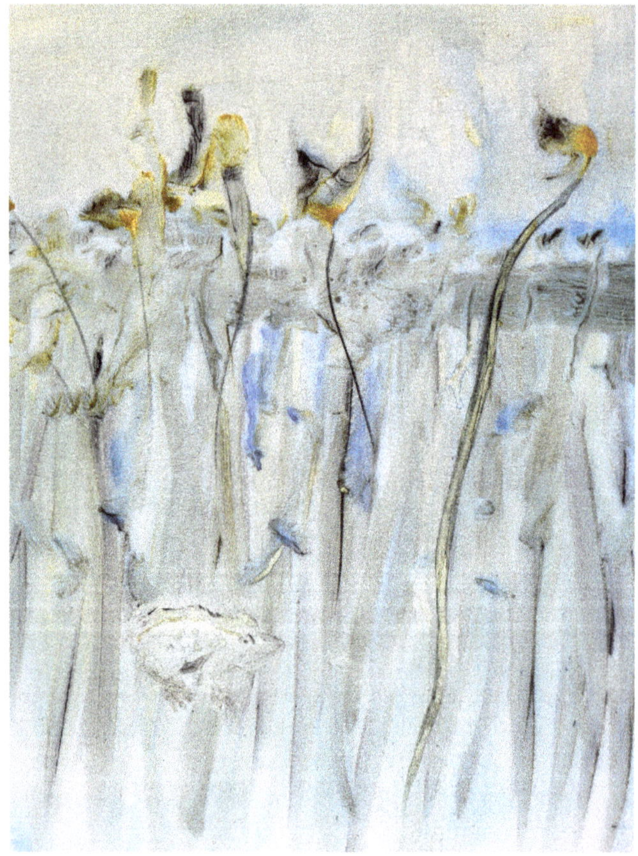

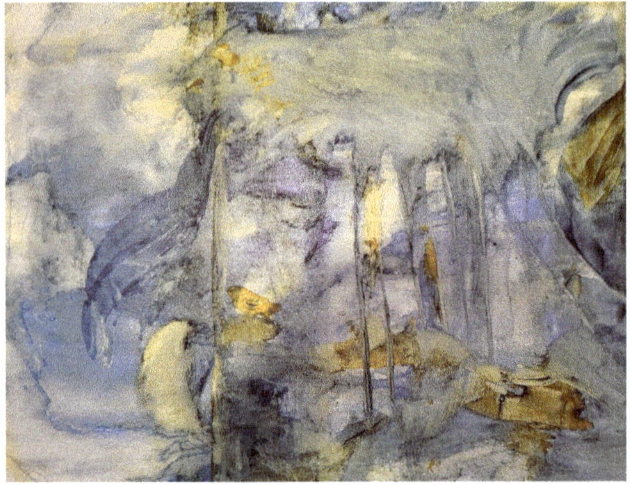

The Forest, 2022, Placrylic paints. 50x60cm

Wetlands, 2022, Placrylic paints. 50x60cm

TOTI CUESTA

Spain | toticuesta.com

Toti Cuesta is a watercolor artist based in Madrid. She studied law and languages and for many years worked in the international field, but art has always been her great passion and the driving force of her life. Art arises from her spiritual need to create, to go beyond the senses. It is an expression of the soul that reflects her commitment to nature, to life and to her inner growth. Her paintings are characterized by the use of symbol and color. The symbol allows her to express and transmit the message of art. Color radiates the light of each human being, allows me to highlight the beauty of their features and transmit the essence of their emotions. Art unites Heaven and Earth and has the power to change the world through creation. It allows us to represent reality in a different way than we perceive it. She defines herself as a watercolorist, although she has numerous works made with other techniques such as oil and pastel because watercolor is the most luminous and transparent technique, the one that can best represent the vibration of other dimensions and capture it in colors that transmit joy and light.

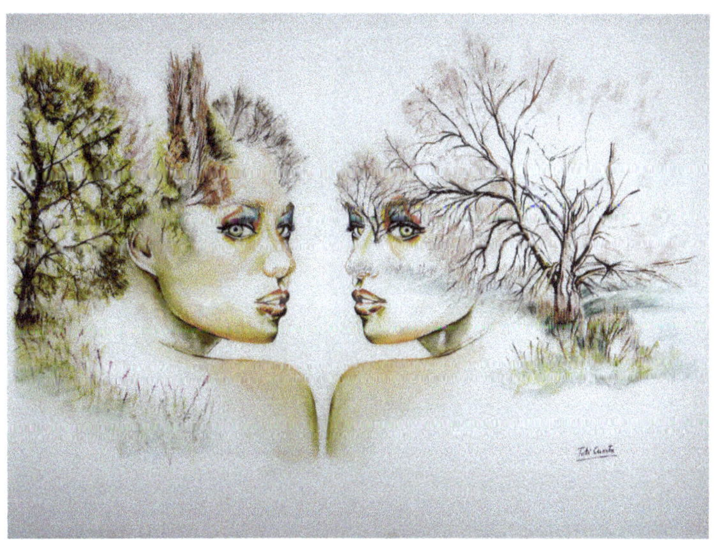

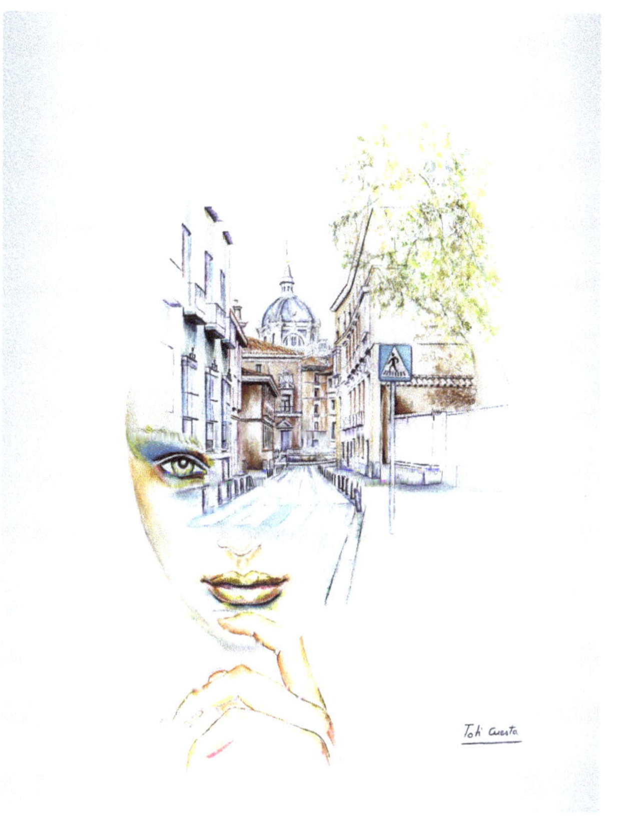

I am nature, Watercolor, 2022, 56 x 76 cm

Sacramento Street Madrid, watercolor, 2022, 68 x 53 cm

MARIA GRANADINO

Sweden | mariagranadino.com

Maria Granadino is an emerging visual artist whose works are distinguished by her abstract and contemporary approach to different influences, from geometric shapes to the fluidity of modernist art. Born in Sweden with a multicultural heritage that delicately influences the art, she started her professional career as an artist in 2016, after graduating from Regent's University London – with an interdisciplinary B.A. (Hons) in art and media. Granadino has studied art history & aesthetics at a master's level and will graduate in 2023, which has influenced her current work. Drawing on influences such as fragmentation, the subconscious, and the balance of nature – a play between soft and structured, or what are traditionally referred to as feminine and masculine qualities; is a recurring theme that are continually deconstructed. Other references include everyday experiences, music, nature, and concepts of mysticism through an abstract lens. Her work is also rooted in avant-garde and modernist tradition of the early 1900s but also influenced by neolithic art, Pre-Columbian Mesoamerican art, minimalism and more. Most recently, she has been exploring the depth of warm earthly color tones and the shapes and movements that they exist within. The reduction and fragmentation of geometric and biomorphic shapes into abstract forms also represents an element of mystery and exploration of movement. Her work has been exhibited in countries, such as the United Kingdom, the U.S.A., South Korea, and Sweden.

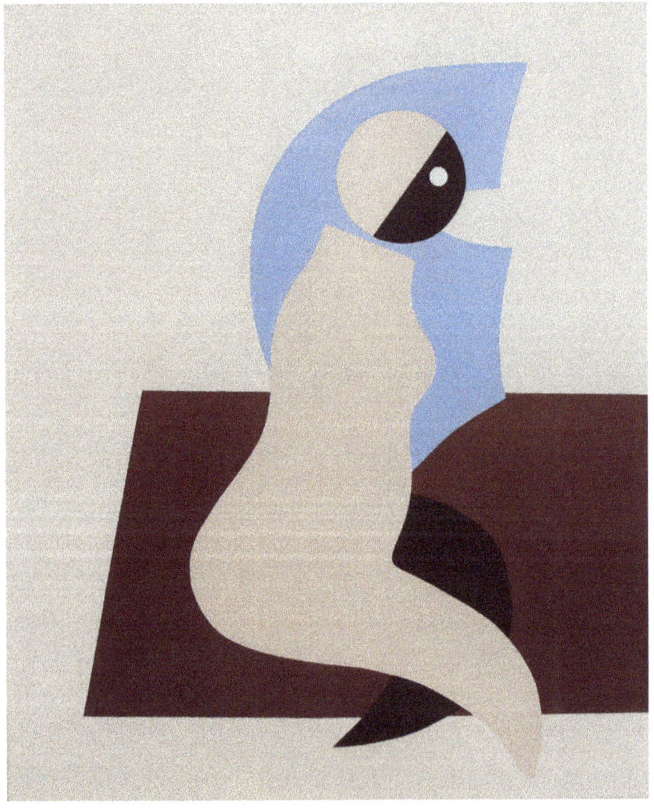

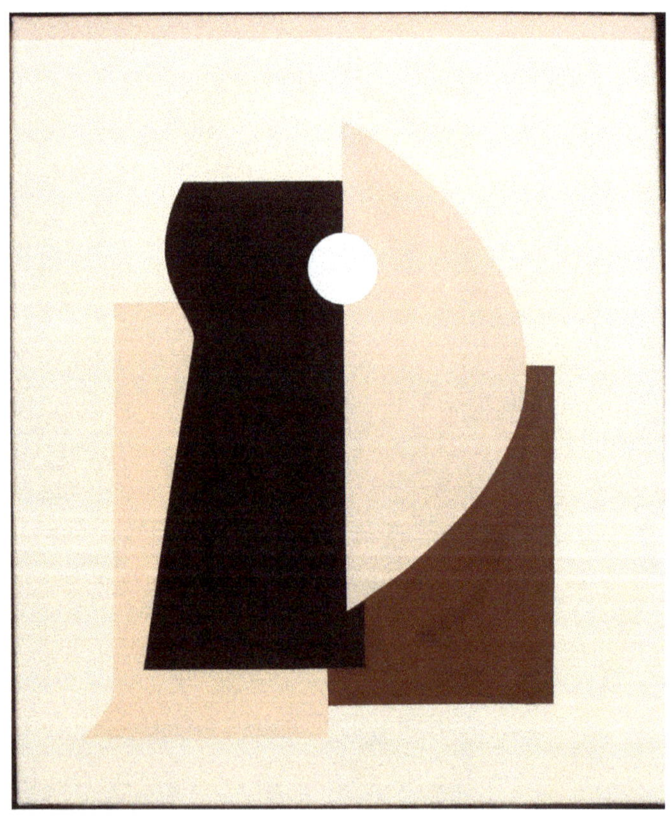

Untitled (movement22), 2021, Acrylic on canvas, 65 x 54 cm

Untitled (love_hyphen_). Acrylic on Canvas. Size:46 cm x 54 cm

LINGMUKI

China | lingmuki.com

Ling Lin (artist name Lingmuki) was born in Nanjing, China. She moved to Hong Kong at the age of eighteen to develop her artistic talents. She has been studying not only in Hong Kong, where she was awarded her degree and master's degree in art and design, but also in Japan and Italy. Ling has experience in different medium including oil painting, Chinese painting, watercolour drawing, digital drawing, etc. Ling's artworks have been exhibited at art fairs and galleries world-wide, among them is important to mention Oxford, Bangkok, Sydney, Shanghai, and many appearances in Hong Kong and native Nanjing. Ling Lin reimagines the possibilities of traditional Chinese landscape painting and its Taoist foundations. She interprets the genre's aesthetics with an innovative range of mediums, using palette knives and oil paint to simulate the varied textures of nature. Ling's investigation of these thematic and formal possibilities surpasses her canvas surfaces: delving into the traditional Chinese landscape genre, she analyzes her own roots, exploring her personal and cultural identity.

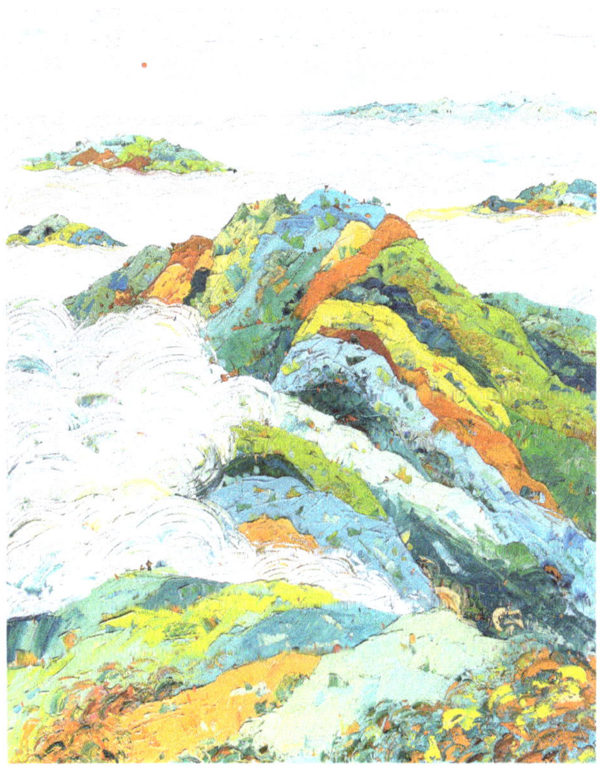

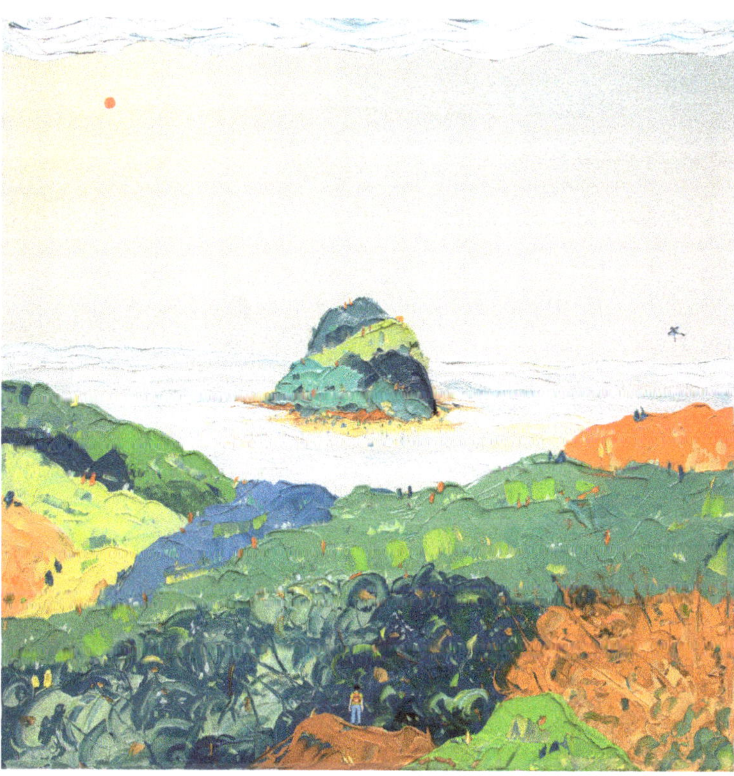

Mountain in the Clouds, 2022, oil on canvas, 80cm x 100cm

Spring Hiking, 2022, Oil on canvas, 40cm x 40xm

SUSAN PLATT

United States | sgplattimages.com

Be prepared to be inspired, delighted, and visually stimulated by images that speak to the heart and the mind. Susan Platt is a fine art photographer that captures the world as only she sees it. It may be the silhouette of a rock formation sinking into the sunset or the simplicity of dewdrops dancing in the wind. Her images stir up the unexpected emotions and thoughts in the viewer. Susan began photographing at the age of 8 and has not put the camera down since. Her keen eye for details developed throughout her 25-year career as a portrait and wedding photographer. Her photographic journeys, also known as #Lightstalking adventures, have been the catalyst and inspiration behind each and every photo. Take a journey through her lens and experience the world as only she sees it.

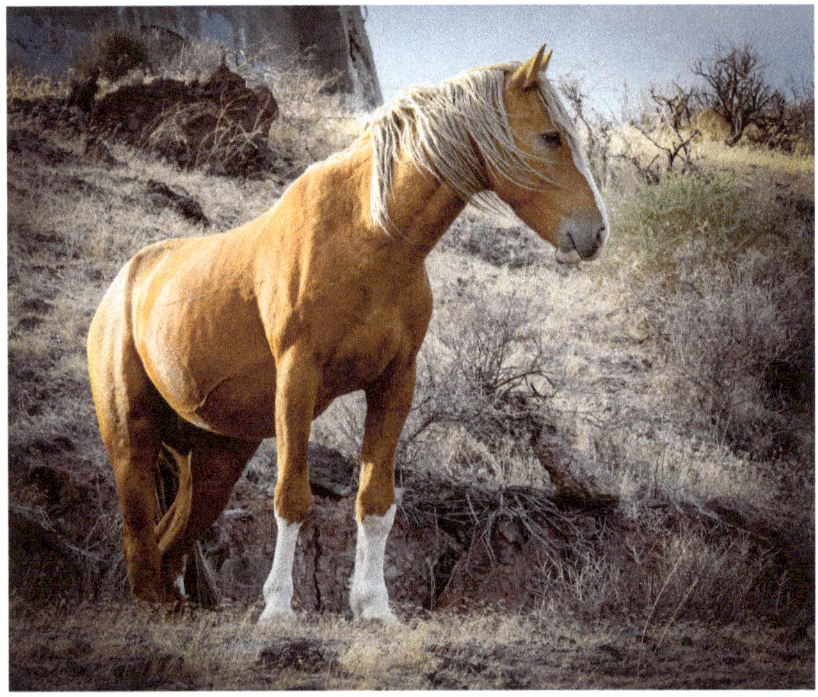

Majestic Golden Casino, 2020, Digital Photograph, 24x20 in

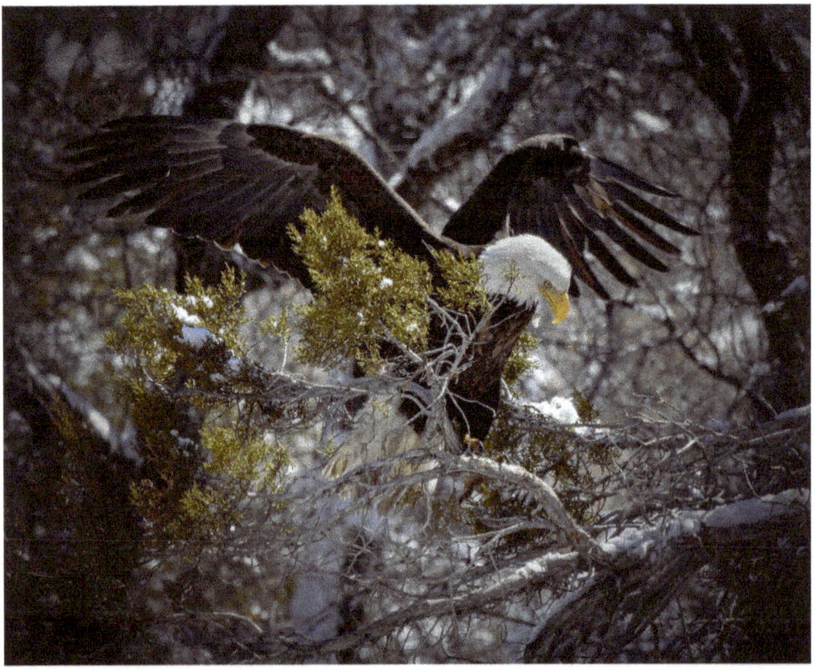

Preparing For Takeoff, 2022, Digital Photograph, 20x16 in

GAYLE PRINTZ

United States | GaylePrintz.com

Although it seems impossible to anyone who has seen her work, Gayle Printz picked up her first paintbrush in May of 2020. By July, two of her paintings were on exhibit in Europe. Now, Gayle is a World Master Artist considered "One of the most important contemporary artists of our time." Her work is on Permanent Exhibit in France at Le Musée de Peinture de Saint-Frajou and, having won over 750 juried international art competitions, every painting in Printz's modern art portfolio is an international award winner. Soaring in value on the walls of prominent art collectors, investors, and art lovers around the globe, Printz paintings rank among the most sought-after art investments in the world. Using color, flow, three-dimensionality, and distinct brushwork, Printz creates paintings that transcend the familiar. There is great meaning in each piece, but because she believes the importance of any artwork is based upon the emotion it evokes, Printz wants to give viewers the freedom to feel and experience the world in unanticipated ways. Her paintings are famous for drawing you in and inviting you to assign personal meaning and universal context by merely listening to the whispers of your imagination. For Gayle, creating these remarkable works of art during the pandemic helped bring lightness and beauty back into a darkened world. Now, by encouraging each of us to use our imagination as the lens through which to find meaning in her work, Printz hopes to inspire all People to celebrate the beauty in life.

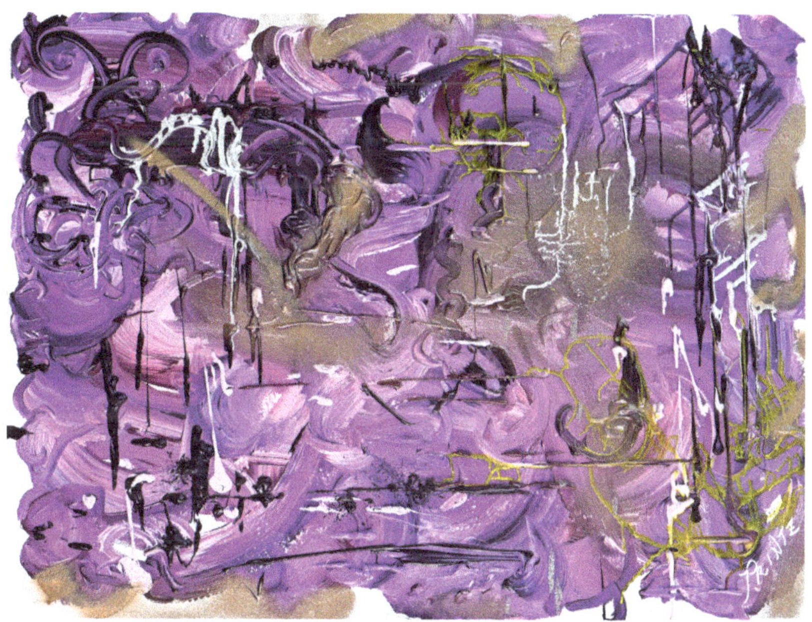

"Music" 2021, Acrylic on Canvas, 76.2 x 101.6 x 3.5 cm

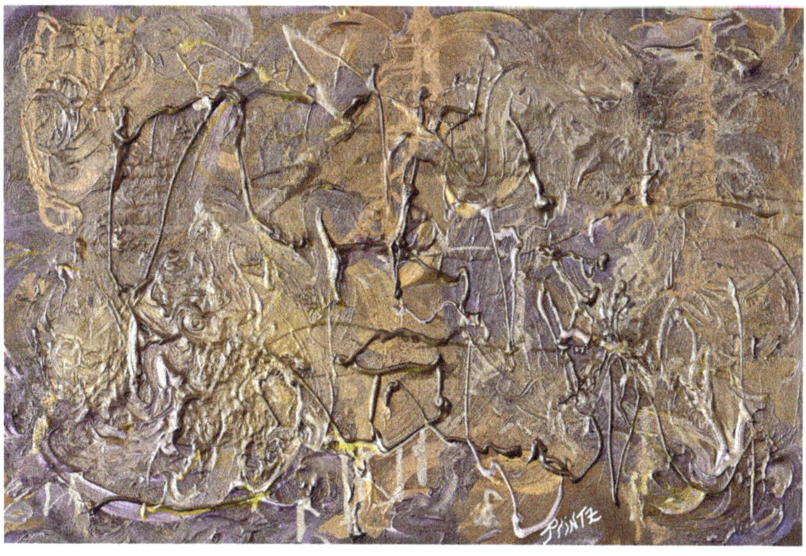

"Ethereal" 2021, Acrylic on Canvas, 60.96 x 91.44 x 3.5 cm

CLAIRE DAVENHALL

Australia | clairedavenhallvisualartist.wordpress.com

Claire Davenhall is an International Artist who graduated from the oldest established Fine Art Institution in Scotland, Gray's School of Art in Aberdeen with a BA (Hons) in Fine Art Sculpture, she has studied at both North Karelia Polytechnic in Finland and Athens School of Fine Art. She migrated from the UK to Western Australia at the end of 2007, where she exhibits her work locally, nationally and internationally. Her work observes the environmental crisis that we live in, where the world is changing and the extraordinary weather events, we see around us is a reflection that it's time to take action. This impact has been significant, revealing the fragility and inequalities buried within many systems and processes, resulting in a call for change. The need to live a sustainable life, to nurture and protect our environment has never been so strong. Creative activism isn't a new thing, but objects hold more words than can ever be spoken, they can travel further, and sculptures provide a voice to make a different in tomorrow's world. As she reflects on the events of the past, the events that have threatened our existence, to gain a greater understanding of the critical need for a happier and more balanced way of living. Where we seek to live a more sustainable life, learn to listen to the warning signs, take responsibility for our actions and correct the imbalances we see around us to protect the fragility of our environment.

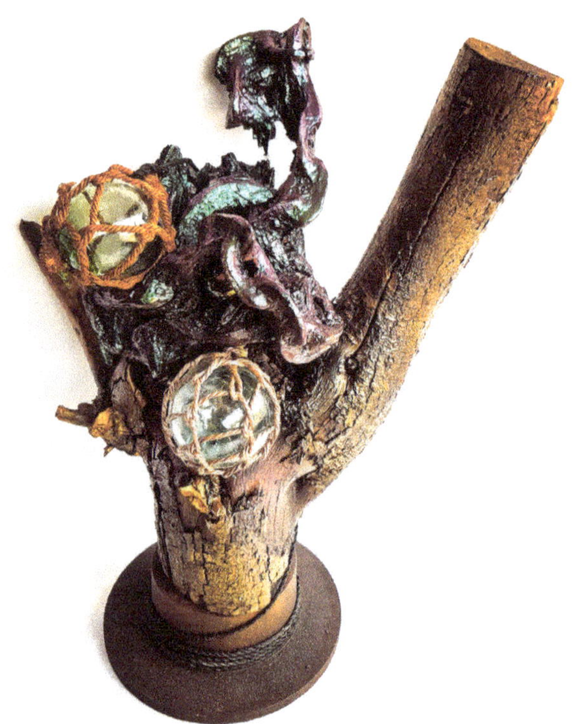

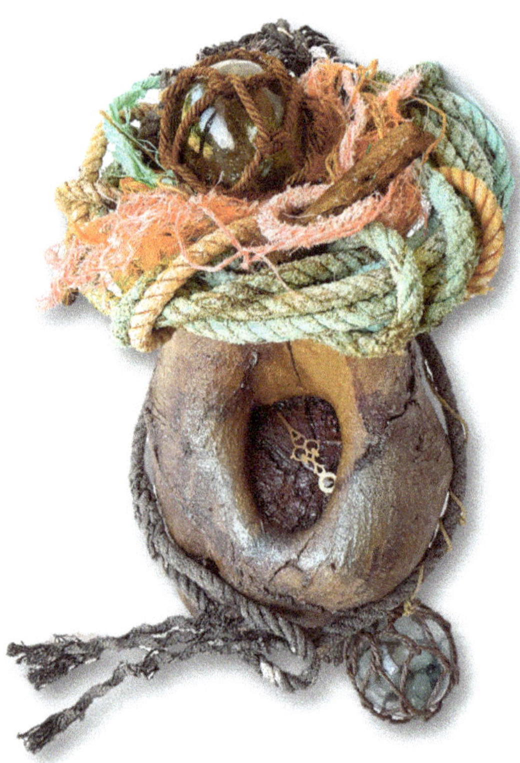

Balancing Act, 2022. Wood, metal, marine rope, glass sea floats, resin, colour changing pigment in automotive paint, h60 x w45 x d30cm

Nesting in the Floods, 2022. Wood, marine rope, glass sea floats, brass hour hand, resin, colour changing pigment in automotive paint, h40 x w30 x d30cm

PAV SZYMANSKI

United Kingdom | hypnoticrepetition.com

Szymanski is a fine art painter and video artist with 30 years of experience.   His current research project is based on creating visual responses to his observations of people, who are suspended in the vacuum of hypnotic repetition. He has travelled the world interviewing and recording individuals, who genuinely struggle with their existence in the context of their survival. He has gathered substantial primary sources and evidence from destinations across the globe. Perhaps, his most significant research findings were from Haiti and Myanmar and resulted in the production of the most spectacular paintings. They have inspired him to develop new and innovative ways of working and experimenting with image making, which are appropriate to the subject. They combine the best of traditional achievements and the power of contemporary thinking and deep reflection. He works full time as a Programme Co-ordinator for Art & Design at a large institution offering a broad range of Further and Higher Education qualifications. He is also an external examiner for the University of The Arts, London and Academic Qualifications Alliance. He has been awarded the International Vision Collector's Award and the Power of Creativity Art Prize by the Contemporary Art Curator Magazine.

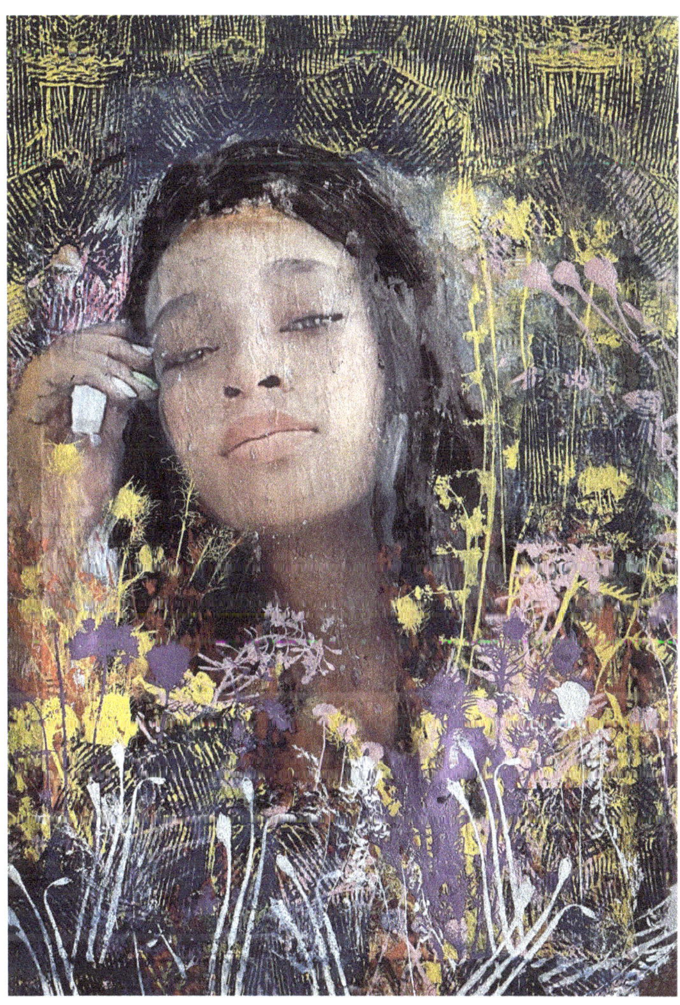

Beautiful Colombian Girl Waiting for Love, 2022, mixed media on canvas, 96.5 x 62.5 cm

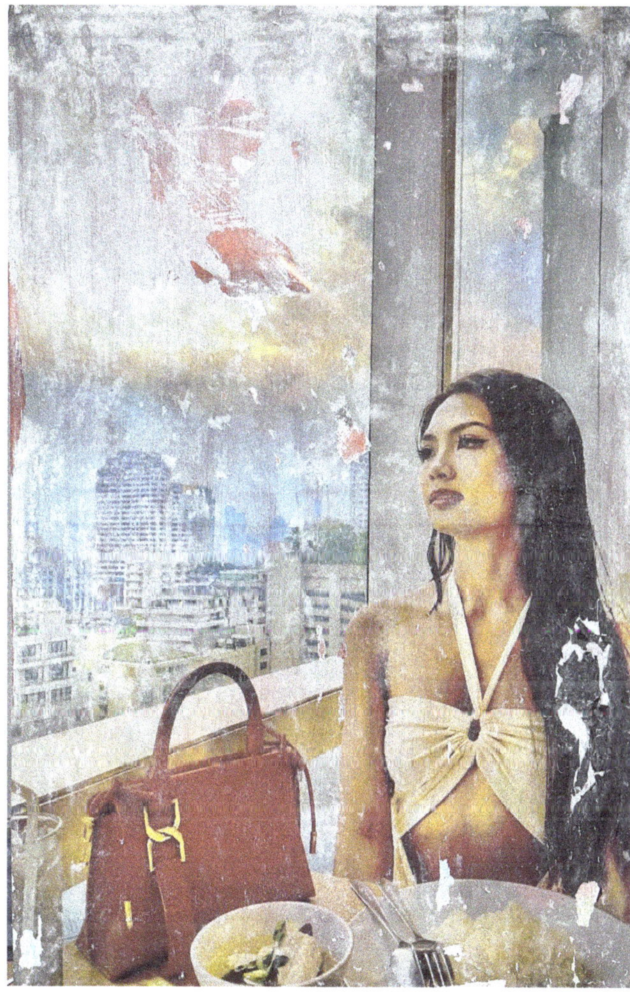

Lamai Refuses to Eat Again, 2022, mixed media on canvas, 96.5 x 62.5 cm

JEONG-AH ZHANG

South Korea | jeongahzhang.com

Jeong-Ah Zhang is a contemporary artist that specializes in painting and works from Seoul Korea, where she was born and raised. Jeong-Ah Zhang, Painter, Photographer, and mixed-media artist, push us to the edge of our own undress ourselves and the world for more meaning than surface deep. And her surrealist paintings connect us to a world that exists inside-out and outside-in of our consciousness.

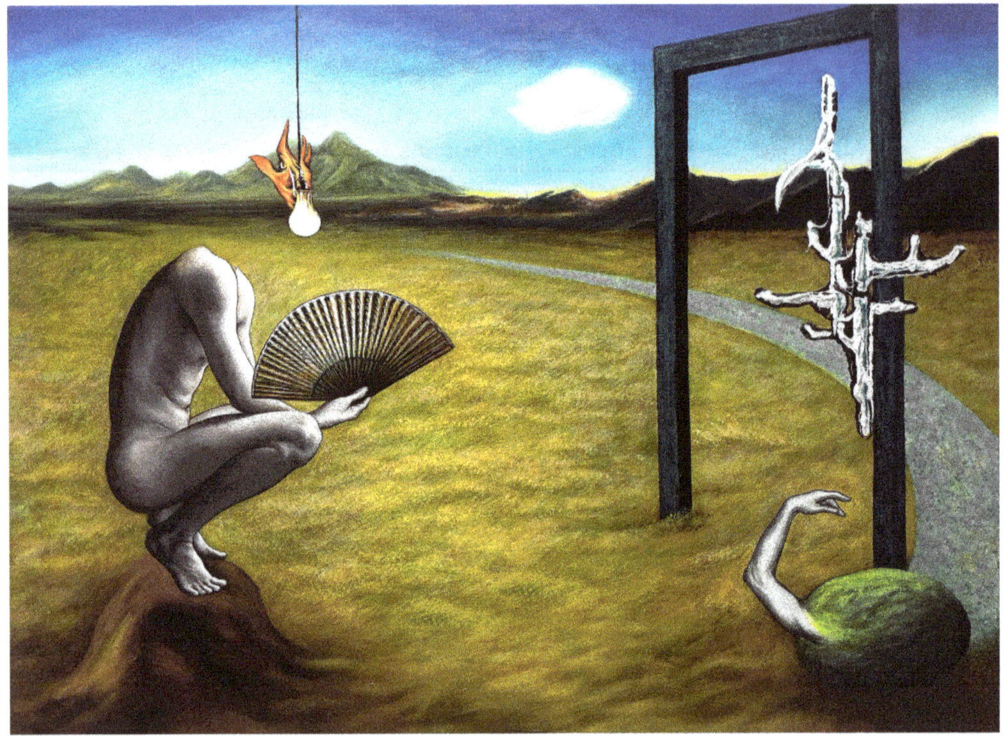

The no-boundary moment. Acrylic on Canvas. 2021

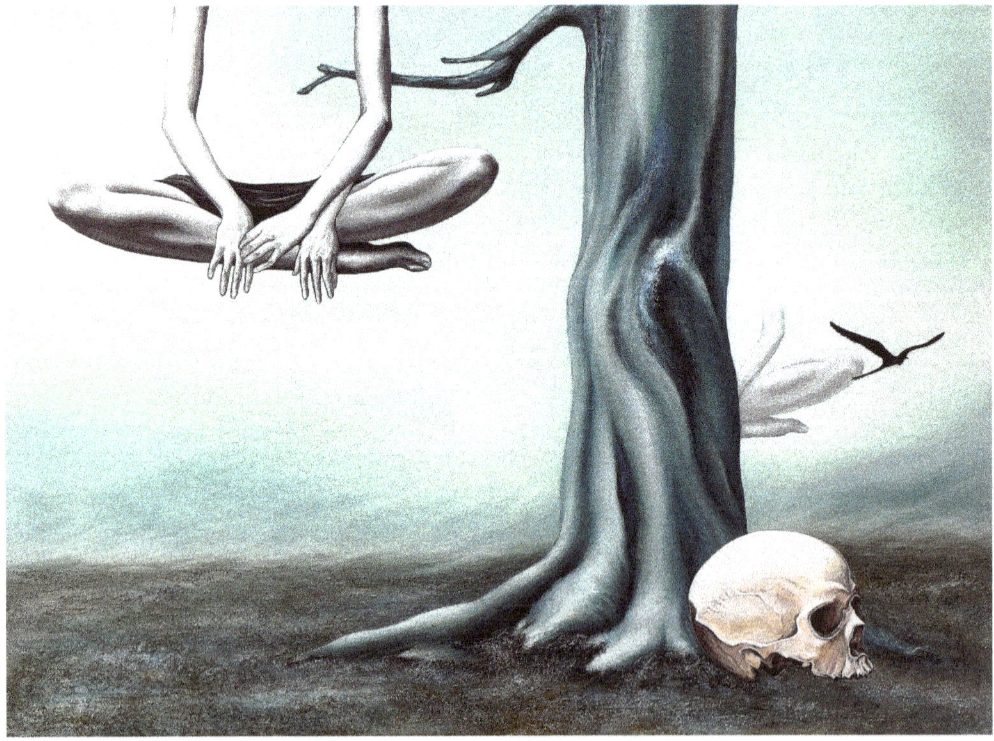

The spirit of the fragrance. Acrylic on Canvas. 2021

NANCY ANNE WOOLF-PETTYJOHN

United States | nancyannewoolf-pettyjohn.com

I am an artist with a natural God given talent from which I can paint any genre. My works are vast and diverse from residential, commercial to investment. As I love history and research several series of paintings will have been made with prior copyright permission. Known to global curators as the only artist in the world to hand paint copies of actual textiles found in museums with prior permission. Honored with Marquis Lifetime Award in 2017. Member of Marquis Who's Who in America. American Art and in the World representing the top 3% of world professionals alongside head's of countries. Past member of National Museum of Women in the Arts as a "Champion of Women Artists" and the White House Historical Association. Works have been exhibited at Lisbon, Portugal and Honiton, England. Published works in MUSA's We Contemporary, Circle Foundation for the Arts Spotlight Magazine, Piecework Magazine, Art Collector Magazine and to be included in Contemporary Art Curator Magazine's Voices of Tomorrow Art book published winter of 2023. Ran for city council and mayor. My Mom also an artist said the famous line..."can you see it, if you can see it then you can paint it"! Like my work? Thank God for my talent that I can share it with you. Daughter of Lucy and Homer Woolf, wife of Matthew Pettyjohn.

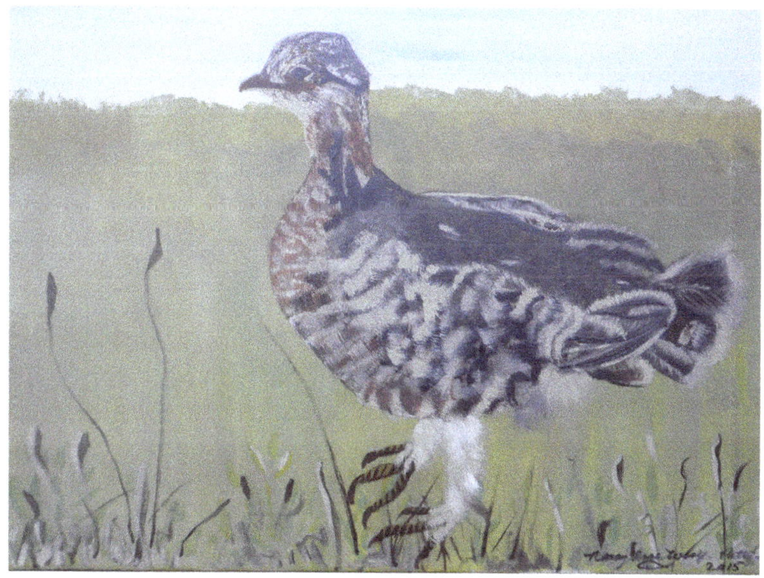

Prairie Chicken Stroll, Medium: Acrylic, Size: 40.64 cm X 50.8 cm

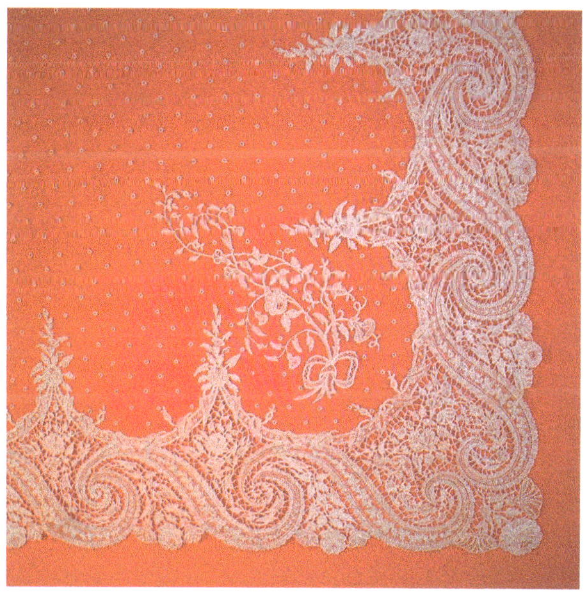

Allhallows Museum Collection # 54 Part of Ladies Hankie 1869, Medium: Acrylic, Size: 60.96 cm x 76.2 cm

WOWSER NG

United Kingdom | jayneanngwz@gmail.com

Zhen Wu, known as Wowser Ng (b.1998), is a China-born, London-based visual artist. He sells artworks in the Japanese gallery "TRiCERA". Wowser gets a letter of recommendation from Steve Brodner in 2019 then he continues to study at UAL for his Master's degree in 2021. His artworks are selected for the 5th Fida Awards Final List, jungle illustration award 2021-New Talent in 2022. He designs fashion illustrations for many brands, including YSL, L 'Oreal Paris, and Chery Automobile, and co-designs artwork□Mirror Garden□with Florentia Village in 2021. Wowser exhibits globally, including including Shanghai exhibition center, Beijing 798 Art District, The Holy Art galley, TRiCERA ART, Tableaux Voices of a NYC Victorian Salon, Central Saint Martins Museum. His works are collected by Central Saint Martins Museum and collectors in Shanghai, Wuhan, Tokyo and London. In the 2022, His artworks are featured in Contemporary Art Curator magazine and Contemporary Art Collectors. Wowser's works combine fashion, illustration and fine art. Art can be a trend, but it can't just be a "commodity". Through narrative context with fashion style, he constructs paintings with personal concepts. With fashion products and commodities that are easy to understand by the public, a series of social issues worth reflecting on, including consumerism and feminism, are discussed. Criticize and reflect the influence of fast fashion and trendy culture.

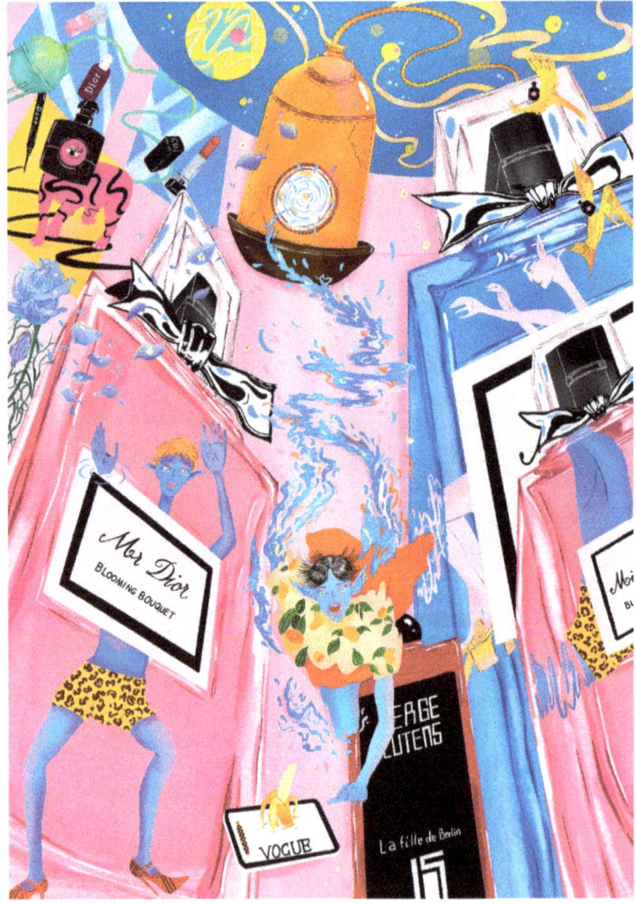

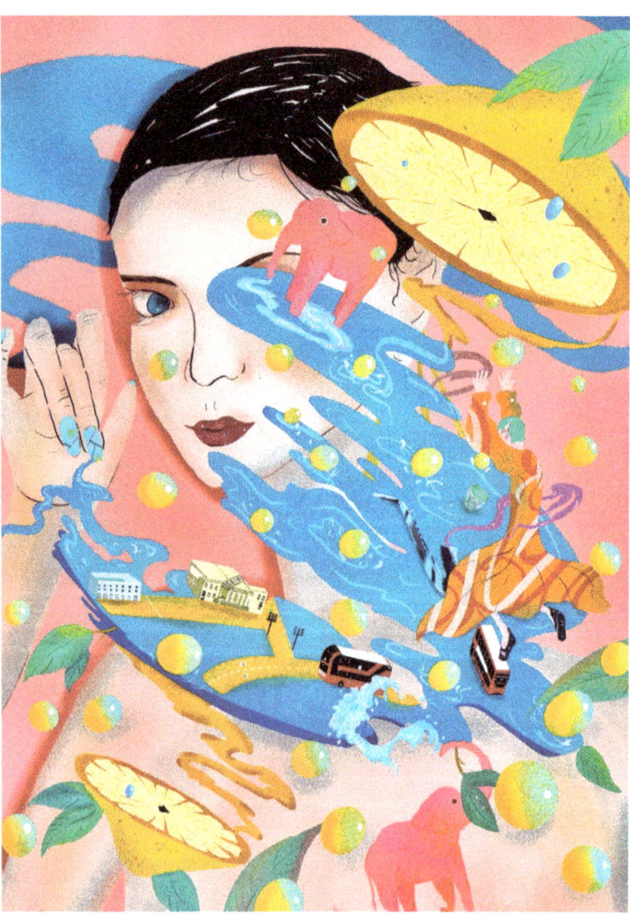

Prison Break, 2022, Limited Art Prints of 30 (Digital Painting)
52.00 × 70.00 × 4.00cm

Pray for rain, 2022, Limited Art Prints of 10 (Digital Painting)
52.00 × 70.00 × 4.00cm

"

GUSTAVS FILIPSONS

Latvia | gustavsfilipsons.berta.me

I was born in 1974,Riga. When I was a child, I was deeply inspired by the cities old architecture and its different moods in different seasons.At that time everything seemed to live its own life and had its special spirit. Dark Jugend style houses in Autumn evenings became alive in feeble lamplight,which was swinging in the wind above the street.Those mythical siluets and symbols at that time had much greater influence on me than the bypassing Soviet Era. In 2004 I acquired Masters degree in painting,Latvian Academy of Art. Abstract Art is the means for me to let the spectator widen his or her perception of ones self and the spiritual Universe it inhabits.The sole intention and porpose of my work is to communicate the unknown in my subcounscious mind, to find the connection with our ,as humans, true self, which I believe is something in common, we all posess.Dr.phil.Ingrid Gardill on my art: We appreciate this artist because he executes his paintings with open working methods and with techniques that he is always developing. His large-format, abstract paintings are convincing because of their radical formal language, which is characterized by vitality."

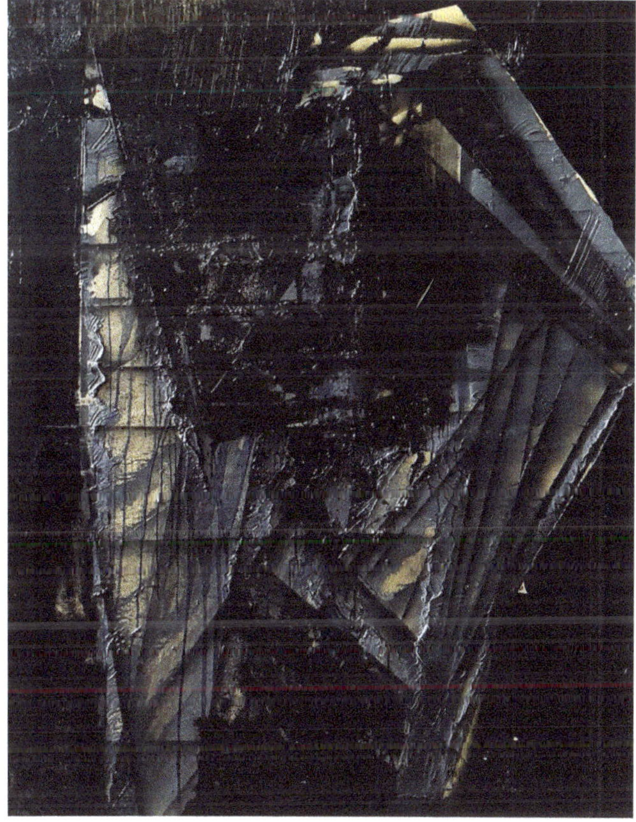

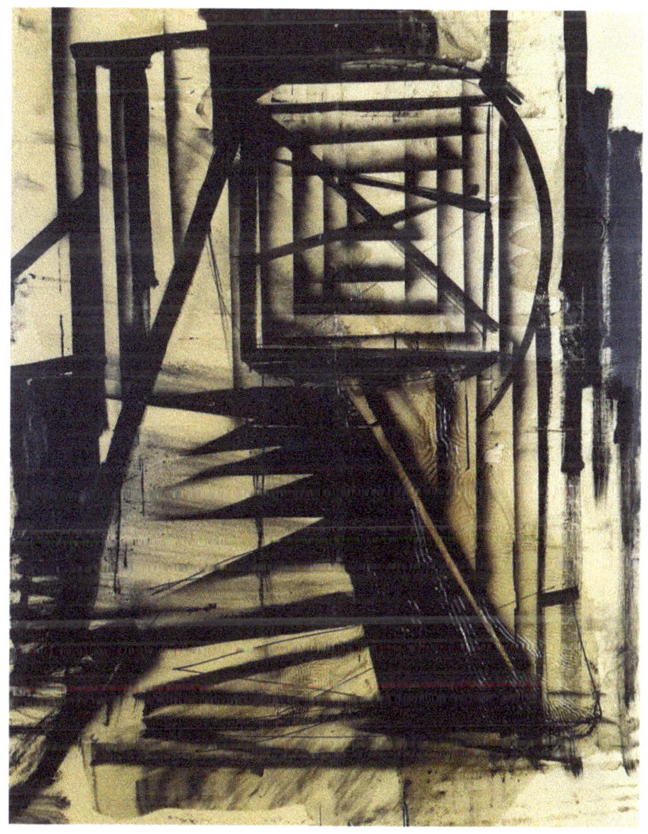

'Construct, 2022, oil, acrylic on canvas,110x140cm

'Observer, 2022, oil, acrylic on canvas,110x140cm

CAROLINE BOFF

United Kingdom | carolineboff.co.uk

Caroline Boff is an emerging contemporary artist who exhibits internationally. Her artwork has been seen in Vogue, Tatler, Vanity Fair, House and Garden and London Life. Her work is a result of the joys of expression and a celebration of what it means to be alive. Caroline has recently exhibited in London, New York, Miami, Greece and San Diego and has upcoming exhibitions in London and New York. Recently she has also been featured in the Collector's Choice, China, Volume III. Caroline is a fellow of the Royal Society of Arts and sponsored the National Social Media Awards in London this year. Caroline feels that she is so lucky to be doing what she loves and that art has given her purpose and her life back.

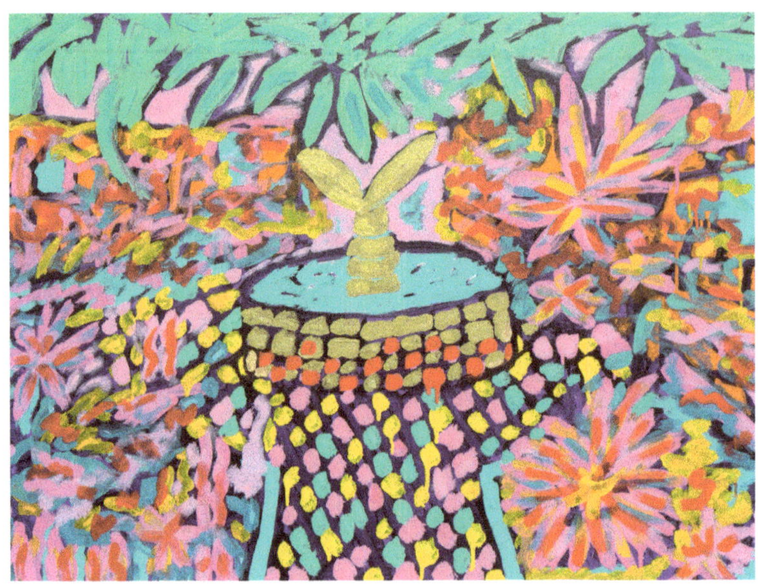

Granada to Extrano, 2020, Acrylics on Canvas, 101cm x 76cm

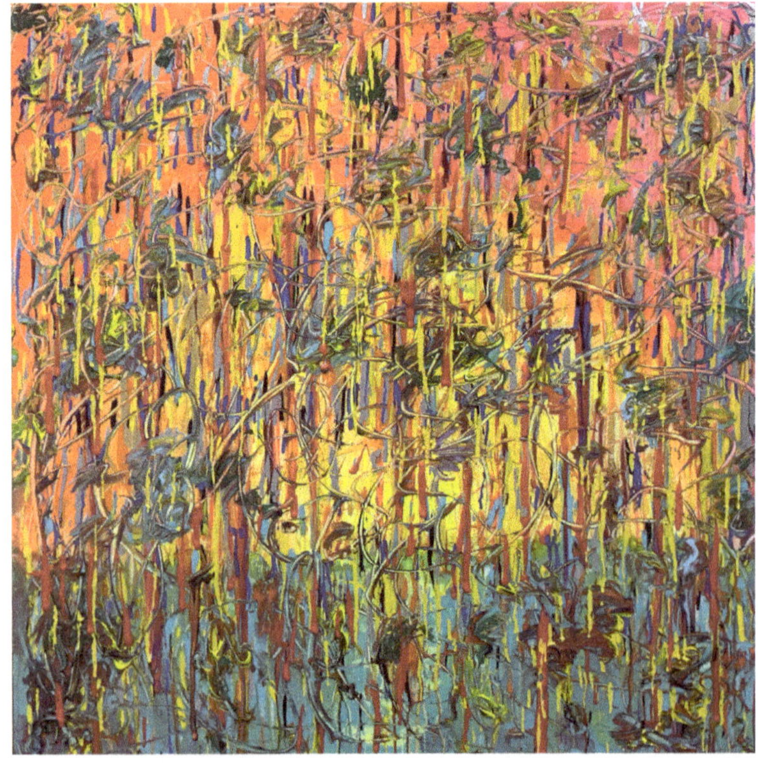

In Actual Search of Sunrise, 2021, Acrylics on Canvas, 101cm x 101cm

MARÍA ISABEL DE LINCE

Colombia | mariaisabeldelince.com

María Isabel Salazar de Lince, is a colombian artist. Studied Art & Arquitecture Design and Psychology, Javeriana University, Bogotá Colombia. Drawing and painting in Cooperartes Workshop, and with Masters David Manzur, Fernando Dávila, and Miguel Moyano. Has participated in several exhibitions, here are some of them: Museum of Hispanic and Latin American Art. Florida - USA, Euroamerica Galleries. New York - USA, Beijing Art Fair - China, Carousel of Louvre. Paris - France, 1st International Modern Art Austria Biennale. Viena - Austria, International Fine Art Masters. Viena - Austria, International Prize Colosseo. Brancaccio Palace. Rome - Italy, Attimi di Luce. MXM Arte. Pietrasanta - Italy, Leonardo Da Vinci Award. Galleria La Pigna. Rome - Italy, Casanova Award. Flangini Palace. Venice - Italy, The best modern and contemporary artists. Palais Sternberg. Viena - Austria, I Segnalati. InArte Werkkunst Gallery. Berlin - Germany, Small is beautiful II. Alliance Francaise. Dubai - United Arab Emirates, International Biennal of Flanders. Bruges - Belgium, International Prize Velásquez. MEAM Museum. Barcelona - Spain y III Bienal de Arte de Barcelona. MEAM Museum. Barcelona - Spain. She has won several national and international awards. In 2014 she was awarded the Moments Lifetime Award. She currently lives and works in Bogotá.

Water we love you 2022 oil on linen 96 x 140 cm

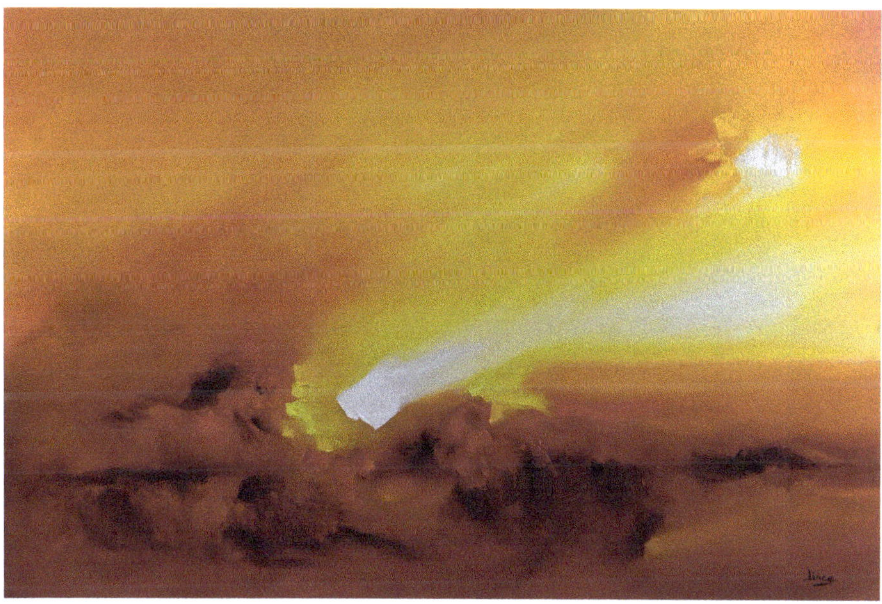

Light 2011 oil on canvas 100 x 150 cm

SHUAI XU

China | shuai-xu.com

Xu Shuai graduated with a BFA in Painting from Tianjin Academy of Fine Arts and an MFA in Fine Art from Claremont Graduate University in California. As a multi-medium artist traversing multiple boundaries of culture, geography, and disciplines, Xu's works engage with human emotions and life against the broad background of vanity and universality independent of identities and temporalities while exploring the possible alternatives for observing and living the macrocosm. In his artistic practice, the universe, science, and perception are recurring themes throughout every process of making and performing. With a current commitment to the contemporary experiments of oil paint and ready-made installations, Xu questions in a theatrical manner the fixated realities of Western societies while returning in a poetic way to the Chinese traditions of relativity and naturalism.

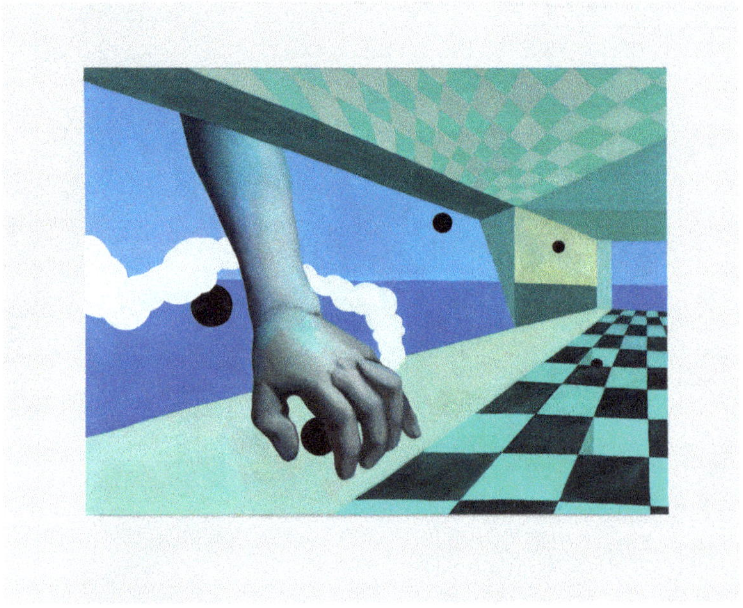

'OJ 287' 121.22x91.44cm   Oil on canvas 2022

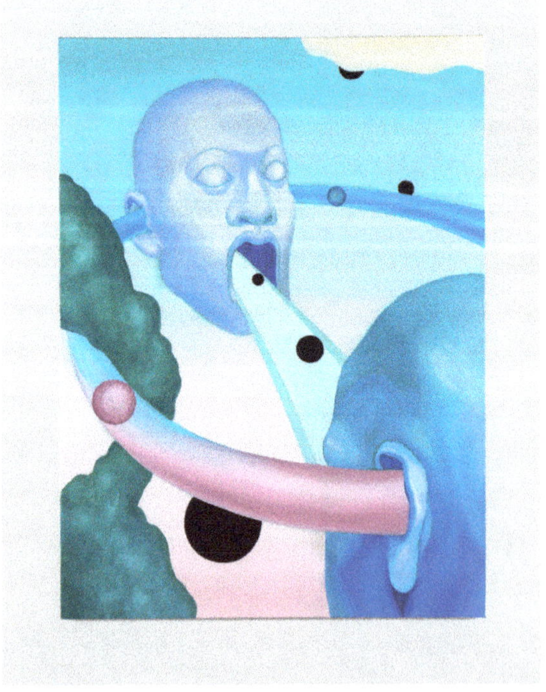

'OJ 287' 121.22x91.44cm   Oil on canvas 2022

DAVE THOMAS

United Kingdom | phantomart.online

Currently based in the UK Bedfordshire countryside, Dave's previous professional career had taken him throughout Europe, where he loved meeting new people and immersed himself into different cultures. Dave believes these life experiences have helped him overcome boundaries and enhance his creative approach with his long-term passion for art. Now as a full time international award-winning self-taught artist, Dave's artwork explores the relationship between figurative/abstract techniques and the balance between vibrant colours and monochrome tones. Dave is a member of the fine art trade guild and frequently exhibits his artwork internationally. Dave has been awarded the "Collector's Vision International Art Award", "Power of Creativity Art Prize" and "Voices of Tomorrow", in addition to appearing in "Power of Creativity" art book from the International Art Curator Magazine. Dave has frequently exhibited his artwork internationally in Milan, London, Parls and USA. "My paintings are all about emotion, light /shadow and capturing "the moment". I strive to blend abstract and loose realism to create a piece that provokes thought and reflection of memories or aspirations in the eye of the beholder. Each time I look at a piece I have created I can always recall a soundtrack I have listened to which helped shape the artwork's direction.... a bit like having my own playlist in paint."

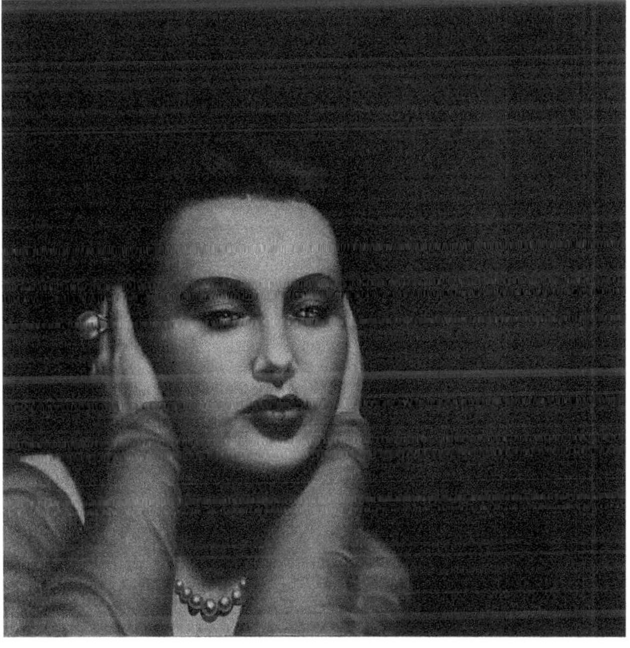

Silent Reflection, 2022, oil 18" x 24" canvas

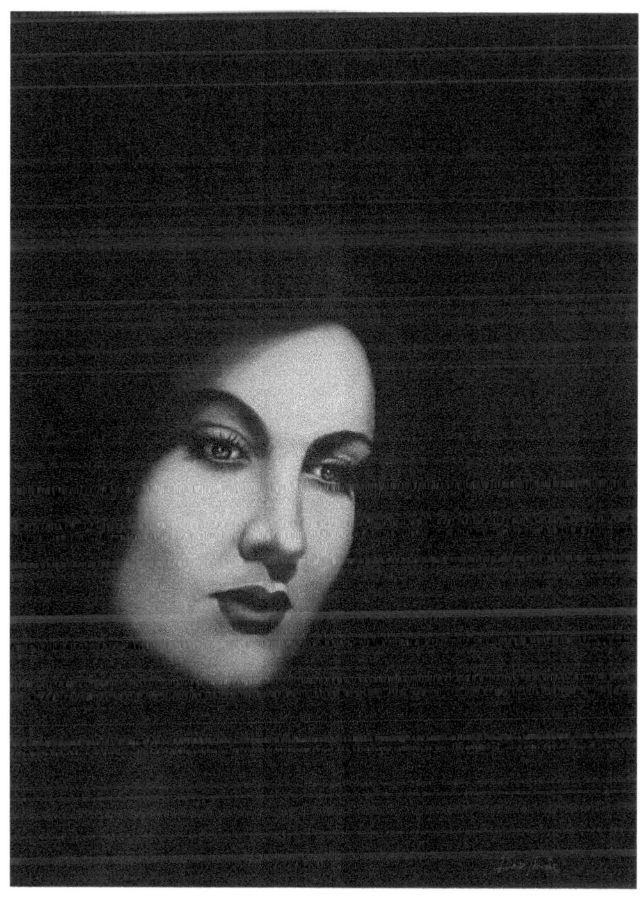

Into The Light, 2022, oil on 18" x 24" canvas

REYDEL ESPINOSA

Cuba | espinosa.art

Reydel Espinosa was born in Cueto, Cuba in 1985 and grew up in the countryside. Thus, nature is very inspiring to his creation since the early stage of his artist career. He was determined to become an artist at the age of 14 years old through a self-taught process. He graduated in 2004 from an artisan school where he learned how to hand-make jewelry but had to learn how to paint in his own free time. Although Reydel is a self-taught artist, he has outstanding painting techniques. His major breakthrough was when he moved to Havana in 2005. He visited frequently the National Museum of Fine Arts in Havana and gained his painting techniques through intense observations, analysis, and emulations of great art masters' artworks. Together with his own imaginative mind, he gradually shapes his signature style of surrealism, especially in the animal themes. He knows well how to marry observation and imagination. He has demonstrated unconventional and liberal ideas in his paintings. He considers the originality of an artwork's idea is far more significant than the techniques. He said: "Instead of imposing my ideas on the spectators, I would rather they are empowered to interpret what they see in my artworks. I consider myself a storyteller, and the story comes from my imaginations." The remarkable influence since the beginning of his surrealist creation is from the painter Hieronymus Bosch. Other artists that inspire him are Max Ernst and Salvador Dali. Reydel feels there seems to be a linear line that unites their styles, especially the liberty in creation that he resonates with them. The moment he creates with complete freedom, he has an automatic mind to paint any figures appearing, like a poem of surrealism. He thinks the creativity and the rareness, that no one ever painted before, is what is interesting. For this reason, he is passionate to create what is unique and what is never seen before. However, he does not like to create surrealist figures for the sake of creating ones. Instead, he is more on the path of breaking the rules and owning total freedom in creativity. Besides Cuba, his artworks has been exhibited abroad in Miami, New York City, Paris and Taipei. He currently lives in old Havana and paints at the Carmen Montilla Gallery. In 2023, He will move to Taiwan to live with his family and continue his creations there.

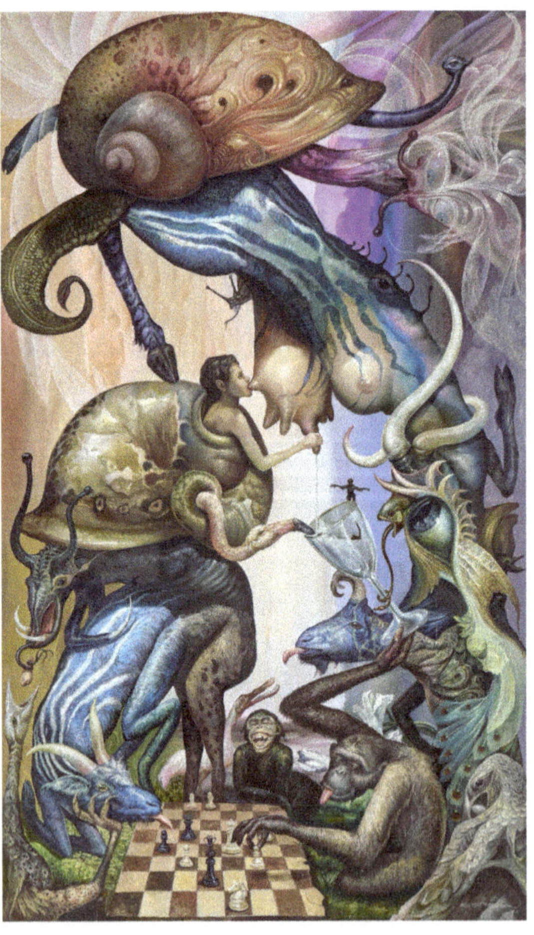

Delusion, oil on canvas, 125x73cm, 2021

Back Cover by Li Ning.

Published by the Contemporary Art Curator Magazine.
All of the images are subject to copyright by the artists represented in the book.
2023 © Contemporary Art Curator Magazine.
Cover and back cover artwork copyright by Li Ning.

ISBN: 978-84-19526-48-9
DL: GR 163-2023

Imprime: Lozano Impresores S.L.
Distribuye: TORRES EDITORES
Tel.: 958 80 05 80 - Fax: 958 29 16 15
www.torreseditores.com
info@torreseditores.com

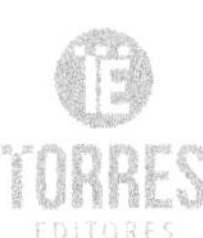

VOICES
OF TOMORROW

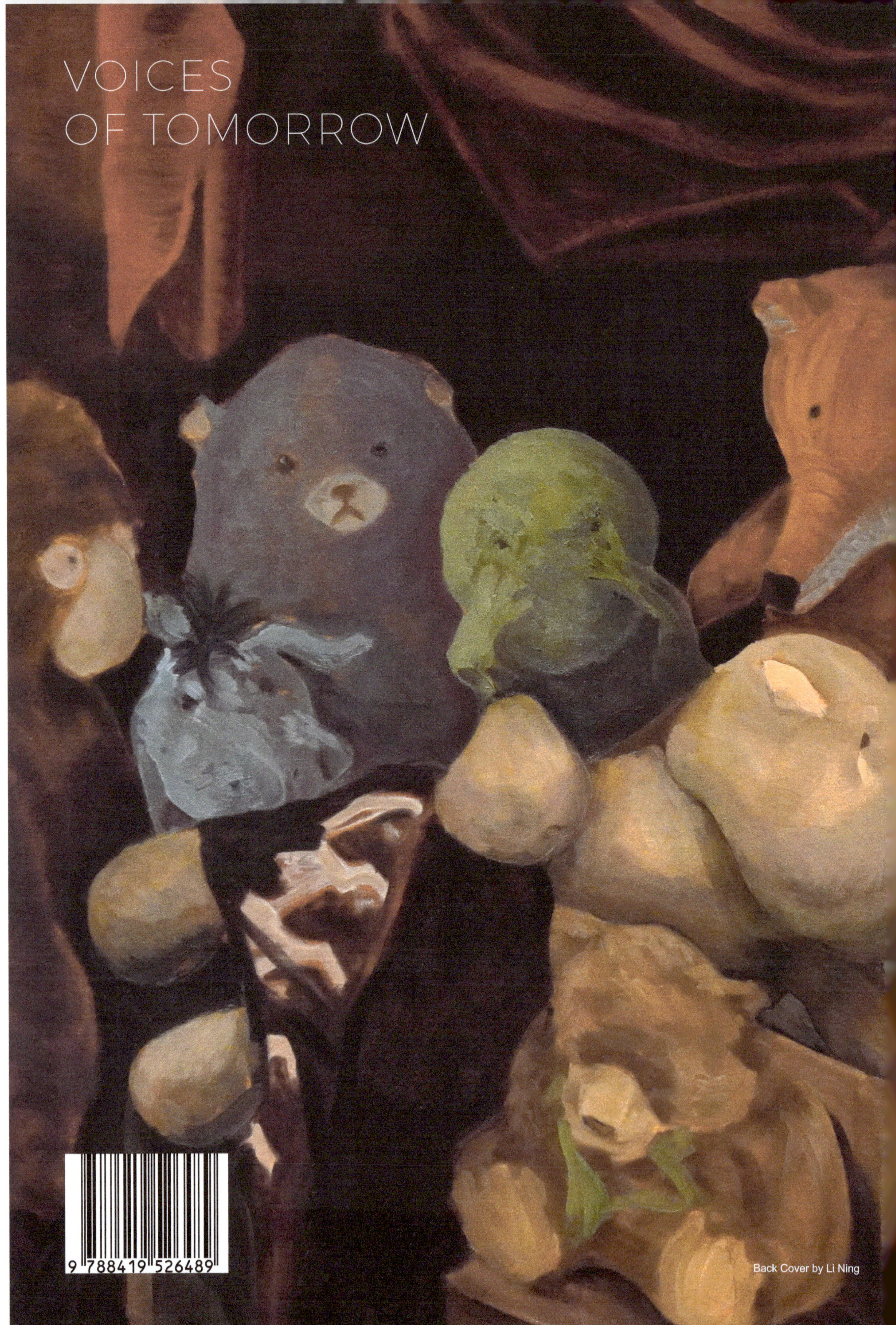
VOICES
OF TOMORROW
9 788419 526489
Back Cover by Li Ning